S0-AYE-309

BOAT MAINTENANCE BY THE AMATEUR

BOAT MAINTENANCE BY THE AMATEUR

Michael Verney

C.Eng., M.I.C.E., M.I.W.E.

Drawings and photographs by the author

WINCHESTER PRESS
NEW YORK

Published by
Winchester Press
460 Park Avenue, New York 10022
1971

Copyright © Kaye & Ward 1970

All rights reserved. No part of this publication may
be reproduced, stored in a retrieval system or
transmitted, in any form or by any means, electronic, mechanical, photocopying, recording or
otherwise, without the prior permission of the
copyright owner.

Library of Congress Catalog Card Number 70–16539
ISBN 0 87691 058 4

Printed in Great Britain by
C. Tinling & Co. Ltd
London and Prescot

CONTENTS

5

BRITISH-AMERICAN TERMS COMPARISON TABLE

BOOK	U.S.
Afco	Stow-A-Vent (Lipton Marine Inds.)
Algicide	Unipoxy by Petit
Araldite	Gluvit, Polypoxy
Avigel 300	CRC soft marine seal
Bottle Jack	Hydraulic jack
Blake	Wilcox-Crittenden
Bluebell	Noxon
Britect	Metal Life
Calfa or PRC	Life Calk by Boat Life or Petit Seam Compounds
Cascamite	Polypoxy
Cascover	Mactac
Decolay	Interlux polycaulk
Dekaplex	Techno-tuf
Domestos	Ajax
Evomastic	Petit Canvas Adhesive
Flexible Caulking Composition	Caulk-Tex
grp	Fiberglass
Galvafroid, Kurust	Drygalv or Nevoxide
Gibbs' Black Rubber Sheathing	Flopaint Inc.'s Rub-r-cote
Glass-reinforced plastic	Fiberglass
Harpic	Comet
Henderson	Dart Union's Guzzler
Hilmor	Blue Dot
Hydra	Seaclo
Isapon or Crystic	Polymender
Jeffrey's Mendex	Boat Life's fill and sand
Jeffrey's Seamflex or Detel spreading paste	Petit sealers and adhesives
Jenolite	Naval Jelly
Jubilee clips	Hose clamps
Kempsafe	Washington
Knotting	Shellac
Lavac	Ball-Head
Limpetite	Liquid Seaprene
Marlow Multiplait	Samson Braid

7

BOOK	U.S.
Osotite, Hermetite	3-M Scotch Seal or Grip
PRC	(see Calfa)
Pentechloraphenol	Samuel Cabot Inc.'s Penta Wood Seal
Perkins	Shipmate
Perspex	Plexiglass
Pithers	Princess
Plus Gas Formula B	Sparcote
Polyclens	Cabot's
Polyseamseal	Calabama: Plastic Seal All
Revon	PVC Flex-Vent (Nicro Fico)
Rippingill	Shipmate
Rozalex	Protek
Ryland SP	Petit
Rylard	Z-Spar
Samcolastic	Techno-tuf, Boatex
Scrim	Woven roving
Sealastic	Coast Pro-Seal's Sealant and Adhesive
Seamflex	Dow Corning's Silicone Sealant
Sellotape	Masking tape
Semtek	Mactac
Shell Ensis Oil	Sea Guard
Skarsten scraper	Scraper
Simpson-Lawrence	(see Blake)
Spinnaker	Cowspar
Sturdee	NRG Braid
Swarfega or Dirty Paws	Flash
Talurit	Nicropress
Talurit ferrules	Nicropress sleeves
Tannoy Ventair	Wilcox-Crittenden mushroom type
Terry Clips	'Holdall' Spring Clips
Terylene	Dacron
Thermofit	Ampsulation
Trakmark	Nautolex
Ulstron	Yacht braid
Ventilite	George H. Allen Sky-light, Dry-vent
Waterloo, Headmaster, Hydra	Seaclo and Graco

PREFACE

Boat owners should have no difficulty in finding books to teach them nearly all they should know about handling their craft on the water. There are excellent volumes available covering seamanship; navigation; dinghy sailing; ocean racing; cruising under sail and power; storms at sea; powerboat racing; or sailing around the world.

However, the tyro who is just about to become an owner, or the experienced yachtsman who can no longer afford to have his boat maintained professionally, has hitherto found it impossible to obtain a single book telling him all he needs to know about the care of craft in all sizes, types, and constructions, when in harbour, laid-up ashore, or being prepared for a new season. This book is intended to fill that gap in the amateur sailor's fund of literature.

Many owners learn to enjoy the practical side of boat maintenance and for them yachting lasts all the year round. For those who prefer to stay at home and watch television I have included comparative costs of professional and amateur work, to give them some encouragement.

Those owners with dinghies or small cruisers that can be trailed home for the winter are in many ways fortunate, as they can choose the right weather for each task and all the required tools and materials are close to hand.

However, when one lives in the big city and owns a craft laid-up near the sea, winter trips to fit her out can be very pleasant breaks in the drearier months. The time is fast approaching when boatyards will be unable to take on further clients for winter work, so that newcomers to the sport may be forced to do all maintenance work themselves. This has long been the case with sailing dinghies, and the number of new boatyards appearing is small in comparison with the increasing number of cruising boats.

If the amateur books all his time and charges it at £0.50 ($2.50) an hour he will probably leave the water and take up golf, for it rarely proves wise to calculate the cost of yachting. Hobbies should not be priced. As the main preventative for insanity and various diseases caused by mental and physical stagnation, hobbies are cheap at any price! If you find your boat costs £10 ($50) an hour of actual sea-time, do not get rid of her unless the bailiffs insist!

Where cost comparisons are important, averages have been calculated based on contemporary prices (Summer 1970), and equivalents in dollars for American and Canadian readers are given. These represent costs in those countries and may bear little relation to the rate of exchange.

Metric and American units of dimension are included so that this work can be of benefit to the boating fraternity in most corners of the World.

MICHAEL VERNEY

CHAPTER 1

OWNERSHIP ECONOMY

When taking to the water for the first time most people choose a dinghy or small powered boat. Before deciding to buy a sailing dinghy, it pays to join a yacht club at the chosen location or to contact that club, in order to find out what classes of dinghies they race. One is sure to embark upon racing sooner or later and activities may become very limited if the dinghy chosen is not a class raced at the club.

The most popular form of small power boat is the inboard or outboard runabout, but it should be remembered that the majority of these are designed for high speed and the speed limit of 5 or 6 knots on nearly all inland waters render such craft quite unsuitable for most rivers and lakes.

The Right Cruiser
When considering the purchase of a cruising yacht, one may have no difficulty in deciding whether she should be primarily a sailing craft, a motor cruiser, or a motor/sailer (also known as a 50/50). The problem arises when considering questions of speed, comfort, choice of rig, type of engine and fuel, availability of moorings, method of laying-up and the amount of time available for maintenance work.

Arranging for a mooring is essential before choosing a yacht because the draft and construction of the hull may be dictated by the type of mooring. Moorings which dry out at low tide are considerably cheaper to rent than deep water moorings and demand the choice of multi-hull, bilge keel, centreboard, or other shoal draft vessels. Such craft are often easier to trail on the road for laying-up but, if exhilarating sailing is what you require, an ex-racing yacht such as a *Dragon* or a *6-Metre* with deep keel may prove considerably cheaper to buy.

11

An old fashioned gaff-rigged yacht may be slow to windward, but she will be cheap to buy secondhand and may be
superbly comfortable at sea. Furthermore, craft of this type
have a great deal of character which is completely lacking from
the modern range of mass-produced yachts. As such a craft
may have a fishing-boat finish, this makes her maintenance as
well as her first cost the lowest possible. The owner with little
time for maintenance work might be wise to purchase a
glass-reinforced plastic (grp) yacht, but he may have to pay
twice as much for her in capital cost.

An outboard motor makes a passable auxiliary engine for a
small sailing cruiser, but an inboard engine is much more
convenient and should not take up too much space. If one is
engineering-minded, a petrol (gasoline) inboard auxiliary has
many advantages provided careful maintenance ensures no
possibility of fuel leakage.

Although a diesel engine is cheaper to run, this is hardly
worth considering for auxiliary use, while new or secondhand
diesel-engined craft have a higher value than their petrol-
engined counterparts. Diesels are more noisy than petrol
engines but they do have the advantage of not requiring
electricity for starting or running, and the fuel is less explosive!

With power boats the above notes do not necessarily apply.
The question of running costs is the major consideration and
this is closely linked with the question of speed.

Taking a 32 ft (10 m) motor cruiser as an example, a craft
built in 1938 with twin petrol engines (installed in 1955) and
capable of 8 knots may be purchased for £1,500 ($6,000), while
her running costs will be perhaps £1.00 ($1.50) an hour. A
similar vessel built in 1962 with twin diesels producing 9 knots
may cost £4,800 ($20,000) to buy with a running cost of £0.22
($1.00) per hour.

A twin-engined diesel cruiser having almost identical
accommodation to the previous one, of the same age, but
capable of 18 knots, will command a price of about £6,500
($32,000) while her running costs will be £1.00 ($4.50) an hour.
Thus the relationship between speed and fuel and age can be
assessed. Motor cruisers are nearly always of shoal draft construction, but many of them have twin propellers which are
vulnerable to damage on a mooring that dries out. Craft with
single or twin Z-drives (out-drives) have a big advantage here,
as the propellers can be hinged-up and there are no rudders.

Picture 1. Old gaff rigged boats can make very satisfactory cruisers, and are cheap to buy and maintain. A powerful engine helps to overcome their wind-ward inefficiency and makes them more suitable for impatient owners.

Picture 2. There is a lot to be said in favour of a sound Bermuda sloop built in the 1930s and similar craft are still built in wood. Craft converted from gaff rig to Bermuda often prove under-canvased off the wind.

Outboard-engined cruisers have the same advantage, with the additional benefit that the motors can be removed and taken home during the winter period. However, it should not be forgotten that large outboard motors which are normally left in position are easy prey for thieves.

The popular motor/sailer type of craft falls between the two above categories. The more modern versions sail remarkably well and have a turn of speed under power equivalent to a conventional medium speed motor yacht. Those built prior to around 1955 tended to be under-canvased and under-engined.

With a reliable engine a motor/sailer is an excellent first choice for the yachtsman who is taking up cruising, especially when he wishes to take his family to sea. The enjoyable silence of sail can be experienced, when conditions are favourable, and the powerful engine is always available to extricate one from awkward situations. When a certain amount of sail is used while motoring, fuel economy is greatly improved and so is the rolling motion of the ship.

There is a lot to be said for large multi-hulled craft for family cruising. With the exception of motor cruisers fitted with expensive stabilizers, cruising catamarans and trimarans are less subject to rolling and heeling than any other type of yacht. Such craft command fairly high secondhand values, and they have two other disadvantages: moorings are difficult to find and expensive owing to the large beam, and fitting inboard engines may prove difficult or even impossible.

Construction Materials

The foregoing notes should give the beginner some idea concerning the type of craft he can afford but two further considerations tend to complicate the choice.

Firstly, there is the question of the yacht's construction. Modern open boats such as sailing dinghies and runabouts are almost all built from plywood or grp (glass reinforced plastics) while the older dinghies and launches are planked with solid wood. At the other end of the scale, motor cruisers over 60 ft (18 m) in length are invariably built of steel while the largest auxiliary sailing craft and ocean racers are mostly of wood, still frequently the cheapest method of construction for large one-off yachts of complex shape.

In between these two extremes the types of material are numerous. Wood and metal have always been used, but grp is now almost universal for mass-produced designs while ferro-cement is gaining ground and other materials are being tested.

In addition to the above, composite construction may be found in which timber planking and decking is laid over steel frames and beams. A wooden hull may be planked, plywood, or moulded, while metal includes steel and aluminium alloys. Some yachts are built entirely from grp while others have grp hulls with timber decking, superstructure and interior.

Secondly, combined with all these possible variations the prospective owner will discover that there are roughly three categories of finish, as follows:

(a) Absolute perfection. The vessel appears at all times as she did after the launching ceremony.

(b) Well-cared-for. Preservation of all parts taken care of: exterior appearance good early in the season.

(c) Workboat fashion. Owners of such craft usually sail at every opportunity (perhaps even during the winter) and use paint only when things get really shabby.

The vast majority of yachts fall into Category (b) and as long as the preservation jobs are not ignored there is little need for

Picture 3. Modern high speed motor cruisers permit owners with limited leisure to explore distant cruising grounds, but they can lead to bankruptcy! Note the wide dark painted sheer band and deep boot-top which help to conceal the vast freeboard.

the impecunious amateur to transfer from (b) to (a). Some keen types (who do little sailing but take a great pride in their dreamships) manage to transfer, and great satisfaction can result from buying a badly cared for ship and gradually rejuvenating her from (b) to (a) or from (c) to (b). It can be done!

The owner of a Class (c) boat is perhaps the happiest fellow afloat. Few yachtsmen may realize it, but to own a boat in Category (a) is not always good for the nervous system. Unless one is sufficiently wealthy to ignore large insurance premiums and the cost of a safe berth in tideless water with a watchman constantly on duty, great psychological agony can be caused by watching a jewel of a ship battered about by beginners in hired boats, or stained continuously by oil-polluted waters.

The Class (c) owner avoids all such cares. His ship may not be a jewel but she may be fast, weatherly, and reliable, giving her owner nothing but enjoyment and satisfaction. The only time this blissful existence may be shattered is when he attempts to come alongside a Class (a) yacht for a well-earned night in a strange harbour and is received by black looks and a lack of co-operation!

15

A very good comparison in everyday terms is the man owning a smart new car worth £1,800 ($3.000) and insured for £50 ($300) a year, who lives in fear of a first mysterious dent or scratch in a parking lot. His carefree pal has a ten-year-old car worth £100 ($200) and insured for £10 ($100) a year, but the older car may be in excellent condition and almost equally reliable.

Short Cuts to Economy
The main purpose of annual fitting-out and painting is to ensure that every item of gear is reliable, that all wood (and other material liable to deterioration) is preserved for the ensuing year and that a well-cared-for appearance is given to the whole ship.

The owner of a grp, ferro-cement, or aluminium alloy hull may not be worried about preservation, but he will have to examine every part if he wants to keep out of trouble during the season, while painting and varnishing will crop up eventually unless the yacht is allowed to drift from Class (a) to (b), or from (b) to (c).

The cost of maintaining a Class (c) boat presents no problem at all, but numerous owners would like to know how to keep a class (b) appearance with the same low expenditure of time and money.

The first obstacle to this goal is, perhaps, adhering to the traditional idea (in Great Britain, Canada and large parts of the USA) of commencing fitting-out work as soon as Spring weather arrives.

Most yacht insurance policies run from April to September inclusive in commission, though the weather is often more suitable for sailing from May to October inclusive. Whichever system is preferred it only leaves a few weeks in March or April to complete all paintwork, as well as the other tasks which one rarely feels like doing in wintry weather.

This means that many owners are forced to hire labour or put some work in the hands of a boatyard in order to get to sea in reasonable time.

The first rule for cutting costs is therefore to do all the fitting-out work yourself. Forget the traditional routine and complete most of the painting and varnishing in October or November when the weather is usually far more suitable than in February and March. Treating the inside of the bilges should be

16

left around to the spring, to ensure a complete drying out, but most of the other chores (including engine work) can be done at leisure during suitable spells of weather in the winter.

Painting topsides in the autumn makes a big difference to the smartness of a boat as fenders rubbing newly applied paint can roughen the surface and cause a dirty appearance throughout the season.

The same thing applies to decks. If a thick layer of paint is applied to them two weeks before launching, the surface is sure to get ingrained with dirt and footprints before the craft is afloat. Even a mast is best varnished in the autumn so that it will not be marked when rigging is tied around it before being stepped in the spring.

Interior paintwork should also be done early on to ensure that there is no smell when next in commission, although an additive such as *Petal* will reduce the offensive odour. Some owners like to leave a certain amount of inside paintwork to do while on moorings during rough weather as there is normally much less condensation in May or June. This leaves only the bilges and perhaps the outside below the waterline to treat just prior to launching.

This reorganization of the traditional fitting-out procedure means that no hired labour should be necessary and more time can be found for achieving a really good Class (b) finish, costing very little more in materials than for Class (c).

There should be no deterioration in enamel or varnish work throughout the winter provided a craft is laid-up in a shed or well-covered-up outside.

When the latter course is adopted, however, all sheeting must be secured firmly to prevent it chafing against the topsides or rail. Such parts can always be touched-up in the spring if there are any marks. Where tarpaulin ropes are tied around a grp hull these must not be allowed to come loose and create chafe, as grp is not very resistant to abrasion and can become permanently scored.

There are other ways in which costs may be cut and time saved without recourse to Class (c) appearance. For instance, the cost of antifouling paint is high but quite variable, depending upon quality. As weed growth is not likely to be severe early in the season, the application of antifouling can be left until May or June so that even a cheap antifouling can be made to last through the most important months.

17

Although a Class (a) yacht invariably has a bright-coloured boot-top stripe around the waterline, Class (c) vessels simplify this by extending the antifouling to the upper boot-top level. There is no reason why a Class (b) boat should not copy this idea as a proper boot-top enamel is expensive and much time is needed to apply it properly. Red antifouling often looks best in this position and it requires no more frequent scrubbing than a normal boot-top to keep it looking bright.

Remember that weed always grows most prolifically close to the waterline where there is strong light, so you may be able to heel the vessel over a few degrees by shifting some ballast or by leading a halyard from the masthead to a distant anchor or mooring pile. If done in hot weather the surface will soon dry off especially if first douched with fresh water. On a 30 ft (9 m) yacht, the whole process of antifouling a strip one foot wide from the boot-top along one side can be done in an hour working from a dinghy with *guest warp* fore-and-aft.

Smartness

Some short cuts to economy can actually make the yacht look smarter. The varnished masts on old boats often appear discoloured with unsightly stains in the wood. Planing spars down to new wood is a big job and, unless one knows how many times this has been done before, serious weakness could result. Painted spars can look very attractive, especially when white, light gray, or pale ochre, so it may pay to adopt this method when rejuvenating an old craft.

Much the same applies to coamings and other brightwork. When these are made of mahogany instead of teak, the wood may become indelibly weather-stained due to neglect, so it may be wiser to paint this than to plane off the surface. Teak can nearly always be brought back like new by hard rubbing down, but with mahogany a layer of wood must be taken off.

Try to keep some varnish work as a relief from large expanses of paint. Many all-plastics yachts suffer from this defect and remind one of an operating theatre! Hatches, handrails, and small areas of trim are easy to keep in good condition when varnished, so these should be retained.

Many small cruisers and motor yachts have too much freeboard for good appearance and this fault can be lessened considerably by making the boot-top a little higher than usual and also by having a wide band of contrasting colour just

Picture 4.   Most pre-War power craft were slow with a tendency to roll, but good ones can be bought at a quarter the cost of fast modern counterparts.

below the sheer from stem to stern. Simple ideas such as this help to transform a boat from Class (c) to Class (b) inexpensively.

Some ways of reducing the amount of labour and therefore the cost involved in yacht maintenance have so far been discussed but if smartness is any consideration, some decorative work may be necessary. The narrow gold leaf or painted line along the sheer plank may take a little time to do properly but it does make a tremendous difference to the appearance of a yacht.

If there is no proper cove to house this line and prevent it being rubbed off, this can be formed on a planked hull by nailing a temporary batten in the correct position and running a moulding plane along it.

This cannot be done on a grp or metal hull although the gold leaf or painted line can be added by running two strips of masking tape the full length of the line and working in between these. If you do this, make sure that the topside enamel underneath is not too tender, or it may be pulled away in places when the masking tape is stripped off (see Chapter 4).

If you wish to find out what a narrow paint line would look like without wasting a lot of time, a reel of narrow coloured PVC tape can be used. This is self-adhesive and will last many months if carefully applied.

There are several other minor jobs which take little extra time, but make a big difference to smartness. For instance, where the deck paint is cut in along the numerous varnished parts and trim normally found on a yacht, many amateurs leave a ragged line which completely ruins the appearance.

Anyone with a shaky hand or in too much of a hurry would be wise to use one of those handyman sheet metal or cardboard shields as these avoid the need for care when cutting in to an edge. For perfect results, it pays to wipe the edge of the shield with a piece of rag occasionally during use. Without a shield, if surplus paint running over an edge is not wiped clean immediately with a turps-soaked rag, the answer is normally to let it harden and then touch up with the other colour. Where the other colour is varnish work, a touch-up paint to match can be mixed as described in Chapter 4.

If inexperienced ladies are called in to help out with the deck painting, much time and trouble can be saved by running masking tape along all the edges to be cut in!

On an old boat with galvanized deck and mast fittings, smartness can often be improved by giving these two coats of aluminium paint including pulpit; lifeline stanchions; tabernacle; rigging screws; windlass; ventilators, and fairleads. Some people dislike the appearance of aluminium paint and in this case one can use two coats of grey zinc rich paint such as *Galvanite* or *Metagalv,* though these are not so hard-wearing as aluminium paint.

Perhaps one of the best short cuts to economical maintenance is to remember the *stitch in time* proverb. If small areas of surface damage to paint and varnish are touched up rapidly moisture will not get into the wood and jeopardize the adhesion of larger areas, while future coatings will be more speedily applied.

Working on a boat is so much more pleasant in the summer than in some draughty shed with snow falling ouside, that it seems a pity that more owners do not forgo a bit of sailing to keep the yacht in good trim. Such chances may arise when one cannot find a suitable crew and in this way a vessel can be made to look her best at mid-season (perhaps during the annual holiday), while at laying-up time she will be little shabbier than when launched.

Do not forget that the interior of a cruising boat can also be classified (a), (b) and (c). Many of our modern mass-produced cruisers have very poor plywood joinery work below decks. The handyman who enjoys a bit of furniture making can easily renew the whole of this piece by piece, producing a Class (a) effect below, which is always a great pleasure to live with.

Counting the Cost

Although yachtsmen are told that grp yachts need no maintenance this is only true when they are new. After a time a well-built teak planked copper sheathed boat can prove cheaper to keep smart externally than a similar grp craft. In the tropics, plastics can be damaged by the continuous action of strong ultra-violet rays, so painting is then advisable from new.

Detailed schedules are given in Chapter 4 quoting typical amateur and boatyard maintenance costs for most types of construction over a period of years. The Table on p. 22 is a breakdown of the annual cost of owning fifteen different craft between 13 ft (4 m) and 60 ft (18 m) in length. Costs vary greatly from yard to yard and coast to coast but the prices shown are typical.

When a yacht requires a really major refit the cost of this would bear no relation to the annual upkeep costs shown in the Table. Labour costs at shipyards are major items when such work has to be done, and the impecunious amateur can save himself large sums if he is prepared to put in a lot of time.

It should never be forgotten that although nearly all modern yachts have stainless steel rigging and fittings, *Terylene* (Dacron) ropes controlled by beautifully made winches, and a load of expensive electronic equipment down below, the older methods and materials which were used with every success on small craft over a long period of time, are still suitable for use today. They are cheaper to make and maintain, but they may require more maintenance and keener attention during use.

Amongst these older items one could list galvanized rigging screws and wire rope; tackles instead of winches; hemp rope instead of Terylene; deadeyes and lanyards; ash blocks instead of *Tufnol* and stainless steel. In addition to this a good set of cotton sails, if well-cared-for, may well outlast Terylene and would not always require annual professional repair work to replace chafed stitching.

Although a modern grp boat may be cheap to fit-out, the annual loan interest on her capital cost might easily pay for the professional maintenance on an older wooden-hulled yacht,

21

TABLE 1
Typical Annual upkeep costs in U.K. and U.S.A.

Type of Boat (Lengths in feet and metres)	Insurance 12 months		Mooring (6 months)										Yard Storage (6 months) including slipping				Amateur Lay-up				Yard Refit (Including painting, rigging, cleaning, piping, engine check, stowage)		Amateur Refit (Including painting, cleaning, engine check, stowage)	
			Trailed to water		Pen ashore		Half tide		Deep water		Marina		Under cover		Open air		Mud berth		Trailed home					
	£	$	£	$	£	$	£	$	£	$	£	$	£	$	£	$	£	$	£	$	£	$	£	$
13ft (4) Runabout	12	70	3	10	20	45	5	12	20	32	—	—	22	40	10	15	—	—	1	2	12	100	2	10
14ft (4.3) Dinghy	8	40	3	10	20	45	5	14	20	35	—	—	24	40	10	15	—	—	1	2	17	115	3	15
17ft (5.2) Launch	12	50	5	12	22	50	6	25	30	40	80	200	35	60	15	20	5	10	1	3	24	140	5	25
18ft (5.5) Sloop	15	160	8	18	25	60	10	35	30	45	100	210	60	70	30	40	5	10	2	6	32	200	7	35
20ft (6) Outboard Cruiser	22	200	8	20	27	60	15	38	32	65	120	230	60	150	28	30	5	10	2	6	25	150	6	30
23ft (7) Aux. Sloop	38	250	—	—	30	75	22	40	35	82	130	270	80	200	44	60	6	12	10	40	66	320	10	50
25ft (7.6) Power Cruiser	40	300	—	—	35	75	26	60	38	90	150	300	75	220	40	54	10	15	12	50	70	340	18	90
27ft (8.2) Catamaran	36	320	—	—	—	—	37	85	80	120	200	450	140	470	80	100	20	30	—	—	65	310	17	85
30ft (9.2) T.S.M.Y.	50	480	—	—	—	—	30	65	45	100	170	350	105	360	50	75	13	15	50	150	90	500	20	100
36ft (11) Motor/sailer	55	500	—	—	—	—	35	70	47	140	190	420	150	400	62	85	16	20	70	250	110	620	26	130
38ft (11.6) Trimaran	55	600	—	—	—	—	40	100	110	250	260	550	230	850	110	150	30	40	—	—	120	660	30	150
40ft (12) Fast Cruiser	100	950	—	—	—	—	42	85	53	160	230	480	190	500	84	100	20	30	90	300	140	750	25	125
45ft (13.7) Ocean racer	90	1000	—	—	—	—	—	—	65	200	270	530	230	600	100	200	25	35	—	—	145	800	37	185
50ft (15) Motor/sailer	150	1400	—	—	—	—	—	—	74	240	300	590	280	700	125	250	30	40	—	—	170	950	45	225
60ft (18) T.S.M.Y.	250	2000	—	—	—	—	—	—	90	300	370	750	350	800	170	350	40	60	—	—	260	1300	60	300

Picture 5. Chafe on permanent shore-lines can be eliminated with the aid of plastics tubing, but chafe through fair-leads and over toe rails may cause more damage than around bollards.

Picture 6. Safety to the fore! Good stowage system for horseshoe lifebuoy. Guardrails high and safe. Anti-chafe tubing through fairlead.

when one prefers that type of vessel and has no time to do fitting-out oneself.

The important conclusion to be drawn from all the above information is that the practical yachtsman, who is willing to care for an unfashionable type of yacht, can own her for about one-half the capital cost and one-half the running cost of the norm for a modern craft which will do much the same job. Provided he does not become unpopular at home he should, in addition, derive much greater pleasure and satisfaction in the pursuit of his hobby.

Boat Care and Etiquette

The claws of bureaucracy have not yet completely enveloped sailing and if only more newcomers to the sport would train themselves sufficiently before taking part in it, the wonderful freedom permitted may yet be preserved.

Therefore, everyone concerned should endeavour to master the ways of the sea and encourage those in need of guidance. Particular attention should be given to *safety*, to ensure that the minimum demands are made on rescue services. Such incidents are invariably given much publicity and attract the

23

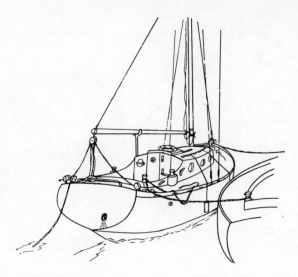

Drawing 1. If you want to annoy your neighbour or invite vandals, moor up like this. No springs. No shore lines. Fenders too small and too low. Halyards left slack. Topping lift too taut. Main sheet slack and trailing overboard. Boom not lashed to crutch. Warps not coiled down. Cabin unlocked. Compass, taffrail log, winch handles and lifebelt left out. No anti-chafe gear on warps or lanyards. No identification on transom.

attention of those who would like to bring in bureaucratic control.

It seems a pity that many more beginners to cruising do not sail for a few seasons with an experienced yachtsman before forsaking racing dinghies for decked craft. Unlike the dinghy owner, who just pulls her ashore and departs with his burgee still flying, the cruiser owner who wishes to receive the approval of the local pundits should carry out a careful routine before leaving his ship.

If a hurried disembarkation has to be made, it is essential that the ensign and burgee should be lowered; all mooring ropes properly adjusted; the tiller or wheel lashed amidships; the mainsheet belayed tightly; the boom scissors or crutch made fast and the topping-lift slacked well off.

When there is no hurry it should take at least 20 minutes to make a sailing cruiser shipshape after mooring up and, when doing so at the end of a cruise or a week-end, one hour is nearer the mark.

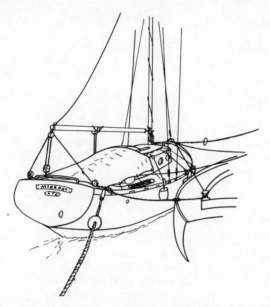

Drawing 2. The owner of this boat has a knowledge of seamanship. All the faults in Drawing 1 are rectified and he has a few additional ideas—effective cockpit cover rigged, shore lines have anti-rat discs, halyards are frapped round mast and falls coiled, plus fore and aft springs and full anti-chafe gear.

Frap the running rigging to the mast by winding the fall of the main halyard spirally around everything, or secure these ropes to the shrouds with shockcord. If you neglect this when you have a metal mast do not be surprised if you find a neighbouring yachtsman has done it for you in his pyjamas before he could attempt to get any sleep. Metal masts with electric wiring or halyards running inside them are also prone to rattles which may be very difficult to cure.

Having lowered the burgee, always hoist a short staff of dowelling or bamboo in its place to prevent seagulls roosting on the masthead and fouling the deck.

Although most of the above notes apply to sailing craft, there is a similar but simpler routine for power craft, sailing dinghies, and all open boats. When moored alongside another yacht, one must make sure that one's vessel is pointing the right way (against the ebb tide in most harbours, but in any case in the same direction as the other moored craft) and that adequate bow and stern warps are run ashore or to the mooring piles.

25

As well as breast ropes there must be two springs to keep the yacht in her station and relieve the breast ropes and fenders of undue load. All warps passing through fairleads should be wrapped around with old canvas or fed through polythene tubing to prevent chafe.

A bow fender should always be kept on board for use when at anchor or when on a swinging mooring with chain bridle. This prevents the chain from scraping the topsides at slack tide or during wind-against-tide conditions. Ordinary fenders for use when moored alongside must be of cylindrical shape and hung vertically. Square fenders (or old scooter tyres wrapped with canvas) cannot roll with the movements of the ship and soon roughen a shiny paint or glass fibre surface.

Check that all loose gear on deck is properly lashed, including the boathook, mop, anchors, boarding ladder, lifebuoys, whisker pole, etc. if you have time, coil down all spare ropes which are in view and make sure an inflated rubber dinghy is lashed to prevent her from taking off in a wind.

Unfortunately the incidence of thieving from yachts and using them without permission is on the increase, but much can be done by owners to mitigate this nuisance.

All open cockpits (even when self-draining) should have a waterproof cover fitted over a central ridge pole (or *strongback*) to ensure rainwater flows off. Such a cover is a nuisance to rig when departing, but a thief will think twice before attempting to find a way in. To do the job properly, one can make up waterproof covers to fit over all hatches, skylights, D/F aerials, radar scanners and even a wheelhouse.

The amateur who looks after his boat by himself will appreciate that all these covers not only ensure that the ship can be left secure and well-cared-for, but the varnish will be so well-preserved throughout the season that a minimum amount of work will be required at fitting-out time.

Any cruising yacht needs a good wash down after being at sea. The old hands will tell you that the decks should be washed with sea water, not fresh water, the reason being that any leakage through the deck will not tend to create rot below, as sea water is a mild disinfectant. However, fresh water must be used for the varnish work, windows, skylights and portlights, as sea water always leaves these smeary.

All rubbish should be taken ashore and not jettisoned overboard. Although it has always been customary to dispose

Picture 7. Quick release harness for circular lifebuoy mounted between twin backstays. Stern light on the same batten is at an ideal height. Neat cockpit cover with ridge pole.

Picture 8. By all means start 'em young, but remember personal buoyancy at all times plus a lifeline on short scope, when not under constant supervision.

of cooking waste overboard while at sea, great care should be taken not to dispose of polythene wrappers (and things that float for ever) in this manner. If glass jars and bottles have to be thrown overboard, they should always be filled with water beforehand.

A walk around the dinghy pen at a yacht club will reveal the lack of care shown by many owners of racing dinghies. Waterproof covers are left holding huge pools of rain water which discolour the material and put a great strain on the eyelets. Burgees are seen left at the masthead to wear themselves to bits needlessly in the wind.

Before sheeting over, a dinghy should always be hosed down after being at sea and the hull left on an incline to allow surplus water to drain away. Inspection ports to built-in buoyancy compartments should be left open occasionally and all sails, spare clothing and other wet gear should be taken home.

If the boom is arranged as a ridge pole for the waterproof cover, care should be taken to insert a sponge or other padding underneath where it rests on the deck, coamings, transom, or mainsheet track.

27

When it blows a gale, many sailing dinghies are knocked over and this hazard can often be mitigated by rigging old motor car tyres under the chines or the turn of the bilges. When ashore, the masts on many modern sailing dinghies are unshipped and laid on a rack in the dinghy pen. This is a very secure idea, provided the racks are properly designed and carefully used.

Dinghies

Most cruising yachts require a dinghy to serve as a tender. Inflatable rubber dinghies are becoming popular for this duty, as they are so easy to stow aboard for long cruises when deflated. However, the old traditional clinker dinghy and its more modern counterparts in grp or moulded wood, are still preferred by many owners.

All tenders other than rubber ones must have an all-round fender. You will not be welcome aboard other peoples' vessels unless you have this and you are likely to get ostracised at a club if you moor a fenderless dinghy at the pontoon to chafe the sides of the other dinghies during a high water lop! An all-round fender should extend over the top of the gunwale as well as around the sides. Rubber dinghies have the great advantage of needing no such protection.

To prevent the loss of ordinary rowlocks (crutches), they must be equipped with lanyards made fast around the thwart by looping through a large soft eye spliced at the bitter end. Remember that the lanyard must be spliced to the recessed neck of the rowlock not to the little hole at the end of the shank. This little hole is provided for wiring a pair of rowlocks together when hung up on the wall of a shed.

Lanyards are useful also to wind around the oars when going ashore for a short spell. Do not forget to keep a dry swab in the dinghy for wiping the thwarts, especially when there are ladies aboard.

Safety

Safety in small open boats is always of prime importance and lives have been lost through overloading a dinghy on a dark night.

In case a dinghy should go adrift – or for more mundane reasons – a name-plate is absolutely essential. This should be marked with the name of the parent yacht and the initials of one's Yacht Club, though an address or telephone number is even more useful. Numerous small runabouts exist with no means of identification whatsoever, making them ideal prey for thieves. Many large cruising vessels have no clearly visible name-plate, and such behaviour only expedites bureaucratic control.

Some cruising yachts display their name in huge letters painted on canvas dodgers attached to the guardrails alongside the cockpit. This may be admirable from the ocean racing viewpoint, but permanent dodgers ruin the appearance of many a handsome craft. They should only be used at sea during rough weather as they limit visibility from the cockpit (especially when the boat is heeling) and a good lookout at all times is imperative for safety at sea. Dodgers can be made with transparent panels.

A grp or alloy yacht's tender will sink without trace unless equipped with buoyancy (see Chapter 11) and there should be hand grips fitted to the bottom in case of a capsize. Nearly all cruising yachts need hinged or rigid steps on the transom or rudder to enable a person (perhaps fatigued) to climb out of the water or out of a dinghy without assistance. Further notes on safety are included in several of the subsequent chapters.

Most people take to the water for peace, quiet and relaxation, so always try to limit unnecessary noise. Try rowing out to the mooring late at night instead of using the outboard motor. Choose the right moment for operating the generating plant, watch the tinkling metal spars and keep the transistor radio below decks.

When visiting other people's boats, make certain you are wearing deck shoes. If you happen to have walking shoes on, remove them even if the owner says it does not matter.

Make the effort to learn about the use of flags at sea, especially before you attempt to go foreign. Some newcomers to sailing take years to learn all the necessary etiquette, while others master it in one season. Try to do it the latter way and you will find yourself welcomed everywhere you sail.

CHAPTER 2

TOOLS AND MATERIALS

Although many people nowadays do painting and repair work around the house, in most instances the family tool-kit is a disgraceful example of neglect. The all too familiar sight includes paint brushes with rock hard bristles left in jam jars from which the water or turps has long since evaporated; a saw red with rust; a screwdriver mangled by years of opening crates and cans of paint; a wire brush with bristles crumbling into a heap of red dust.

One cannot do good work with tools in this condition and it pays to allow a little time after the completion of any job, to clean, sharpen, or oil and put away any tools which have been used. Few tools are needed for normal yacht maintenance work, but tools make excellent anniversary gifts and it usually pays to keep adding to the tool kit throughout one's life.

The primary tool kit should, perhaps, consist of the following items:

(1) A set of good quality paint brushes of widths $\frac{1}{2}$ in (12 mm), $1\frac{1}{2}$ in (37 mm), and $2\frac{1}{2}$ in (62 mm). Extra brushes are useful in case any helpers come along. You may also want a paint roller.
(2) 1 lb (450 g) claw hammer and one of those plastics wallets containing a few nail punches and a small cold chisel.
(3) One pair of pliers with wire cutting jaws.
(4) Cabinet screwdriver with $\frac{1}{4}$ in (6 mm) wide tip.
(5) An 8 in (200 mm) smooth flat file with handle.
(6) A 6 ft (2 m) spring rule.
(7) A Junior hacksaw.
(8) A Skarsten scraper, bradawl, putty knife, long-handled scrubber, and cork rubbing block.
(9) For a steel hull, a chipping hammer and wire brush.

Picture 9. A minor engine tool kit as illustrated is normally carried on board by the do-it-yourself enthusiast. The range of tools depends on the size and type of engine. For the unpractical yachtsman a tool kit is still necessary for emergency repairs. A competent helper might come along but he may not be carrying a tool kit with him.

Much useful work can be done with these few tools and the manner in which the range needs increasing should be apparent well before the first launching date, according to the type of craft and the limits of the owner's enthusiasm. If the intention is to burn off paint, caulk seams and carry out alterations or additions to the joinery work, or to the deck and rigging fittings, a proper carpentry tool kit including a plane (or *Stanley Shaper*), panel saw, hand drill, small ratchet brace, tenon saw, sets of chisels and drills, mallet, tool bag, cramps, pincers, oilstone, oilcan, marking gauge, try square, caulking irons, spirit level, blowlamp (with prickers and nipple key), and a stripping knife.

The engine tool kit can be divided into two separate sections. The first kit is intended to cater for normal running adjustments and minor repairs and is still supplied with certain makes of marine engine when new, though rarely seen in the world of automobiles nowadays.

The minimum contents should consist of:

(1) A full set of open-ended spanners and box spanners (with tommy bars) to fit all nuts and bolts on the engine, including spark plugs.

(2) One small and one large adjustable spanner.

(3) Screwdrivers with $\frac{3}{16}$ in (4 mm) and $\frac{5}{16}$ in (7 mm) tips.

(4) A $1\frac{1}{2}$ lb (680 g) ball-paned hammer with a set of punches, drifts and centre punch.

(5) Some small tools including carburettor jet keys, magneto or distributor tools, feeler gauges for contacts and spark plugs, and a pair of pliers.

(6) The kit should also contain an oilcan, a little graphite grease, and jointing compounds such as *Osotite* and *Hermetite*.

For more serious engine work including top overhauls, sump removal and pipe work, the following items should be added:

(1) A full set of socket spanners to fit all nuts and bolts. A torque wrench to fit these can probably be borrowed when required.

(2) A full set of ring spanners to cover the same range as above.

(3) A 10 in (250 mm) Mole (Elmo) grip.

(4) Two Stillson wrenches, one 10 in (250 mm) and one 18 in (450 mm).

(5) A full set of keys for Allen recessed-head screws.

(6) A hammer with one copper face and one hard rubber face.

(7) A full set of feeler gauges, a cold chisel with $\frac{1}{2}$ in (12 mm) tip.

(8) An assortment of files including a few warding and needle files and the necessary handles.

(9) One or two bearing scrapers.

(10) A blowlamp or blow-torch, with equipment for soft and silver soldering.

(11) A 12 in (300 mm) steel rule, to serve also as a straight-edge.

(12) A valve lifting tool, a valve turning tool, and a supply of grinding paste.

(13) A $\frac{1}{2}$ in (12 mm) 2-speed breast drill with a full set of twist drills, and a small can of cutting compound.

(14) A small roll of 1 in (25 mm) wide emery tape, Grade 0.

(15) Two wire brushes, one two-row and one four-row.

(16) A 10 in (250 mm) hacksaw with spare blades.

(17) A pair of small long-nosed pliers, metal shears, pairs of internal and external circlip pliers.

(18) A bench with fitter's vice (and fibre jaws), a 4 in (100 mm) hand operated grinder with fine grade emery wheel, and a chunk of cast steel (such as an old diesel engine crankshaft balance weight) to use as an anvil.

The Bosun's Store

Unless all the above tools are kept on board, any yacht larger than a dinghy should have its own tool kit in the bosun's store to serve all duties at sea from unscrewing shackles and touching up paintwork to clearing away a broken mast or sealing a leak below the waterline.

The minimum tools to be kept on board a 30 ft (9 m) cruiser would be approximately as follows:

(1) Carpentry tools including a hammer and a saw, two screwdrivers, a small hand drill with wallet of suitable drill bits, a 4 in (100 mm) G-cramp, wood rasp, rule.

(2) Metal working tools. Assuming you keep the engine maintenance tool kit listed above on board, you would need in addition a junior hacksaw, oilcan, large Stillson wrench, $2\frac{1}{2}$ lb (1 kg) club hammer, cold chisel with $\frac{1}{2}$ in (12 mm) wide tip, an assortment of files, and, if possible, a portable vice.

(3) Miscellaneous tools. Large yachts often carry a small axe and a pair of bolt croppers on board, to be used for cutting away a broken mast. There should always be a sharp knife, two shackle keys, several funnels, small and large marline spikes, a fid, a roll of heavy PVC tape and a sail repair kit (see Chapter 8). An assortment of paint brushes may also be carried.

For each of the three sections of tools listed above a range of materials and spare parts will also be required on board. With the carpentry tools should be small cans containing as wide a variety of marine screws, nails, roves, tacks, screw eyes and screw hooks as possible. Then there should be a range of oddments of wood, including some small sheets of marine plywood, one or two 3 ft (1 m) lengths of 2 in (50 mm) × 1 in (25 mm) and 6 in (150 mm) × 1 in (25 mm) pine, an assortment of hardwood chocks and wedges.

In the metal working department there should be small cans (all labelled) containing a wide range of steel and fibre washers, nuts, bolts, set screws, split pins, hose clips, packing for stern gland and pumps. In addition to these things, one requires a roll of 24-gauge (0·6 mm) sheet copper for making tingles,

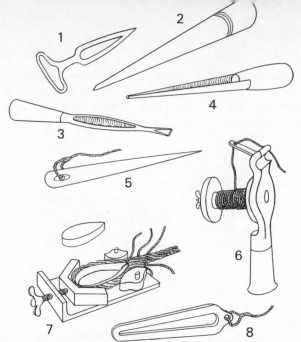

Drawing 3. Some common and some unusual rigger's tools:
1. The Easy Splice made by Brookes and Adams. Tucks can be passed with tool left through the lay.
2. Lignum vitae fid. Essential for splicing big ropes, also for fitting thimbles.
3. Wire rope spike. Similar in action to the Easy Splice but flat tip gets through stiff wire lay easily.
4. Swedish Shell Spike. Same idea. Is normally big enough to tackle cordage of any size.
5. Steel marline spike. Traditional, heavy, and dangerous!
6. Patent Serving Board. Essential for veterans with stockholm tar running through their veins! Saves an extra hand to pass the ball of spunyarn when serving long runs.
7. Riggers' clamps. Can be home-made with adjustment for big range of wire-rope eye sizes. Without a thimble, the separate heart is placed inside the eye.
8. Shackle key. If standard size will not fit your big anchor shackle, a marline spike should do it. A lanyard is essential to prevent loss overboard. Will not float!
some small pieces of brass shim, some coils of copper wire from 8-gauge (4 mm) to 20-gauge (1 mm), a roll of emery tape, some sheets of *Hallite* (or similar jointing material) $\frac{1}{32}$ in (0·8 mm) and $\frac{1}{16}$ in (1·5 mm) thick, some sheet cork $\frac{1}{8}$ in (3 mm) thick, a roll of asbestos tape, and a large quantity of rag.

In the miscellaneous department aim towards a supply of abrasive paper; some lengths of shockcord; rolls of old canvas and sail-cloth; small quantities of all paints and varnishes for touching-up work, a few pieces of leather, a variety of corks, a lot of spare rope, some rigging wire, spare shackles, rigging screws, thimbles, wire rope grips, some trowel cement for stopping, a ball of caulking cotton, spools of whipping twine, marline, sail thread, codline, some Vaseline, anhydrous lanolin, turps, raw linseed oil, spare butane cylinder and Primus prickers.

All the above items are, of course, in addition to distilled water, the usual oils and greases for engine and sterntube, and the supply of spare parts appertaining to engine; pumps; electrical and radio equipment, stoves, refrigerator, and all the other complicated apparatus which abounds on our sophisticated modern yachts. Last but not least, always keep a suit of overalls on board in case a dirty job has to be done in a hurry.

In the Workshop

Few things are more infuriating than to find during the precious weekend of leisure that the supply of turps has run out, or that there is no fuel for the blow-torch. Most of the materials needed are not expensive and it pays to keep a fairly large supply of everything in the home workshop to avoid disappointing delays.

As well as keeping often-used materials in old lemonade bottles on a shelf, it proves wise in addition to keep half-gallon (2 litre) cans of turps, linseed oil, petrol (gasolene), paint remover, washing detergent or bilge cleaner, meths (alcohol), cellulose thinners, trichloroethylene (or other degreasing agent), and any other liquids which one likes to have ready at hand.

Note that cellulose thinners make an excellent brush cleaner for use with all types of paint, but if one habitually uses polyurethane paints or grp materials, it would be as well to have a supply of acetone or other recommended cleaner. The owner of a steel-built yacht may wish to keep phosphoric acid (*Jenolite*) or other rust removers and inhibitors.

Also in the liquid department comes the question of paint. To minimize the range held, it proves wise to decide from the outset on a certain paint maker and whether one proposes to stick to the cheaper *alkyd* paints or to go for the more expensive but longer-lasting *catalyst* materials.

If the ordering of top coats is left until fitting-out time, there may be difficulty in obtaining the shades required locally so try to obtain these well in advance. The same applies to anti-fouling paints and, to a lesser extent, to varnish, primers, sealers, undercoats, black varnish, bitumastic paints, fillers,

35

stoppers and bedding compound. The owner of a smart new craft may require only top coat and varnish for some years while other owners will need to keep the full range of materials. Dinghy owners may want special graphite paint for use on centreboard, rudder and bottom.

When a hull has to be stripped down to bare wood, a little shellac varnish (knotting) will be required to seal off all knots prior to priming. For treating stripped aluminium alloy a special self-etching primer helps while each paint maker has his own specification for treating steel.

Any yacht chandler will advise on the choice of an anti-fouling paint, but it should be remembered that antifouling containing metallic copper cannot be used on alloy hulls or in the presence of galvanized underwater fittings.

Buying paint in bulk is not always an ecomony as once a large can has been opened it may lead to wastage due to skinning. This problem can be obviated by decanting the paint into smaller cans when the large one is opened for the first time. When washed and dried, empty air-tight cans as used for syrup and molasses are ideal for holding paint and varnish.

A large roll of 1 in (25 mm) wide masking tape should always be kept in the workshop. This is most useful for labelling containers of paint, fluids, screws, nails and other materials. A strip of the tape should be run right around the container to ensure that it will not come adrift even when left in the moist atmosphere on board a yacht.

The contents may be written on the tape with a ball-point pen or crayon. Try to avoid using undecipherable codes or abbreviations which no one else can understand. This may prove awkward one day when you require a friend to hunt for something. Never have any containers in the workshop without labels, as this is important for safety reasons.

The list of materials which different yachtsmen hoard goes on indefinitely. For some craft you may require a book of gold leaf plus a little Japan goldsize adhesive. Aluminium paint is useful for keeping galvanized fittings looking smart and the owner with laid teak decks will require caulking cotton or oakum, marine glue with ladle or a supply of one of the more modern synthetic rubber caulking compounds such as PRC. You may like to keep a stock of *Teak-Brite* on board to ensure that your scrubbed teak decks always look smart.

In case of canvased decks it may be wise to keep a supply of

Picture 10.   Using a butane torch for burning off paint. For such an infrequent job it may pay to hire this equipment. The torch weighs little and will stay alight in a breeze, but several small gas bottles often prove easier to transport than one heavy one.

Picture 11.   To burn off the bottom of a big boat, a flame gun as used for weed destruction works at great speed. A second operator with the long handled scraper is essential to keep pace with the gun.

mastic cement (e.g. *Polyseamseal*), also perhaps some spare canvas and copper tacks for repairs. A supply of matching non-slip deck paint will certainly be required at home, if not also on board.

Note that where decks (or below the waterline) have been nylon sheathed with the *Cascover* Process, a special vinyl paint may have been used and a supply of this ought to be kept. For grp sheathed decks and hulls a small amount of matching resin for patching-up marks and damage is needed, while for a craft built entirely in grp a fair sized repair kit consisting of some sheets of chopped strand mat, some cellophane, polyester resin (with catalyst, accelerator, and colour pigment) and some glass fibre putty should be kept. A *Stanley Shaper* or a *Surform Plane* is useful for cutting down to a smooth surface after using these materials or epoxy stopping.

If you recover your decks with *Trakmark* or a similar plastics material, always keep the offcuts and some adhesive to use for any future repairing. Excellent liquid plastics coatings (such as Dekaplex) are now available for use on canvas, plywood, and old planked decks. A supply of the correct shade is useful to keep, and a small amount is handy on board to enable the *stitch-in-time* motto to be fulfilled.

For maintaining a very old boat supplies of *Black Rubber Sheathing* and *Fibrous Caulking Composition* should help in eliminating leaks (see Chapter 3).

One must never run out of abrasive paper for rubbing down varnish and paintwork. This should always be of the wet-or-dry type (w.o.d.) as the cheaper varieties absorb moisture under marine conditions and are then useless when needed. Grit numbers of about 180 and 250 will cover most needs in w.o.d. paper. When used with water and a little soap each sheet lasts at least five times as long as ordinary sandpaper and some of the coarse sheets may be kept after use as they will then serve again for fine rubbing work.

Racing dinghy owners who use graphite paint may need some 500 grit paper for burnishing the surface. This will also be needed for removing blemishes on polyurethane or grp gel coats prior to polishing.

Some people prefer to use stripper blocks instead of abrasive paper. These are used wet and one fine and one medium grade block should last a year.

Miscellaneous Items

Ladies' nylon stockings are ideal for straining paint and varnish, a process which is well worth while when a can has been opened more than once or whenever a skin, however thin, has been formed on the surface. With the supply of nylons there should be a few large rubber bands as these are ideal for securing the stocking over the top of the empty can or paint kettle.

Few amateurs ever use a proper *paint kettle* made of galvanized iron with a nice handle. Most of us prefer to use empty food cans for holding in the hand while painting (and for holding turps for cleaning out brushes) as these can be thrown away after use instead of having to be cleaned out. Therefore, always keep a cardboard box full of clean empty food cans.

Remember *Big* brush, *Big* can, or the bristles will be spread out every time the brush is dipped in. When a new can is brought from the house into the workshop, check that the inside of the rim is clear of those sharp pieces of metal which some can openers leave. For safety reasons it is advisable to knock these down with a ball-paned hammer before use.

An adequate supply of old rags is a must. Non-absorbent materials such as nylon and rayon are absolutely useless for rags so one needs to be quite choosy. A few pieces of old towelling should always be kept for the special purpose of washing down after rubbing with w.o.d. paper.

While on the subject of rags the question of what to wear while messing about on a boat should perhaps be mentioned. The ideal is to have three separate outfits. The first can be quite smart, to be used around the home during the odd carpentry jobs; when sharpening and cleaning tools; preparing materials to take down to the boat; or for jobs like rope splicing or canvas sewing. Wearing this rig you will not look too much of a tramp should a friend call unexpectedly.

The No 2 outfit should be composed of garments that will not matter too much if marked with paint or grease. This will be the rig most often worn when working on a dinghy at home or on a larger yacht in a mudberth or shed. These clothes can be things you enjoy wearing as they may be the ones most often used. From the practical viewpoint a navy-blue boiler suit is ideal if you feel comfortable in overalls. A white boiler suit is smarter but shows dirt marks rather easily.

The No 3 rig is only for use when cleaning bilges; applying antifouling paint; or cleaning down the engine. Naturally, No 1 clothes can be relegated to No 2 when too old, and eventually items from the No 2 set can go to No 3. Rubber soled canvas deck shoes are ideal wear for most jobs on or around a boat.

If your craft is laid-up in a shed with earth floor or in a mudberth, an old pair of canvas shoes can be secreted within reach of the boarding ladder so that a change from rubber boots to these can be made on arrival. Well-worn deck shoes have the advantage of not holding dirt in the non-slip sole. Trousers (pants) should never have turn-ups (cuffs) as these catch on cleats unexpectedly and are positively dangerous. Creams such as *Rozalex* are useful when working with resins to prevent skin diseases and, as these creams are applied before work starts, they prevent hands looking grimy for weeks after undertaking very dirty jobs.

A small container of *Swarfega* or similar hand cleanser is ideal to rub into greasy hands before washing. An additional container of soft soap will ensure that hands can be cleaned to perfection even in cold sea water, before leaving for home or having a meal.

An item so far not listed, though absolutely essential, is an ordinary household bucket. This should be of large size to enable it to be used for carrying tools and materials. Although the plastics type is nice to handle, a galvanized one has the enormous advantage that it can be used for heating water by using a blow-torch on the outside. Perhaps the ideal way is to have one of each type which will fit snugly one inside the other.

The steel bucket is best for washing down decks, for when equipped with a lanyard for lifting water from overboard, its weight makes it capsize easily on hitting the water. Where a plastics bucket is used in this way it floats about on the water unless thrown very precisely. A canvas bucket is ideal for holding tools and parts when working aloft on a bosun's chair, or when shopping (see Chapter 8).

The list of miscellaneous items one requires might never end if one incorporated all the peculiar things which people hoard. The requirements depend largely upon the size and type of yacht concerned. Although a dinghy requires almost the same list of tools and materials for annual painting and varnishing as a medium size cruising yacht, the latter must naturally demand a much longer list of equipment to cater for work below decks, engine, caulking, ballast, etc.

A few brief items which one may consider worth keeping handy are as follows: A sheet of 22-gauge (0.77 mm) sheet steel or tin plate for making protective shields for varnish work when burning off paint; two or three funnels to assist in decanting liquids: various Aerosol cans (containing such things as touch-up paint, rust inhibitor, lacquer for brass and chromed fittings, moisture inhibitor for engine ignition systems, releasing oil, and ether for starting obstinate engines in cold weather); eye shield and nose filter to wear when using a power sander or spraying paint; one of those metal shields to use when cutting in an awkward paint line; industrial gloves for handling pigs of ballast; tack-rags for dusting off before varnishing; grinding paste; resin glue; oxalic acid; neatsfoot oil for treating leather; caustic soda for boiling out exhaust systems; naphtha for cleaning black varnish brushes.

Care of Tools
Although every handyman knows that good work cannot be done with tools in poor condition most of us are occasionally guilty of allowing insufficient time at the end of a job for

Drawing 4. A few useful home made tools:

1 & 2. Bent and straight scrapers made from old files.

3. Long drill bit. Many sizes can be made as and when needed from old car brake rods or silver steel rod.

4. Serving board. No need for a shaped head as marline can be rove through the holes to get correct tension.

5. Paint or resin mixing paddle to fit in drill chuck. Use a narrower paddle for a high speed electric drill; bigger paddle for a hand drill.

6. Sheath knife made from old power hacksaw blade.

7. Paint brush with extended handle. Useful in bilges, underneath ballast keel, or behind bilge keels.

8. Wooden box for oilstone. A rubber band will keep lid in place when a sloppy fit.

9. Chisel scabbard. Looks silly, but is more convenient than a canvas wrapper and rubber band. Prevents injuries as well as protecting the tip.

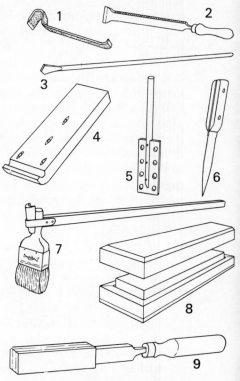

cleaning and sharpening tools. Luckily most of this work can be done at home to avoid wasting precious time while actually on board, but the owner who trails his yacht or dinghy to the house for the winter has no excuses in this respect.

If brushes are carefully wrapped around with rag after painting or varnishing, they may be kept for several hours before cleaning. If they are left too long and are found to be stiff, cleaning can often be done quite effectively by using hot turps, but do not use a naked flame for heating it. Cellulose thinners can also be tried. Should a brush be too hard for this treatment submersion in paint remover or a special brush cleaner will have to be used.

If *catalyst* paints are used, brush cleaning should be carried out without delay as once such materials have hardened the brush must be thrown away. Cleaning is necessary every half-hour when painting in hot weather.

The advice given to amateurs on the care of brushes is often confusing. Most instructions on the subject tell you to drill a little hole through the thick part of the handle. After use the brush is wiped out, a short piece of wire is pushed through the hole and the brush can then be suspended into a pot full of brush cleaner with the tips of the bristles clear of the bottom. When there is no hole, a spring clothes peg may be used to balance a brush at the side of the pot.

In this manner sludge collects at the bottom of the can while the bristles are not distorted by the weight of the brush.

Although this is an excellent method to use for storing brushes overnight (using thinned varnish in the case of the varnish brush, or turps for paint), cleaning a brush out completely after use is so easy that it would seem prudent always to do this.

It just needs a little training to allow time for it, remembering that a $\frac{1}{2}$ in (12 mm) brush takes 2 minutes to clean, a 2 in (50 mm) takes 5 minutes and a 4 in (100 mm) 10 minutes. There are two excellent ways of cleaning brushes;–

(1) By using numerous sheets of newspaper. Pour a little turps on to the brush while held on the paper and work the brush vigorously as though painting all over the top sheet. When the brush is almost dry, discard the wetted sheets of newspaper and repeat the process with some fresh turps several times until no more colour washes out. Cleaning the roots of the bristles can be assisted by slapping the brush on to the surface.

(2) Pour about 1 in (25 mm) of turps into an empty can and press the bristles firmly into this many times in different directions. Wipe the bristles with a rag applying a considerable pressure to the roots of the bristles and then repeat the washing process in fresh turps. Continue washing and wiping until all trace of colour disappears.

Either of these methods ensures that brushes are always in first class condition and ready to use for any change of colour. To complete the job properly all turps should be removed by washing the brushes twice in warm water with soap or detergent, finishing with clean water and a few quick flicks of the wrist before leaving in a warm room to dry.

Although turps is the most often used brush cleanser, others such as *Polyclens* may be advantageous. The 'turpentine' used for paintwork nowadays is always *white spirit* or *turps substitute*. When using ordinary marine varnish a 50/50 mixture of turps and raw linseed oil should always be used for the initial cleaning as turps causes the varnish in the bristles to congeal into a myriad tiny particles which emerge on the next surface you varnish as minute hard *nibs*. Once the initial wash in linseed/turps mixture has been completed subsequent washing out of the bristles can be done with neat turps.

It should not be unusual to make a good quality brush last for ten years using the above treatment and old brushes are often better than new ones. If brushes are kept in cardboard boxes the outer bristles will not become damaged.

Some yachtsmen like to keep a special brush for varnish but this should not be necessary if all brushes are properly cleaned. Although various types of brush can be bought (such as round, oval, flitches, wall brushes) most amateurs make do successfully with standard flat ones. A long-handled tar brush may prove useful at times. If the handle of a brush should break, do not discard it, as by screwing the stock to the end of a 2 ft (600 mm) piece of batten at right angles, you can make a useful tool for painting underneath the keel or behind bilge keels.

People who are not prepared to look after brushes as detailed above should buy cheap brushes and throw them away after use. However this is a retrograde method, as good quality brushes are so much easier to use and they produce superior results.

New brushes of the modern vulcanized and resin-set type should not need soaking in water before use. It pays to stroke a new brush over a clean brick wall to remove any loose bristles.

New brushes in the sizes $\frac{1}{2}$ in (6 mm) to $1\frac{1}{2}$ in (37 mm) often work best with half the bristle length bound around with masking tape or twine, especially where edges have to be cut in. This method has the added advantage of making brush cleaning quicker, and it lessens the possibility of paint hardening in the roots through incorrect cleaning. The binding must be tight and must be removed after use.

It takes a lot of turps or other fluid to keep brushes properly cleaned and one needs to keep a good sized can of this rather than relying on those little 8 oz (220 ml) bottles sold by hardware stores. Kerosene (lamp oil) will sometimes serve for cleaning brushes, and is cheaper.

Great economy with turps can be effected by storing used turps in a separate container. Most of the paint particles form a sludge at the bottom after standing for a week and fluid decanted from the top can be used repeatedly for brush cleaning leaving new turps for the final wash. A new container is advisable once a year to eliminate all the sludge. This economy can be extended by having a further container of even dirtier turps for cleaning brushes which have been used for dark colours or bitumastics.

Paint rollers demand a lot of care in cleaning and, because of the trouble involved, they are only worth using when much time can be saved covering a large surface area. Although the more expensive lambswool or moquette rollers are the nicest to use, the cheap plastics foam rollers may be discarded after use and many amateurs prefer to do this.

To clean a good quality roller the simplest way is to wipe the sloping tray used to hold the paint and then use successive doses of turps in this with a rolling action and hard pressure, wiping off each time by rolling on sheets of newspaper or with rag held in the hand. When all traces of colour have disappeared the roller should be cleaned in warm water and detergent as for a brush.

Little maintenance is required for the majority of the tools listed earlier in this chapter but care is needed to keep them clean and free from rust. This process is simplified considerably if all tools are kept in proper tool boxes as VPI paper (such as *Banrust*) can then be inserted to inhibit rust. Remember to replace this twice a year.

Tools having a sharp edge such as planes, knives and chisels must always be kept sharpened on the oilstone to ensure that they are ready for immediate use. It pays to keep planes and chisels wrapped with pieces of old canvas to protect the edges though special moulded caps are made to fit over the tips of chisels.

If the grinding angle is maintained correctly on a grinding wheel only a few strokes on the oilstone are necessary to hone the tips correctly. The amateur is recommended to use a honing gauge to ensure that the angle is correct and not rounded. Always keep the oilstone in one of those special boxes made for the purpose. Use light machine oil rather than heavy lubricating oil and wipe the stone with a piece of old rag before putting it away.

Skarsten and triangular paint scrapers need to be kept razor sharp to the original bevel using a fine warding file or the coarse surface of a combination oilstone. Wrap them in canvas

Picture 12. When sharpening a Skarsten scraper keep the grinding angle exactly as on a new blade. A fine file is essential to avoid wasting the metal and finishing with a carborundum stone will make a perfect job.

to avoid accidents and remember to keep a few spare hooks (blades) for the Skarsten.

A little care may be needed in the way paints and other materials are stored. To avoid a skin forming on the surface of paint or varnish while stored, some people leave the can upside down. This is not a very good idea because once a can has been opened a skin is sure to form and it proves wiser to have this on top where it can be cut around with a knife and removed in one piece. On no account should skin be stirred up with the paint and this is sure to happen when a can is stored upside down. Vacuum sealers are available to remove the air from partly filled cans, thus preventing the formation of a skin.

Home Made Tools
Many useful tools can be made at home at zero cost and some handymen become quite enthusiastic about this. Old flat files can be made into excellent scrapers for rough work, while the tangs of files can also be formed into useful shapes especially as raking hooks for removing old caulking cotton from seams. To shape the files in this way the metal must first be heated to bright red and hammered into any desired shape while still hot.

When the steel has cooled, a scraper tip may be ground to a 25° bevel. The tip must then be tempered or it will soon get blunt during use. To do this the metal is made dead hard by heating to bright red and quenching in water. Then make a bright area on the tip by rubbing with emery paper and heat the tip slowly in the cool part of a gas flame. The bright piece of metal will be seen to change in colour through amber to deep straw to blue. When it reaches straw colour immediately quench in a can of cold water held close by. If the flame is too vicious and the colouration uneven return the metal to the dead hard condition and try again with a cooler flame.

Many tools can be fabricated in this way but you must use tool steel, not ordinary mild steel as often found in bolts and reinforcement rods. Suitable metal can be obtained from old automobile parts such as valves, gear box shafts and king pins.

Extended drill bits can be made from wire wheel spokes and brake rods by hammering a spade shape on to the tip while red hot and then grinding this with a 120° 'V' on the end. Layshafts and loom spindles can be turned into screwdrivers, bearing scrapers and punches.

Lawn mower blades can be cut to form the ends of triangular (and other shape) paint scrapers, while scrapers to deal with hollowed cove lines around the sheer can be fashioned by sharpening the tips of old egg spoons! Excellent sheath knives can be fabricated from thick power hacksaw blades, the handle being formed by riveting pieces of hardwood on either side, duly rounded off.

From various sorts of timber one can make such things as caulking and carpenter's mallets, cramps, tool handles, serving boards and a bosun's chair, while the handles from old dish mops should not be thrown away as with the heads cut off they make excellent paint stirrers. Another most useful tool is a bench hook which rests on the edge of the bench and supports strips of wood when sawing them off to length.

If one likes to make use of the sail repair kit in the bosun's store, useful items such as canvas buckets, fenders, and tool bags can be sewn up from the offcuts of canvas sometimes available from sailmakers, upholsterers, and awning makers as explained in Chapter 8.

Numerous other small items can be home made. A simple paint mixing paddle to fit into an electric drill is useful, especially when large quantities of resin are to be mixed for sheathing. If a marine engine or outboard motor is to be stripped down at home, a stand of convenient height can be fabricated in wood or angle steel.

Power Tools

All normal boat and maintenance work can be accomplished without the need for any power tools. It will certainly be advisable for the amateur of limited means to invest in a complete kit of hand tools before considering power tools. Electricity is not always available where a yacht is laid-up, but it proves handy to have, at least, lighting and the use of a vacuum cleaner.

An electric drill of $\frac{3}{8}$ in (9 mm) capacity is always a useful tool for the handyman especially when equipped with a drill stand to fit on the bench, plus a *thyristor* variable speed control and other attachments. For engine overhauls a set of wire brushes and burrs is handy for decarbonizing while a large size wire brush wheel is useful for cleaning off iron ballast and rusty steelwork.

However, the popular disc sanding attachment is not a good tool to use for rubbing down paint and varnish work as it leaves whorl marks which show up on a glossy surface. The orbital sander attachments tend to be rather slow in use and generally speaking a rub down by hand with w.o.d. paper is better. Always keep the chuck key attached to the cable by means of a short length of light chain, or much time may be lost in hunting for it.

If rubbing down must be done by power, a 4 in (100 mm) belt sander should be hired for a day. If electricity is not available it may be possible to hire a portable generating set. Other useful items of equipment which can be hired include a paint sprayer, butane or propane torch, flame gun, electric paint stripper, shot blasting equipment, or a space heater.

Other rarely used tools can sometimes be hired from friends or perhaps from a boatyard. Such tools might include stud extractors, taps, dies, reamers, a torque wrench and a nut breaker for engine repairs, plus things like a blowlamp, sealer gun, serving mallet, electric drill, or eyelet closing tools.

When using power tools at a boatyard, remember to check whether the supply is correct, as some yards work at lower voltages to eliminate accidents. Naturally one must obtain permission to use yard tools and equipment and any item borrowed should be cleaned and returned promptly.

CHAPTER 3

SURFACE PREPARATION AND CAULKING

Even the owner of a so-called maintenance-free cruiser or dinghy is sure to have to prepare surfaces for painting or varnishing at some time, if the boat is to remain smart, while details of repairing surface blemishes (and more extensive damage) applying to grp craft of all sizes are given in Chapter 11.

Good surface preparation takes much longer than the subsequent painting. Unless the preparation is thorough, not only will the finished surface be poor, but the paint adhesion might be so weak that it will all have to be stripped off again the following year!

Surface preparation is a lengthy job, but it need not become too tedious if tackled in the right way. As newly prepared surfaces should not be left exposed to the air for long, especially in winter, it usually pays to work in limited areas and get a coat of primer on before commencing further preparation.

In one instance, however, this cannot be done, i.e. when a paint solvent stripper has been used. Some of these solvents have to be killed by washing the surface with fresh water and some with turps. In either case (and especially with water) a complete drying out must be achieved before applying a primer. Drying out may be hastened by wafting a heating torch over the surface, and this is a worthwhile precaution during cold moist weather even when the surface has not been washed.

When and How to Strip
Some yachtsmen never seem to own a craft more than about five years old and they are never faced with the task of stripping off all paint and varnish. Those who manage to keep a yacht no older than ten years, may encounter the necessity to strip off a

few areas of varnish but are not likely to have to take off the outside of the hull.

When a craft is fifteen or more years old, the time for complete stripping may not be too distant, though a well-maintained yacht over twenty years of age may not require this if the correct amount of paint has been taken off by thorough rubbing down each year and the adhesion is good.

A grp hull will probably require painting when about six years old to keep it looking smart. As a catalyst paint (such as polyurethane) should be used for this, repainting may not be required more often than once every two years. Provided the adhesion is good, stripping might not be required for twenty years.

As complete stripping is a big task it should not be undertaken until really necessary. Quite large areas of flaking paint can be scraped away and made good with trowel cement without the necessity for complete stripping, so the full process is only essential when more than 30 per cent of the surface is poor, due either to roughness caused by many years of bad painting workmanship, or to flaking, cracking, crazing, blistering, or bonding failure.

Varnish work may need stripping much sooner than paint because defects such as bond failure are visible immediately they occur, showing discolouration of the wood. Furthermore, as trowel cement is no good on brightwork, if small areas are scraped clean it may be necessary to apply ten or more coats of varnish with careful rubbing down to build up to the surrounding depth. This means that complete stripping is often the quicker alternative.

Whereas paint may remain quite sound with forty or fifty coats in position, brightwork looks too dark with more than twenty coats and therefore needs more frequent stripping to retain its fresh and lively colour.

Latent rusting on a steel boat may not show through a thick paint covering so it pays to strip a few small test areas every year to ensure that all is well.

There are three main methods in use for stripping paint completely:
(1) By burning off with a torch and scraper or with an electric tool.
(2) With the aid of a chemical stripper and scraper.
(3) By dry scraping or with some form of power sander.

(4) On thick steel a chipping hammer may be used to remove
     completely any number of coats of paint.

Burning Off

Although the oldest method of removing paint, even today,
burning off has many advantages over the newer methods on all
types of wooden hull. It must not be used on a plastics boat, or
on thin metal. Plastics laminates can be severely damaged by
heat. It may distort thin plates of steel or alloy, and it will also
blister any interior paint as metals are good conductors of heat.

Burning off is a delightfully easy process for the amateur to
carry out although the speed and excellence of the work is
likely to improve considerably with practice. The object is to
melt the paint over an area about 6 in (150 mm) long and 3 in
(75 mm) wide and then to turn the flame away from the work
before the wood underneath becomes charred, peeling the
paint off while still soft by means of a flat stripping knife. The
process is then repeated continuously.

The common kerosene blowlamp (or blow torch) is the most
frequently used tool for applying the heat, but a butane or
propane gas torch is a superior tool for the job in every
respect.

For small areas the type with integral interchangable
cylinders is convenient although for serious work it pays to use
a fairly large burner head on the end of a rubber hose fed from
a 14 lb (6 kg) cylinder resting on the ground. These torches are
lighter to wield than a blowlamp and the flame is more stable
in a strong wind.

When using a blowlamp in a strong wind it may be necessary
to erect some sort of windshield nearby but it should be
remembered that a little wind is advantageous to carry the
fumes away from the operator's face.

The butane or propane torch is almost immune from block-
age, but if this should occur, an ordinary adjustable spanner
can be used to remove the nipple for clearing the gauze filter
after simply unscrewing the burner head. When using a
kerosene (paraffin oil) torch one must always be fully prepared
for blockages. A long nipple key should be carried together
with two or three prickers.

A butane torch can be ignited instantly with a match but a
kerosene lamp requires preheating and this is best done by
igniting a small quantity of meths (alcohol) in the reservoir

Picture 13. For preparing and painting topside surfaces on most yachts laid-up ashore, some scaffold planking speeds up work tremendously.

Picture 14. Burning off in the traditional manner is often the best way. Note that a triangular scraper is being used on this chine dinghy.

provided. An old oilcan is convenient for supplying the meths, though special containers are available which meter out the correct dosage when tilted. Neat kerosene from the jet can be used for igniting but makes a smoky flame. In winter weather it may be necessary to preheat twice for the vaporizing coil must be really hot before pumping air into the tank.

When using a torch to remove paint adjacent to a varnished rail or rubbing strake, much worry can be saved by bending up a shield from light gauge tin plate which clips over the varnished part and can be slid along as the work proceeds.

For burning off below the waterline on a large vessel, work can be speeded tremendously by using a flame gun with a helper to do the scraping by means of a stripping knife wired firmly to the end of a 4 ft (1200 mm) long broom handle. The flame gun is like an enormous blowlamp and is marketed primarily for destroying weeds.

Very large propane burners are, of course, available to do the same job but the fuel is noticeably more expensive than kerosene when using large quantities. Much care is needed when using a flame gun on old tar or black varnish as this is liable to flare quite viciously. A mains water hose with nozzle is therefore a wise precaution to have ready. If no mains supply is available, an ex-wartime stirrup pump with a couple of buckets of water should suffice.

Always be careful to avoid heating the transducer fitting of an echo sounder, or the impeller of a log/speed indicator which may be withdrawn into its housing.

Another great advantage of burning off compared with other methods of stripping is the fact that the wood is warmed up considerably during the operation. This ensures that the surface is dry and thus ideal for receiving a priming coat. In cold or moist weather one should therefore stop burning every ten minutes or so, rub down the exposed surface and apply knotting and primer.

If the stripping knife is held in the right hand, burning off is normally accomplished working from right to left along a surface. However if the wind happens to be in the wrong direction for this it may be advisable to work from left to right. Should you have to manage without a proper broad-bladed stripping knife, an ordinary triangular paint scraper will answer the purpose.

Electric paint strippers have a shielded heating element which moves close over the surface. A scraper is fitted to the end of this so that melting and scraping of the paint is continuous. These tools are not quite so fast as blowlamps but they are better for removing thin coatings with less tendency to char the wood and they are also ideal for working up to varnished parts which do not need stripping.

Chemical Strippers
Most paint makers supply chemical removers. These are normally suitable for stripping all types of paint and varnish including polyurethanes and cellulose, but check the wording on the can before buying. As chemical strippers will dissolve one's fingers as well as the paint, protection in the form of barrier cream (or PVC gloves) is advisable. Alternatively have a pail of warm water with some soap nearby so that any solvent splashing on to the skin can be washed off immediately.

Plan your work carefully. Chemical from a varnished rail must not be allowed to run down on to grp topsides. Work from the top down to avoid getting stripper on a part already painted. Use paper and masking tape to prevent the chemical splashing on to the deck when stripping coamings or a deckhouse.

52

Picture 15. To avoid damaging a varnished beading or rail, bend a sheet of tinplate in the form shown and slide this along as work proceeds.

Picture 16. Dry scraping on large areas with a Skarsten is a heartbreaking task and can score the surface. A chemical stripper reduces the effort needed but may take longer.

These removers can damage a grp gel coat seriously but although they do not harm *Cascover* nylon sheathing they can soak through it and damage the glue unless neutralized rapidly.

A large quantity of stripper is required to remove numerous coats of paint or varnish. One thick application of stripper spread on by means of a brush or a spatula will, after an interval of five or ten minutes, cause the top two or three coats of paint to soften for easy removal in the form of shavings with a triangular or *Skarsten* scraper.

As there could be sixty coats of paint on the outside of the hull, it will be appreciated that a considerable quantity of stripper could be necessary so these materials are normally used only where a blowlamp will not suffice, i.e. on brightwork or on hulls which must not be heated.

Having continued to apply stripper, pausing, and then scraping off the required number of times to get down to bare wood, the chemicals must be neutralized before a primer can be safely applied. Read the notes on the outside of the can to find out whether it should be neutralized with water, turps, or some other fluid. A quantity of this should then be flowed over the surface with a brush or cloth and the surplus wiped away after a few seconds.

Although water is the most convenient neutralizing agent, there are times when any moisture on the surface is anathema. However, if work can be planned so that application of paint or varnish can be delayed for at least a day, or preferably a week, there should be ample time for the timber to dry out. This problem will hardly arise on a non-absorbent metal or a ferro-cement hull, but note that bare steel tends to hold moisture in its surface pores and this will not often be visible until the surface is heated.

Dry Scraping and Sanding

A well-sharpened Skarsten scraper will remove old paint and varnish dry but much energy is required especially on large surfaces, while extreme care is needed when close to the wood to prevent score marks being caused by the ends of the blade. Serrated blades are available for the Skarsten and, although faster in action, they are more liable to cause surface damage to wood.

Dry scraping is quite effective on narrow brightwork parts such as mouldings, handrails, cleats, and surrounds. On paint-work it proves useful for removing areas of loose, blistered, or flaking paint. The method has the advantage that it can be done at odd moments without the necessity for opening cans of stripper or hunting for brushes which later need cleaning. Also, it keeps the wood dry so that, after sanding, a priming coat may be applied at any time.

Dry scraping is particularly welcome on a cold day as the effort keeps one beautifully warm. It works well on round masts and spars and a traditional method of doing this is by dry scraping with a piece of broken glass!

Using an 8 in (200 mm) disc sander with a coarse aluminous oxide disc, numerous layers of paint can be removed very quickly. This tool is quite different from the normal handyman's 5 in (125 mm) disc on an electric drill, this latter tool being of use only for light sanding jobs.

Heavy duty disc sanders are abominable things to use, especially on overhead surfaces such as one finds below the waterline of a large yacht. Not only are they heavy to manipulate for any length of time, but they throw poisonous particles from the surface at an alarming speed making it essential to wear an eye shield, a cap and a nose and mouth filter. When working on the vertical topside surfaces, the weight of the tool can be relieved by means of a suspension spring hung from the lifelines or rail, or simply by attaching a rope lanyard which is controlled by a helper on deck.

As coarse discs rapidly become clogged with paint which has been softened by the heat created, one needs to keep several spare discs ready. The finer grade handyman discs may not clog so readily but they are liable to wear out quickly during use.

All types of discs leave whorl marks on the surface which can never be eradicated unless copious amounts of trowel cement are used. A disc sander is quicker than burning off only where a thin layer of paint is present.

When just power sanding has to be used (as may be the case with a grp hull), a belt sander is the most reliable tool. This weighs even heavier than a disc sander so the suspension spring or lanyard is even more necessary when working on the topsides, while the job is very nearly impossible when working overhead.

Some belt sanders have an extractor fan built in which fills a detachable bag with most of the dust. Although one belt will last two hours when working on wood, this is reduced to about twenty minutes on paintwork due to clogging.

An orbital sander is no use for rough work of this nature and generally speaking the whole process of sanding is a more difficult method of stripping than the other methods mentioned above.

One other type of sanding attachment is available for use on an electric drill. This consists of an *arbor* (shaft) attached to which is a drum about 3 in (75 mm) in diameter and 2 in (50 mm) wide (made mainly from foam rubber) with a layer of garnet paper bonded around the periphery. This tool has an action similar to a tiny belt sander and is suitable for light smoothing work.

Remember when using a disc sander to ensure that the central nut securing the disc to the rubber pad is screwed on tightly. This may be achieved only by means of a special pronged key supplied by the makers. During use only the outermost part of the disc should be used for sanding; the central portion of the disc should never be used at all.

Although stripping by sanding has such limitations, it has

the advantage of being a universal process for use on all materials including steel and alloy. Being the process most frequently used for stripping paint on glass fibre, it will no doubt find increasing favour in this field as the number of grp boats needing adornment by paint grows year by year.

Many amateurs fail to obtain a good key on plastics with polyurethane paint and if these coats start to peel complete stripping by sanding may have to be undertaken much sooner than the fifteen years or so quoted for wooden hulls.

Extreme care is needed to avoid cutting through the gel coat with a power sander. Paint of a colour different from the gel coat helps a lot as the grp can be identified immediately the sander gets to it.

Chipping it Off

Paint chipping is a routine job in the Merchant Navy where few ships have steel thinner than $\frac{1}{4}$ in (6 mm). The method works beautifully on thick metal and forms a good key for the primer by covering the surface with tiny marks showing clean metal, but it must never be used on galvanized or zinc sprayed steel.

The normal chipping or scaling hammer has a horizonal chisel edge on one tip and a vertical chisel edge on the other end. The speed and weight of strokes used depends upon the thickness of paint but normally a light rapid action is most effective as slow heavy strokes could well cause dents in the surface.

Note that, for working over small areas, an ordinary cold chisel used on its own or in conjuction with a light hammer will produce almost as effective a job as a proper chipping hammer.

On completion of chipping, the whole surface should be scoured with a wire brush, preferably a rotary power type.

Other power tools are available for speeding the preparation of steel surfaces. A pneumatic chipping hammer is far too vicious a tool for use on yachts but a *needle gun* which uses a comparatively small quantity of air is a fine tool which leaves a bright steel surface.

This tool has a nozzle from which protrude the tips of numerous hard steel rods like knitting needles. These rattle to and fro rapidly during operation and are held against the surface by hand pressure on the tool.

Shot blasting equipment can sometimes be hired. This will

Picture 17. A chipping hammer is not only essential on steel built craft, but is ideal for scaling the rust off neglected pigs of ballast.

Picture 18. When working on the topsides of a yacht afloat it may be possible to borrow a painting raft to hasten the job.

produce the finest surface known for receiving paint, though it pays to chip off most of the existing paint beforehand.

No tool which chips is much good on aluminium alloy as, due to the comparative softness of this material, severe damage could be caused. On steel, just as with wood, one should endeavour to cover a newly prepared surface with paint at the earliest moment.

Having warmed the surface with a torch, the next operation depends largely upon the condition of the steel and upon the proposed paint specification. If zinc-rich paint is used this should be applied direct on to bright steel whereas if red oxide or similar primer is to be used on a rust pitted surface, phosphoric acid (*Jenolite*) should be brushed on to kill the rust. With alloys the correct primer can go straight on although on new metal degreasing followed by a self-etching primer is normally specified.

Working Position

The owner of a dinghy, rowing boat, or a small cruiser that can be trailed home, should have little difficulty in being able to roll the hull over at will so that all parts can be worked upon without need for acrobatics. Although most craft under three tons in weight can be rolled over on to a couple of old mattresses (or partially over on to chocks under the bilges) with comparative ease using jacks, levers, chocks and wedges (see Chapter 12) some modern bilge keel cruisers are not so simple to deal with as they cannot be rocked on the central keel.

Owners of large vessels which may be laid-up in a mudberth, hauled out on the foreshore, or in a boatyard, may not be able to shift the boat so readily. In a mudberth it may be impossible to reach below the waterline so that any work on this part will have to be delayed until a move on to a grid or scrubbing piles can be arranged.

For working on the topsides when in a mudberth a few wide planks or duckboards will facilitate walking about on the mud, but remember to remove these when you leave, or have rope lanyards attached to them in case they float away on the next high tide. Whenever a ladder is used it should be securely lashed at the top to avoid accidents especially where it stands on soft material.

A raft is useful for dealing with topsides when afloat or in the mud berth. This should have padding attached where it rests against the hull and warps fore-and-aft to assist manoeuvrability.

When treating the topsides on craft larger than about 35 ft (11 m) some form of staging helps to speed work tremendously. Hauled out ashore this can be the conventional yard equipment of trestles and planks or a set of do-it-yourself steel scaffold assemblies.

Afloat or in a mud berth, a short plank, rigged in the style of a bosun's chair, may be suspended from the bulwarks, rail, or lifelines, to allow its height and position to be adjusted during work.

If work is done afloat from a dinghy or raft there is a strong tendency for the dinghy to push away from the parent ship. This can be overcome by rigging a *guest warp* running tightly from stem to stern of the yacht close to the waterline outside the dinghy.

Marking the Waterline
If the lines marking the limits of the boot-top have been lost during stripping they may have to be set out again. This is not an easy job and it pays to ensure that the positions of these lines are scored permanently into the surface.

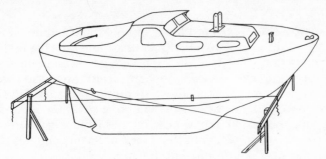

Drawing 5. Striking in the waterline. More often needed on plastics and metal boats as a permanent line can be scribed into a wooden surface. To avoid the need for rails of great length, secure the cord with masking tape at the positions shown, then swing in to stem and stern.

Old score marks in the wood may be discovered when numerous layers of paint have been removed, but if on stripping a trial patch no marks are found, a carpenter's pricker or a nail and hammer should be used to make a series of holes through the paintwork and into the timber to enable the positions of these lines to be picked up again later.

To nick the lines accurately, a long piece of batten should be fastened to the hull with thin wire nails which just enter sufficiently to support it. If a tiny moulding plane with V-shaped cutter is not available a large sharp bradawl can be used.

Nicked lines cannot be used on plastics or metal hulls, so new lines may have to be struck more frequently than with wood. It may be found that the position of the boot-top is incorrect once a new yacht has settled down to her permanent waterline and on many older craft the lines may be too high or too low in certain places.

Although there are many ways of striking-in the waterline using known positions at stem and stern one simple way is to erect a level athwartships rail at each end of sufficient length to allow a tight cord stretched between them to touch the hull at any desired point.

Most dinghies and motor runabouts which are hauled ashore when not in use need no antifouling, waterline or boot-top. If a waterline is required on such a craft, care should be taken to chock her up dead level before starting to mark out the line.

Having marked the line which is the true position of the water when the vessel is left at moorings in normal trim the *lower* boot-top line may be measured off about 1 in (25 mm)

59

higher than this all around for craft up to about 30 ft (9 m) in length and some 2 in (50 mm) for craft around 45 ft (14 m).

The *upper* boot-top line is a curve with its lowest point about three-fifths of the waterline length from the stem rising towards each end. For the above mentioned smaller size craft the boot-top will be about 1 in (25 mm) wide at the minimum increasing to 2 in (50 mm) wide at the stern and 3 in (75 mm) at the bow. For the larger craft these measurements might be 2 in (50 mm), 3 in (75 mm), and 4 in (100 mm).

With grooved lines top and bottom lining in by hand is quite simple, but on a grp, metal, or ferro-cement hull without nicked lines, work is speeded up and improved if masking tape is used.

Priming and Stopping

The available range of primers is almost as bewildering as for topcoats, but the amateur cannot go far wrong by keeping to a certain paint maker's recommendations.

The old type of paint primer made with white lead, red lead, linseed oil, turps and driers, is still considered by some paint makers to be an ideal covering for new or stripped timber under *alkyd* as well as white lead finishes, but most authorities consider that the more modern metallic primers have better adhesion and penetration, while the quicker drying is an enormous advantage. Metallic primers may need thinning before use.

Thinned varnish is the only primer required for ordinary varnish although special primers are available to ensure maximum adhesion on teak and similar oily timbers. Similarly, most *catalyst* paints are simply thinned to form a primer, though special epoxy resin primers are available to improve the adhesion on glass-reinforced plastics.

For priming steel, calcium plumbate and zinc chromate paints are frequently used under alkyds, while the zinc rich preparations (such as *Galvafroid* and *Kurust*) are widely used on bare steel under most types of finish. Self-etching primers are made for use on aluminium alloy while similar preparations can be used on grp to eliminate the need to scour the surface.

After burning off old paint on a hull planked with pine, fir, or larch, knots and other resinous defects should be coated with *knotting* (shellac varnish). This is rarely needed on hardwoods such as mahogany, agba, teak, or iroko.

60

A primer is brushed thinly on to the bare sanded wood to achieve good penetration. If seams are to be recaulked and fastening holes filled, primer is worked into all these places. A small flat seam brush is useful for this job though an ordinary $\frac{1}{2}$ in (12 mm) brush will do if the bristles are bound with tape to make them flatter. Even an old toothbrush will serve for this.

Once primed, depressions and defects in the surface will show up readily, especially if a light-source can be held close to the surface. The correct maker's *trowelling cement* applied with a broad-bladed stripping knife will rapidly take care of most defects. The makers' *knifing stopper* would normally be used for seams and fastening holes, the stripping knife being much the fastest tool for seams while an ordinary glazier's putty knife is ideal for holes.

These materials are normally allowed one day to harden and are then rubbed down dry until dead flush. As the abrasive paper will clog rapidly it may pay to take the bulk off with a 100-grit paper, finishing off with 240-grit, cleaning the paper at intervals with a wire brush.

Instead of knifing stopper, one can use Brummer Green Label stopping. This hardens in less than one hour and rubs down with very little clogging of the paper. It dries up rapidly in the can while in use (and sometimes when stored) but is readily softened again by the addition of cellulose thinners or amyl acetate.

Other makes of stopping cannot always be revived once they harden or skin, so it pays to buy them in small cans and always use fresh material.

For brightwork, stoppers must be a good match, remembering that the colour of the wood and the stopping will be quite different after varnishing.

Never attempt to fill deep holes with stopping in one operation. The first layer should be the thickest, leaving space for a thin final smear to cover any shrinkage cracks. With practice, stopping can be knifed on to leave a slight hump, which, after the inevitable shrinkage during drying, may be rubbed down quickly flush with the surface.

Where the surface shows a multitude of tiny defects the most fluid of all the stoppers, called *brushing cement,* may be applied over the entire surface using a 2 in (50 mm) paint brush. Any defects still showing after rubbing down must be stopped again and if much bare wood shows after a thorough rubbing of the primer a second thin coat of priming paint is advantageous. After a further rubbing down dry, undercoating will probably be applied depending upon the maker's specification. After this all rubbing may be done wet.

For a catalyst specification, or beneath glass fibre sheathing or Cascover, only the correct grades of resin stopper must be used. Some of these become very hard on curing and require the prior use of a *Stanley Shaper* or Surform Plane before finally sanding flush. Some antifouling paints have their own special stoppers and bitumastic putties.

Rubbing Between Coats

Rubbing on bare timber, metal, grp and priming paint, should be done *dry* using common sandpaper or glass paper.

Good adhesion by polyurethane paint is difficult to achieve on grp so that perfect surface preparation with the correct grade of abrasive paper is absolutely essential. Dry garnet paper or silicon carbide w.o.d. paper of about 180-grit used dry cuts the surface to a more efficient paint key than can be achieved when rubbing wet and an orbital sander proves quite useful for this operation. Note that the life of w.o.d. paper when used dry can be extended by scrubbing the paper with hot soapy water after use, or with a wire brush.

However, a wet rub is normally faster than dry, and makes the paper last about five times longer, so one alternative is to rub down the grp gel coat wet using 180-grit, then finishing off with a light rub all over using 240-grit paper without water.

Except for the above advantages of rubbing dry, w.o.d. paper used with water is superior in every way for preparation between coats. Although dry rubbing is more costly in abrasive paper than wet, it should perhaps be mentioned that 6 in (150 mm) wide rolls of used garnet paper of various grades may sometimes be obtained gratis (from joinery works and boat-yards having a sanding machine) with plenty of life left in it for hand rubbing.

Garnet paper as well as ordinary sandpaper should be stored in a warm room for, if used when moist, its surface will disintegrate. For this reason, any abrasive paper kept on board a yacht should be of the wet-or-dry type.

Ordinary sandpaper may not be so accurately made as garnet or w.o.d. and it pays to rub two sheets against each other first to get rid of any grit which might cause deep scratches.

When rubbing large flat surfaces the sheets of the correct grade of paper should be wrapped around a *cork block,* this being superior to an old block of wood. A sheet can be folded and used in the hands for working around narrow parts and into corners but if the hand only is used on flat surfaces, the high spots may not be levelled off as well as they should be.

The above applies whether rubbing dry or wet. Although cork blocks tend to disintegrate gradually when used wet they are cheap, and can be replaced periodically. Much more expensive rubber blocks and other devices are available, but they are liable to get lost and work no more effectively than cork.

If standard sheets of paper are creased centrally and then torn into two, each piece folded in half then makes a convenient size for wrapping around a block. The direction of wrapping should be changed occasionally to ensure that the whole of the paper is used. When rubbing wet, a pail of warm soapy water should be kept near so that the paper can be dunked in this approximately once every minute while rubbing. This knack is soon acquired and work can then proceed rapidly.

An area about 2 ft (600 mm) long and 1 ft (300 mm) wide should first be moistened by means of the paper (or with a swab) and rubbing commenced over this area until a muddy liquid composed of powdered paint and water forms under the paper. Frequent dunking in the pail is necessary to clear this paste away.

As each small area is rubbed one learns to observe where the last panel ended (to avoid rubbing needlessly at each overlap) by reference to landmarks such as blemishes in the surface, scarf joints in rail or beading, visible plank seams and stopping over fastenings. If further reference marks are required a piece of chalk can be used to make marks along the boot-top or rail when working on topsides.

Having rubbed an area about 9 ft (3 m) long and whatever width it happens to be, wipe away the surface paste with a moist swab. Then a clean swab with copious amounts of fresh water should be used to rewash the surface, drying it after wringing out the swab.

Now is the time to renew the warm soapy water in the pail and before using this again for further rubbing, the first swab should be rinsed out in this water ready for the next wiping down.

Used in this way a sheet of w.o.d. paper will last for about one hour's rubbing though it proves a good idea to bring a new sheet into service after half an hour and keep the old sheet for use on smoother work.

Rubbing wet produces a much finer scratch-free surface than is possible with dry paper so that a slightly coarser grade can be used to advantage.

A 100- or 180-grit is suitable for the first rub down on last year's paint or varnish but as subsequent coats proceed it pays to change to a 240- or even a 300-grit, remembering that the higher the grit number the finer the paper. The half worn out coarse paper can well be used for rubbing these later coats.

Be careful to use much lighter pressure when rubbing tender coats than is permissible on old paint. If rubbing is too vicious a whole coat of paint or varnish may be rubbed away in certain places, while heavy pressure (especially when rubbing dry) is liable to peel off the surface if insufficient time has been allowed for complete hardening.

On completion, with all water dried off, a rubbed surface should have a matt frosted appearance with a few small glossy patches still showing where hollows exist. The quality of the work is difficult to judge on a white or light coloured finish, but is immediately apparent on varnished wood or on darker colours.

Amateurs may be confused by the different gradings adopted by various makers for abrasive papers. The table opposite gives a comparison of the most frequently met gradings.

One method of rubbing old or new paint surfaces which has not yet been discussed, is by means of the *stripper block,* sometimes called a soda block or pumice block. Looking like moulded blocks of hard chalk, they are a convenient size to hold with the fingers.

The mode of operation is very similar to rubbing with wet paper. The block is dunked in warm water twice a minute during use and a paste consisting of old paint and composition from the block is formed on the surface as rubbing proceeds. The operator is advised to wear industrial gloves or to include a small pad of rag between the fingers and the block, otherwise the action of the soda and the roughness of the block soon causes raw fingers.

TABLE 2
Abrasive Paper Comparison

Garnet	Silicon carbide	Glass paper	Emery cloth
10/0	400	—	—
9/0	320	—	—
8/0	280	—	—
7/0	240	—	—
6/0	220	—	00
5/0	180	00	0
4/0	150	0	FF
3/0	120	1	F
2/0	100	1½	1
0	80	F2	1½
½	60	M2	2
1	50	S2	2½
1½	40	2½	3
2	36	3	—

Stripper blocks are obtainable in three grades, fine, medium and coarse. Medium is usually ideal for cutting down last year's paint surface while the fine grade is best for rubbing between coats. One medium block will prepare the old topside paint-work on a 30 ft (9 m) yacht before wearing too thin to hold.

A stripper block softens old layers of paint as it works and enables more to be taken off in a given time, thereby preventing the thickness from building up too much over the years. It has an excellent levelling effect on high spots, but is not at all handy to use on hollow surfaces, such as on the forward flared topsides of some modern motor cruisers.

Interior Work
Although surface preparation below decks follows the lines detailed above, great care is needed to avoid breathing the fumes from burning paint or chemical strippers. A through current of air is rarely sufficient to cope with this and, unless a power extractor fan can be installed, the only solution is to treat a small area at a time. By having several other jobs in action there should be no loss of valuable time if stripping work is done intermittently.

Glass fibre boats often have a very rough interior surface which cannot be rubbed down properly. The best tool to use on this is a wire brush, for as long as all flaking paint is

65

Picture 19. A piece of rag on top of a soda block will prevent one's finger tips from getting sore. A copious supply of water is essential to keep the block working efficiently.

Picture 20. Hardening down th caulking cotton in a seam. Note correc manner for holding the caulking iron which averts injury should the mallet g astray.

removed a fresh coat can be applied after a normal sugar soap wash to get rid of dirt and grease.

Treating the bilges is best left until last to ensure a thorough drying out, though it pays to get the bilges washed down with a degreaser while laying-up the boat, see Chapter 12.

Working on a dinghy inside a garage or small shed is rather similar and work should not be continued unless there is adequate ventilation. If weather conditions are suitable, a dinghy or trailer-mounted craft should be hauled out into the open for stripping. This is advisable even if a power sander is used because these tools result in thick layers of dust over everything inside a workshop.

When working in a large boat shed, it should not be forgotten that the smoke from burning off and the dust from a power sander is likely to be most troublesome to neighbouring workers.

Caulking and Paying

The process of caulking hull seams and decks is very similar and is a major item of work for the amateur to undertake. Wide seams in thick planking, especially on old craft, are frequently caulked with oakum which consists of short strands of hemp impregnated with stockholm tar and compressed into a bale.

For paying (stopping) oakum below the waterline, it used to be the practice to brush hot pitch over the seams, but tar putty made by beating whiting and coal tar (or cement and coal tar) together is more convenient for the amateur.

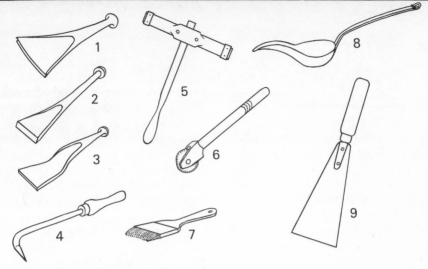

Drawing 6.   A selection of caulking tools:
1. The most useful caulking iron, a single crease.
2. Sharp iron or jerry. Will ream narrow spots in a seam.
3. Bent iron with blunt tip. Useful for garboard seams alongside the keel.
4. Raker. Usually home-made, several sizes useful when raking out old caulking.
5. Traditional lignum vitae caulking mallet.
raking out old caulking.
6. A caulking wheel. This started automation in the boatyard! For feeding cotton into good quality uniform seams.
7. Flat seam brush. Better than a tooth brush for priming seams.
8. Pitch ladle. When paying deck seams with molten marine glue, the operator stands astride the seam and walks backwards.
9. Stripping knife or pallette knife. Not made for the job, but is the ideal tool for pressing putty into seams. Keep blade tip parallel to seam.

Most yacht seams are caulked with white cotton which is usually sold in 1 lb (0·5 kg) balls consisting of eight separate continuous strands. Paint makers produce hard and soft stoppers suitable for paying over cotton.

On modern craft deck seams are normally caulked with one of the synthetic compounds which cure into a stiff rubber. Some of these can be used for hull seam caulking, being especially useful below the waterline. White rubber compounds suitable for topside caulking are made but they are not so easily rubbed down to create a fine finish as the conventional hard seam stoppers.

Flexible Caulking Composition (made by K. M. Gibbs Ltd, Shepperton-on-Thames, Middlesex) is a much cheaper bitumastic putty containing asbestos fibre which is ideal for filling the underwater seams of a working craft (or a Class (c) yacht) instead of using oakum or cotton with conventional stopping and its use saves many hours of labour.

However, it should not be forgotten that hard driven caulking strengthens a planked hull by forcing the planks against each other and this may be especially important on an old vessel with some nail sickness, i.e. the fastenings are slack through the planking, due to slight movements or electrolytic action. On the contrary, driving caulking too hard can distort a weak deck. Old caulked hulls which leak under way may be sealed by painting the bottom with Gibbs' *Black Rubber Sheathing*.

Having removed the stopping, caulking which is in good condition may be hardened down with a caulking iron of correct size to fit freely into the seam. Before doing this some of the cotton should be raked out and checked for soundness. If it crumbles between the fingers it will certainly need to be replaced. Good tools for raking out seams can be made at the tang end of a file as described in Chapter 2. Small strands of cotton which prove difficult to rake out may be left in the seam.

Professionals do not always prime the seams with paint before caulking but priming is a sound idea as there should be no unpainted wood anywhere on a boat. If the cotton can be driven before the priming paint becomes completely hard so much the better.

A little practice is necessary to find out how many strands of cotton a seam will take when driven hard, but a few trials on a short length of seam will soon determine this and the trial pieces should be raked out again before starting continuous caulking.

A rope slightly longer than the seam to be caulked should then be laid-up with the requisite number of strands by securing one end and winding the other end by means of a hand-drill having in its chuck a wire hook to which the cotton is tied. Twisting into a rope while the strands are pulled taut is then only a matter of a few seconds winding.

Using a fairly sharp-edged caulking iron the cotton is pinched into the seam at intervals of about 6 in (150 mm) throughout the length and then the remaining loops are forced into the *Vee* of the seam with the same narrow iron and a wider tipped *crease iron* is used finally to level off the cotton to a depth of about $\frac{1}{8}$ in (3 mm) below the surface.

Where a seam is particularly wide, the same number of strands may be twisted but driven into the seam in a series of loops to make up the required bulk. Butts between plank ends are caulked separately using offcuts of cotton. Be careful not to drive the caulking right through the seam.

Preparing oakum for use is quite different. A large wad is torn from the bale and teased out between the fingers into a loose rope about 3 ft (900 mm) long and this is then twisted up between the thigh and the palm of one's hand. Once the knack has been acquired it can be done very quickly.

For planking thicker than about 1 in (25 mm), considerable force is needed to drive caulking satisfactorily. The professional uses a heavy hardwood mallet with iron ferrules at each end, but the amateur is likely to find this tool troublesome and may be able to get by with the heaviest type of carpenter's mallet.

It pays to watch a shipwright caulking, to observe these points and to note how he holds his caulking iron on the palm of his hand with the knuckles downwards when working on topside seams.

Caulking decks is considerably easier than hull seams as the working position is more restful and the problem of reaching high up, or below the level of one's knees, does not arise. Seams in teak do not really require priming before caulking, but when priming (perhaps on a pine deck), some care may be needed to prevent the paint running right through the seams into the cabin!

Paying (stopping) deck seams appears simple on this almost level surface, but in practice it proves more difficult and takes longer than stopping hull seams. There are many makers of marine glues for paying deck seams and various qualities, prices, and colours are available. The cheaper glues are made for working craft and it pays to use the best quality yacht glue as this is more resilient and clings better.

These glues are sold either in repair sticks or as random lumps in 56 lb (30 kg) kegs. To use they are heated in a ladle with a long fine spout until molten and then run into each seam. The glue should not be boiled, but heated until it smokes. Insufficient heating will cause voids to be left, poor adhesion and overspilling due to the low viscosity.

Shipyards sometimes use thermostatically controlled electric glue ladles mounted on wheels with guide blades to align the spout with the seam. These tools are not very practical in a small yacht for although they may have an offset spout for working close to edges and obstacles, the length of the seam runs is normally too short.

Experts can lay marine glue in one run almost exactly flush with the surface so that the necessity for scraping off surplus is almost eliminated. The amateur will find it much easier to achieve success if he pours each seam with two runs; one to just cover the caulking cotton and the next to bring the glue up flush with the deck.

The best time to scrape off surplus marine glue is on a cold day or early in the morning when the glue is brittle, as a Skarsten or bent file scraper will then clean it off without fuss. Dipping the scraper in water often helps the job along.

Caulking with the modern synthetic rubber compounds is a completely different procedure from the above and, if carried out conscientiously, should make a superior job. There are now many makes of these (in addition to the original P.R.C. made by British Paints Ltd), including *Calfa* by International Paints and *Decolay* by Ralli Bondite Ltd, Waterlooville, Hants.

Decolay is a catalyst preparation activated by mixing equal parts of two differently coloured putties together just before use and this is ideal for doing small sections or working intermittently. Most of the others are now air-curing compounds supplied in cartridges for a sealer gun (see Chapter 5) or in larger kegs for loading into a cylinder type gun with a spatula. Unsealed cartons should be stored in a refrigerator to prevent premature hardening.

All these compounds demand precise cleaning of the seams to reveal bare wood and two coats of the special primer are essential. Complete success is more likely on new wood than old.

Synthetic rubber has the advantage of being used cold and its elasticity, coupled with excellent adhesion, provides for a large degree of expansion and contraction without leakage. The material shrinks slightly on curing which, with careful application, minimizes the amount of surface to be cleaned off for a flush finish.

These rubbery substances cannot be scraped off cleanly like marine glue and a belt sander is quite the best tool to use. A coarse disc sander is a possibility for deck seams as the whorl marks it leaves rarely show up on a scrubbed deck.

CHAPTER 4

PAINTING AND VARNISHING

Few cruising boats escape some damage during a season, the chief culprits being anchor flukes; mooring chains; scraping at wharfs and trots when unattended; racing dinghy bombardment, and the friendly tyro who comes alongside with a dinghy having no all-round fender. Oil pollution plays havoc with topsides, while unsightly stains invariably appear below scuppers and chain plates.

Steel boats resist minor damage the best, followed by alloy and planked wooden craft. Glass reinforced plastics may be tough but the resistance to abrasion is poor. Both grp and plywood hulls can be chafed right through during a rough night on a mooring when a critical fender carries away.

Types of Paint
On account of these knocks and discolourations, most topsides seem to need an annual repaint, making the advantages of expensive long life catalyst paints rather questionable.

The term *catalyst* refers to any paint which has to be mixed with a special hardener before use, the two-can polyurethanes being the most widely used at present.

However, some of these resin coatings are considered ideal for use on grp and they can also be used to advantage on such brightwork parts as coamings and hatches which do not often get damaged. Similarly, the topsides of racing dinghies and other craft which are normally kept on shore or in private boat-houses, can be made to last two seasons with a catalyst coating, burnishing this with a special cutting compound after the first season.

There is always a certain element of risk when expecting a paint film to last for a long duration, as good adhesion is the

71

key to success or failure. Brightwork always seems more susceptible to bond failure, than enamel surfaces. There are three reasons for this:-

(a) Brightwork is often of teak, an oily timber difficult to prime to perfection.
(b) Brightwork is fairly dark in colour and so absorbs more heat than pastel shades of paint.
(c) One can see the yellow patches when moisture has crept under varnish whereas the opacity of paint hides this.

Surface preparation for catalysts must be perfect, especially over an existing coating, and weather conditions must be ideal before any attempt is made to apply a coating.

In competition with catalyst paints we have a large range of one-can materials which are, in general, easier to apply than catalysts and less susceptible to bond failure due to inadequate preparation or adverse weather conditions.

The newest of these ready-mixed paints include the one-can polyurethanes and the acrylics. In addition, we still have available the phenolic resin paints and varnishes which have been with us for over 30 years, and the more modern *alkyd* resins which form the bulk of all the one-can materials in use.

For surfaces which do not have to be glossy, a further range exists, including chlorinated rubber and epoxy resin for steelwork; vinyl and PVC coatings for use on decks and below the waterline; and a huge range of synthetic enamels used for automobile spraying which are also applicable to grp hulls.

Without a fungicide, water mixing emulsion paints are useless below decks in a yacht as they form an excellent culture for breeding mould and mildew under moist conditions.

Choosing an antifouling paint is a bewildering process for the newcomer so it pays to get advice from one's favourite paint maker, from local ship chandlers, or from experienced local yachtsmen.

One-Can or Two-Can

When repainting a yacht the amateur has to decide whether to adopt alkyd paint and varnish with a traditional recoating every year, or whether to go for catalyst finishes at almost twice the cost and try to make these last two or three seasons.

Such materials as one-can polyurethanes tend to fall between these two categories with regard to both cost and

Picture 21. A brush is still the best tool for painting awkward deck areas. Note how the mast has been used as a ridge pole for the winter tarpaulin.

Picture 22. A roller is fast for almost any paint job on a large flat surface. The operator is holding a brush for cutting in along the sheer beading. For a good finish a helper must follow up with a wide dry brush used with light parallel strokes.

durability. They have a harder surface than *alkyd* and can last two years.

The following notes should help one to reach a decision:

(a) Alkyds are much cheaper, easier to brush and lay off into a perfect finish, and more likely to keep in place when conditions for painting are not ideal.

(b) Alkyds are handier for intermittent work. With catalysts, once a quantity of paint has been mixed it must all be used the same day or thrown away. Alkyd brushes can be wrapped up after use and cleaned at leisure, whereas catalyst brushes must be cleaned immediately, or once an hour during normal use.

(c) Catalysts have the advantage of rapid drying. This means less liklihood of dust and flies marring the surface, but it also makes the material difficult to work as it dries before one can join two panels neatly. Some makers supply retardant additives to delay the hardening time slightly and these are especially useful during hot weather.

73

(d) Correctly applied polyurethanes can waterproof a wooden hull completely, preventing the additional weight due to soakage which can be detrimental to a racing craft.

(e) Due to the quicker drying time with catalysts, two coats can be applied in one day when necessary.

(f) Catalysts do not form a skin during storage and do not therefore need straining before use. Although skinning means wastage with alkyds, there is normally more wastage with catalysts due to the difficulty of judging how much material to mix before starting work.

(g) On wide surfaces some expertise is required to produce as fine a surface with a catalyst paint as with an alkyd. The catalyst finish has the advantage that any defects can be burnished out after hardening, but it should be remembered that this process takes a great deal of time.

(h) In general, catalyst paints do not require separate primers, undercoats and topcoats, which simplifies work and reduces wastage. It also means that scratches and scrapes do not reveal a different colour.

(i) Alkyd paints and varnishes usually cover about 500 sq ft per gallon (10 m² per litre), while catalysts cover about 450 sq ft (9 m²).

To serve as a guide on the economics of these two basic methods, four schedules are listed on pages 76–81 showing the total annual cost for amateur and professional work during the normal repainting of a sailing or motor cruiser between 25 ft (8 m) and 28 ft (9 m) in length.

The first schedule covers work on all types of wooden hull; the second, steel which has not been treated with zinc; third, aluminium alloy and galvanized steel; fourth, glass reinforced plastics.

The object of the schedules is to cost the annual painting and varnishing routine, during a cycle of between six and ten years duration, including a complete stripping job at some point in the cycle.

Although the grp hull works out the cheapest for maintenance, this conclusion could be considered unfair as the hull is presumed to be brand new at the start of the cycle whereas the other craft quoted could be older.

Furthermore, one could have a tremendous amount of maintenance done with the extra interest required to cover the higher capital outlay on a modern grp vessel of this size. Stripping a grp hull is so difficult that one should try to avoid it completely by rubbing down heavily before any new paint is applied. This has been allowed for in the schedule.

Costs are given for both alkyd and catalyst materials under each instance of amateur and professional work. In doing this it has been assumed that there is no point in using catalysts unless they are made to last for two years and are simply burnished for the second season. Using this method the cost for alkyd is little different from catalyst, but the alkyd finish would probably be smarter than the catalyst during the second season.

Alternatives do exist, of course. Sometimes one can make do with just one coat of catalyst paint each year. In all cases no allowance has been made for a change of colour. The Catalyst Specification includes the use of the best antifouling paints (such as Kobe, or Marina) whereas the Alkyd Specification includes medium priced antifouling paints (such as Hard Racing or Algicide).

In the following schedules the metal craft are presumed to have decks clad with teak (which is common practice) and therefore little deck maintenance expenditure is necessary. Some steel boats have decks coated with a composition such as *Semtex,* or sometimes plywood cladding covered with *Trakmark* or glass fibre is used. This might make some alteration to the listed annual cost. Where the superstructure and coamings are also in metal there would obviously be less brightwork to maintain.

No costs are included for the maintenance of masts, spars, rigging, sails, engines, pumps, toilet, dinghy, or plumbing equipment as these items need similar attention regardless of hull construction.

The reasons for stripping off an untreated steel hull after five years are two-fold. It will be noted that unlike the wooden hull, the yard cost of external painting increases steadily each year as larger and larger areas start to corrode and need extra treatment. Rust can occur under a perfect film of paint without being detected, so stripping after five years ensures that the hull surface is checked as well as ensuring that maintenance costs are reduced in subsequent re-fits.

A steel hull which was grit-blasted and zinc sprayed to a thickness of about 0·004 in (0·1 mm) inside; 0·006 in (0·15 mm) for topsides and 0·010 in (0·3 mm) below the waterline, when built, should require a similar painting program to an alloy hull for the first fifteen years.

75

TABLE 3
Typical Maintenance Schedules for Wood, Metal and Plastics

A=Alkyd Specification B=Catalyst Specification. Costs in £ (U.K.). For $ (U.S.A.) multiply Amateur Cost by 4, Boatyard Cost by 5.

1. WOOD

Based on Planked Hull. Plywood, or Moulded Hull is Similar.

Year	Task	Amateur Cost		Boatyard Cost	
		A	B	A	B
1st	Topsides – rub, stop, two coats	2	4	14	17
	Bottom – scrub off, scrape loose paint, rub, stop, two coats	2·50	5	12	16
	Boot top – rub, stop, two coats.	0·50	1	3	4
	Painted deck – scrub, rub, stop, two coats.	1	2	6	6
	Brightwork – strip faults, apply three coats. Rub over all, apply two coats.	1	2	7	8
	Total	7	14	42	51
2nd	Alkyd Spec. as for 1st year.	7	—	42	—
	Catalyst spec. Topsides–Touch up and burnish	—	1	—	5
	Bottom, boot top, and deck as 1st year	—	8	—	26
	Brightwork – touch up, one coat	—	1	—	4
	Bilges – scrub, touch up, one coat.	1	2	6	7
	Accommodation – rub, paint, varnish two coats in fo'c'sle.	1	2	5	6
	Total	9	14	53	48
3rd	Alkyd Spec. as for 1st year	7	—	42	—
	Catalyst Spec. Topsides – rub, stop, one coat	—	2	—	12
	Bottom and deck – as 1st year.	—	7	—	22
	Boot top – rub, stop, one coat.	—	0·50	—	3
	Brightwork – as 2nd year.	—	1	—	4
	Accommodation – rub, paint and varnish two coats in saloon.	1	1·50	7	8
	Total	8	12	49	49
4th	Topsides, bottom, boot top, deck, brightwork, and bilges, as 2nd year.	8	12	48	42
	Accommodation – rub, paint and varnish two coats in galley and lockers	1	2	5	6
	Total	9	14	53	48

1. WOOD—*continued*

Based on Planked Hull. Plywood, or Moulded Hull is similar.

Year	Task	Amateur Cost		Boatyard Cost	
		A	B	A	B
5th to 8th	Repeat above program	33	54	197	196
9th	Burn off topsides and bottom, check all caulking and stopping. Rub, prime, stop, three coats.	7	13	48	56
	Strip painted decks, two under, one anti-slip paint.	2	3	14	16
	Brightwork – strip, fill, three coats varnish.	2	4	18	22
	Total	11	20	80	94
10th	As 1st year.	7	14	42	51
	Total over 10 years	84	142	516	537
	Average cost per year	8	14	52	54

2. STEEL

Ungalvanized, Welded or Riveted Mild Steel, with Teak laid Decks

Year	Task	Amateur Cost		Boatyard Cost	
		A	B	A	B
1st	Topsides – chip off rusted or damaged parts, apply five coats with stopping. Rub over all, apply two coats.	2·50	5	18	21
	Bottom – scrub off, treat as topsides.	3·50	6	20	23
	Boot top – as for wood yacht.	0·5	1	3	4
	Bulwarks and coamings – as for topsides.	1	2	9	11
	Brightwork – as for wood yacht.	0·50	1	4	5
	Total	8	15	54	64
2nd	Repeat 1st year program but reduce catalyst spec. to one coat on topsides, coamings and brightwork.	8	12·50	54	57
	Bilges – scrub, chip off rusted parts, apply three coats to these and two coats over all.	2	3·50	10	13
	Accommodation – as for wood yacht.	1	2	5	6
	Total	11	18	69	76

2. STEEL—*continued*
Ungalvanized, Welded or Riveted Mild Steel, with Teak laid Decks

Year	Task	Amateur Cost		Boatyard Cost	
		A	B	A	B
3rd	Repeat 1st year program but touch up and burnish only for catalyst topsides, coamings and brightwork. Accommodation – rub, paint and varnish two coats in saloon.	8 1	8·50 1·50	54 7	17 8
	Total	9	10	61	25
4th	Repeat 2nd year program except accommodation. Accommodation – rub, paint and varnish two coats in galley and lockers.	10 1	16 2	64 5	70 6
	Total	11	18	69	76
5th	Strip all external surfaces. Prepare rusted area with compressed air needle gun. Prime twice, stop, apply three coats (including plant hire). Check and renew teak deck seam filling when required. Brightwork – strip, fill, three coats.	24 1 2	30 1 4	89 8 10	96 8 13
	Total	27	35	107	117
6th	As 1st year.	8	15	54	64
	Total over six years Average cost per year	74 12	111 18	414 69	422 70

3. ALUMINIUM ALLOY OR ZINC SPRAYED STEEL.
Welded or Riveted Hull with Unpainted Bilges and Teak laid Deck.

Year	Task	Amateur Cost		Boatyard Cost	
		A	B	A	B
1st	Topsides – rub, stop, two coats.	2·50	4	14	17
	Bottom – scrub, treat as topsides.	2·50	5	11	15
	Boot top – rub, stop, two coats.	0·50	1	3	4
	Bulwarks and coamings – as for topsides.	1	2	9	11
	Brightwork – as for wood yacht.	0·50	1	4	5
	Total	7	13	41	52

3. ALUMINIUM ALLOY OR ZINC SPRAYED STEEL—*continued*
Welded or Riveted Hull with Unpainted Bilges and Teak laid Deck.

Year	Task	Amateur Cost		Boatyard Cost	
		A	B	A	B
2nd	Alkyd Spec. as for 1st year.	7	—	41	—
	Catalyst Spec. Topsides – touch up and burnish.	—	1	—	5
	Bottom – as for 1st year.	—	5	—	15
	Boot top – rub, stop, one coat.	—	0·50	—	3
	Brightwork – touch up and burnish.	—	—	—	2
	Bilges – scrub only (if unpainted)	0·50	0·50	3	3
	Accommodation as for wood yacht.	1	2	5	6
	Total	8·50	6	49	34
3rd	Alkyd Spec. as for 1st year.	7	—	41	—
	Catalyst Spec. Topsides – rub, stop, one coat.	—	2	—	12
	Bottom – as 1st year.	—	5	—	15
	Boot top – as 2nd year.	—	0·50	—	3
	Brightwork – rub, stop, one coat.	—	1	—	4
	Accommodation, as for wood yacht.	1	1·50	7	8
	Total	8	10	48	42
4th	Topsides, bottom, boot top, brightwork and bilges as 2nd year.	7·50	7	44	28
	Accommodation, as for wood yacht.	1	2	5	6
	Total	8·50	9	49	34
5th to 8th	Repeat above program.	32	38	187	162
9th	Strip all external surfaces, rub, prime, stop, three coats.	8	14	57	66
	Check and renew teak deck seam filling where required.	1	1	8	8
	Brightwork strip, fill, three coats.	2	4	10	13
	Total	11	19	75	87
10th	As 1st year.	7	13	41	52
	Total over ten years	82	108	490	463
	Average cost per year	8	11	49	46

4. GLASS FIBRE
All Plastics with some Varnished Trim and Joinery. Coloured Topsides.
No Boot top.

Year	Task	Amateur Cost		Boatyard Cost	
		A	B	A	B
1st	Topsides – wash down. Build up damaged parts with pigmented resin. Burnish.	1	1	6	6
	Bottom – scrub, rub, stop, two coats.	2·50	5	12	16
	Upperworks and Decks – wash down.	—	—	3	3
	Brightwork – rub, touch up, two coats.	0·50	1	3	4
	Total	4	7	24	29
2nd	Topsides, bottom, upperworks, decks and brightwork, as for 1st year.	4	7	24	29
	Bilges – scrub with detergent. Accommodation – wash down fo'c'sle. Paint and varnish all wood trim.	0·50	1	6	7
	Total	4·50	8	30	36
3rd	Topsides, bottom, upperworks, decks and brightwork, as for 1st year.	4	7	24	29
	Accommodation – Wash down saloon. Paint and varnish all wood trim.	0·50	1	4	5
	Total	4·50	8	28	34
4th	Topsides, bottom, upperworks, deck and brightwork, as for 1st year.	4	7	24	29
	Bilges – as for 2nd year. Accommodation – Wash down galley and lockers, paint and varnish all wood trim.	0·50	1	6	7
	Total	4·50	8	30	36
5th	Topsides – Rub down with power sander, touch up, apply two coats paint (including plant hire).	5	7	16	19
	Bottom – strip all paint, rub down, two coats.	3	5·50	20	23
	Upperworks – wash down, build up damaged parts and burnish.	0·50	0·50	5	5

4. GLASS FIBRE—*continued*
All Plastics with some Varnished Trim and Joinery. Coloured Topsides. No Boot Top.

Year	Task	Amateur Cost		Boatyard Cost	
		A	B	A	B
	Decks – scrub down, one coat paint.	1	2	5	7
	Brightwork – strip, fill, three coats varnish.	1·50	3	9	11
	Total	11	18	55	65
6th	Topsides – rub, touch up. Alkyd two coats. Catalyst one coat.	2	2	14	8
	Bottom – as for 1st year.	2·50	5	12	16
	Upperworks and decks as for 5th year.	1·50	2·50	10	12
	Brightwork – as for 1st year	0·50	1	3	4
	Bilges and accommodation as for 2nd year.	0·50	1	6	7
	Total	7	11·50	45	47
7th	Topsides – Alkyd as for 6th year.	2	—	14	—
	Catalyst, touch up and burnish.	—	1	—	5
	Bottom – as for 1st year.	2·50	5	12	16
	Upperwork and Decks as for 5th year.	1·50	2·50	10	12
	Brightwork – as for 1st year.	0·50	1	3	4
	Accommodation – as for 3rd year.	0·50	1	4	5
	Total	7	10·50	43	42
8th	Topsides, bottom, upperwork, decks and brightwork as for 6th year.	6·50	10·50	39	40
	Bilges and accommodation as for 4th year.	0·50	1	6	7
	Total	7	11·50	45	47
9th	Topsides, bottom, upperworks, decks and brightwork as for 7th year.	6·50	9·50	39	37
	Total over 9 years	56	92	339	373
	Average cost per year	6	10	38	41
	Summary of Average Costs				
	Wood	8	14	52	54
	Steel	12	18	69	70
	Alloy	8	11	49	46
	Plastics	6	10	38	41

The range of marine coatings available (especially for steel work) is so bewildering that the best course open to the amateur is to decide whether to adopt one-can or two-can materials and then stick to the recommendations given in a certain paint maker's data sheets.

The costs in the previous schedules were based on typical maker's specifications, but variations are possible, especially when using alkyds. For instance, undercoats need not be used at all, as two gloss coats (used in the same way as ordinary varnish) will produce a very durable finish, while a single coat of gloss may be all that is required where the old surface is good and when no change of colour is required. Should a single coat fail to produce the desired quality, it might pay sometimes to delay applying a second coat until mid-season.

The catalyst materials allowed for in the schedules are normal two-can polyurethanes. Epoxy resin enamel would be more costly and one-can polyurethane not so durable. Although catalysts are normally slightly less than twice the price of alkyds, the increased wastage to be expected plus lower covering capacity, makes the material cost-ratio about two-to-one. Professional labour charges are also higher for catalysts as weather conditions are more critical and more time is required for cleaning brushes thoroughly at regular intervals.

The craft in the schedules are presumed to be of modern design with very little inside ballast. Although this reduces maintenance it would be advisable to clean the bilges every year to avoid unpleasant smells and to remove the inevitable accumulation of blanket fluff, crumbs, and the odd label off a food can which might wrap itself around the strum box.

The schedules are not intended to represent Class (a) perfection, and to maintain a smart appearance it may be necessary to touch up some paint and varnish during the season.

Referring again to the grp boat in the schedule, coloured topsides are assumed, for white topsides might be made to last for as long as eight years without needing painting. When buying a new or nearly new grp cruiser or dinghy try to find out whether the topsides were sprayed with car paint when built. Many grp boats are sprayed nowadays and this may be advantageous provided one can find out the exact type of material sprayed on, and recoat with this when required to maintain smartness.

Some grp hulls are left glossy below the waterline when new,

Picture 23. Yachtsmen are rarely experienced painters but they can do a faster and better job by making use of aids such as an edge shield.

Picture 24. Masking tape is another aid by no means scorned by professionals. Try to avoid using it over fresh paint in case the tender surface comes away when stripping off the tape.

so where antifouling is to be applied a thorough rubbing down will be required to produce a good key. In the schedule it was presumed that the grp hull was already prepared to receive antifouling when new.

Brushing Technique

There is quite a difference in the brushing action required for applying ordinary alkyd enamels, ordinary varnish, and the whole range of two-can materials. Some makers maintain that their undercoats are self levelling and will not show brushmarks. Under practical conditions this rarely proves to be true, so it pays to apply undercoat with great care laying off each panel with light parallel brush strokes as one would for enamel. Unless this is done, or unless the undercoat is rubbed down very hard afterwards, the erratic brush strokes on the undercoating will show through all subsequent coats.

The technique for applying ordinary alkyd or similar enamels is as follows. One third of the length of the bristles is submerged in paint and the bristles are stroked or gently tapped on the side of the paint kettle so that none drips off while transferring the brush from the kettle to the work.

83

A right-handed person normally works from right to left applying paint to the surface with quick strokes parallel to the seams on a planked boat, or, in general, in the direction of the wood grain. Crisscrossing strokes are then used to ensure that the paint is spread evenly, then this area is completed with quicker strokes in the original direction.

When several of these areas have been completed the whole panel is laid off by using long, gentle, slow strokes parallel with the grain holding the brush lightly between thumb and first finger at an angle of 60° to the work.

Laying off is very important if a good finish is to be achieved. These strokes are always made to terminate on the panel already coated and if done properly no joint should be visible after drying. If each panel laid off is too large, the paint on the previous panel may have started to dry and the strokes in this vicinity will have to be made very slowly to ensure a good join.

The drag on the bristles during each stroke should feel even. If the drag feels variable this means that the paint has not been distributed evenly. Increased drag may mean too thin a coating with poor gloss and durability. A lessening of drag may mean a pool of thick paint which will show run marks or *curtains* before the film dries, plus wrinkles after drying.

Having completed several panels one should always inspect the earlier ones for run marks. If these can be brushed out before the paint becomes too dry it may spoil the gloss a little but this will be preferable to run marks. Any insects which land on the wet paint are best left alone to be brushed off when the surface has completely hardened.

Where a second gloss coat is to be applied it pays to leave the first one as long as possible before rubbing as alkyd and similar enamels take about four days to harden sufficiently for dry rubbing in good weather and about two days for rubbing wet. Some of these paints need three months or more to become sufficiently hard to resist marking and abrasion, hence one of the reasons for the recommendation in Chapter 3 that painting and varnishing should be done in the Autumn.

Ordinary phenolic synthetic varnishes such as *Rylard* and *Spinnaker* are brushed on with a similar technique to alkyd paints, but they do have different characteristics. Having no pigment, varnish flows much more readily than paint. It hardens more rapidly and can be rubbed wet the following day. It tends to foam in the bristles and the tiny air bubbles formed may create imperfections in the surface.

Being so thin the coating is also thin and tends to show up specks collected from the brush and from the surface much more readily than the heavier pigmented paints. Therefore, for first class varnish work, the attention to such details as cleaning brushes, dusting off the surface, and keeping dust out of the atmosphere, needs to be rather more thorough than for paint work.

On the final coat of varnish much of the trouble due to air bubbles forming can be overcome if the foamed varnish in the bristles is stroked off into a separate can before applying any varnish to the surface. Not many people are likely to go to this trouble when covering a large area but for small parts such as hatches and coamings little extra time is taken to do this. After standing for some minutes most of the foam will disperse from the settling can and this varnish can then be strained and used, or kept for rough jobs.

The brushing technique for catalyst paints such as polyurethanes is quite different from the above. These materials have a very rapid drying time in warm weather which almost prohibits any possibility of laying off in sizable panels.

Professionals like to use a wide brush with fewer bristles than normal, a 3 in (75 mm) wall brush being commonly used. Whether paint or varnish, catalysts are best applied with a rapid crisscross action as used in emulsion wall paint. More practice is required than with alkyds to achieve a good technique and when this has been mastered one can use laying off strokes by keeping each panel no larger than about 1 ft (300 mm) square.

The material must not be brushed excessively to ensure an even coating, but this does not matter so much as with alkyds. A thicker coat normally results, but except for reducing the coverage per gallon this does not matter as these materials are slightly *thixotropic* (will not run) and the initial set occurs before runs or curtains can form. If two coats are to be applied without rubbing down between, adhesion is improved if the first coat is not left long enough to get rock hard.

Brightwork
When varnished surfaces are stripped to bare wood it always pays to apply a grain filler and perhaps a wood stain, before

the priming coat of varnish is applied. Each paint maker has his own specification for this job so the recommendation of one's chosen maker must be adhered to.

The grain fillers supplied are normally transparent or stained. The creamy filler is stroked across the grain by means of a piece of coarse cloth and surplus wiped away as the work proceeds. On hardening, a light rub down removes the thin film of filler from the surface and leaves the pores of the wood filled flush. This process saves the need to apply some three full coats of varnish, which would otherwise be needed to obliterate the roughness caused by the grain showing through to the surface.

Filling is not necessary on some softwoods if these have been correctly prepared by planing and sanding, but most hardwoods used in yacht work such as mahogany, teak, iroko and agba have surface pores which should be filled.

After rubbing down the filler flush, a coating of diluted naphtha stain is sure to be needed on most mahoganies to produce a pleasing colour after varnishing. Stain may be applied to the wood before grain filling. Grain fillers combined with stain are available and speed up the two operations. However, care is required to minimize the need for rubbing down a filler/stain to avoid a patchy effect.

Stains are available for mixing into varnish to give it any desired degree of colouration. This saves a lot of time and enables the colour to be built up during several coats, though it does have the snag that where varnish is chipped or rubbed off during use the original pale coloured timber may show through and be difficult to touch up neatly.

Teak should not require staining as its rich golden colour always returns when varnish is applied. All types of mahogany can be ruined by weathering, and very artful staining is required to match in areas which are bleached or blackened. Most species of mahogany, even when new, need staining red for the best appearance while pale timbers like agba and opepe look best if given a mahogany tint.

When the appearance of otherwise good varnish work is marred by a multitude of blackened areas where moisture has crept under fittings and stopping, these can be hidden almost completely by applying matching paint with a small sable hair artist's brush. By mixing together a few drops of different coloured enamels, a tint can be obtained which is almost exactly the same as the varnished surface. For teak, some orange enamel mixed with dark brown will usually do the trick while for mahogany, with its variable shades, one usually needs some signal red, maroon, yellow, and brown.

Although this method is not too successful on areas larger than about 2 in (50 mm) square, it rarely makes matters worse, and on small defects it should be perfect. If the touch up paint is covered by two coats of varnish it will continue to answer its purpose until the next complete stripping.

To achieve the perfect mirror finish normally desirable for a racing dinghy additional precautions not normally considered for average yacht varnishing are necessary. Work must be done indoors and dust must be minimized by plugging all ventilators and cracks; vacuum cleaning; moistening the floor, and arranging that no unauthorized access will be allowed until the varnish has hardened.

Dust excluding precautions should be taken one hour before work starts and for a mirror finish these precautions should be used for every coat not just for the final coat. Straining ordinary varnish through two layers of nylon stocking before use is essential. For mirror-finish work even newly opened cans should be strained. For the final coat specks on the surface are minimized if a new brush is used.

Nibs, or specks have already been mentioned. For a racing dinghy finish (with correct precautions) the average number of nibs should be kept down to about two per square inch (one per 3 cm^2). On normal good class brightwork, the number of nibs averages about 10 per sq in (5 per 3 cm^2), while on rough work where no precautions are taken to strain the varnish and keep brushes absolutely clean, the number may rise to as many as 100 per sq in (15 per cm^2).

Although a mirror finish can always be achieved with catalyst paints by burnishing when hard (and many racing dinghy enthusiasts use this specification) a tremendous amount of extra work is involved and this time can be saved by ensuring cleanliness. *Tack-rags* must be used to wipe the surface prior to varnishing as a dry cloth leaves a myriad unseen particles behind it.

Class (a) work is difficult to achieve in the open air and additional precautions are necessary to guard against rain, dew and frost. Early in the year work should cease before 1400 (or preferably before noon) with alkyd and similar materials, otherwise the surface may become bloomed by moist or cold weather. Bloomed paint is rarely entirely ruined, but has to be rubbed down and recoated to produce a proper gloss.

Even light rain falling on fresh paint or varnish is likely to produce a pock-marked surface which can only be rectified by hard rubbing down after hardening followed by a fresh coat. Rain and dew washing dirt from the decks can mark tender surfaces permanently even after they appear to have dried. This trouble can often be mitigated by pressing rags into deck rail scuppers.

If you find it difficult to strike in an accurate line where a painted surface ends, do not scorn the use of a sheet metal shield, but have some rag handy to wipe its edge clean occasionally during use.

Using Rollers

All the above notes on the care required to produce a mirror finish, apply almost equally to paintwork as to varnish. As speed of application is important to allow adequate time for drying, a paint roller proves useful on very large areas as the work can be completed in from one-half to one-third the time required with a brush. Rollers are not normally suitable for catalyst paints but with ordinary air-drying paints and varnishes first class results can be obtained with a little practice.

A team of two is essential, one with the roller and one using a fairly wide brush to lay off each panel and line in along the edges. If necessary the brush-man can carry a small pot of paint with a $\frac{1}{2}$ in (12 mm) or 1 in (25 mm) brush for lining in, together with a $2\frac{1}{2}$ in (60 mm) or a 3 in (75 mm) brush for laying off. The bigger brush should not need to be dipped in paint.

The roller-man should not hurry or he will get too far ahead of the brush-man and a team of three is not satisfactory as they get in each others way.

With enamel there is more danger of applying too much than too little, creating curtains before drying. The laying off process is absolutely essential to prevent a stippled effect. This effect may not be detrimental below the waterline on most cruising yachts. Information about the sizes and types of roller available is given in Chapter 2.

For use on narrow surfaces a brush is invariably more convenient than a roller, also on grooved boarding or panelling. For coating the bottom of a large vessel rollers with

88

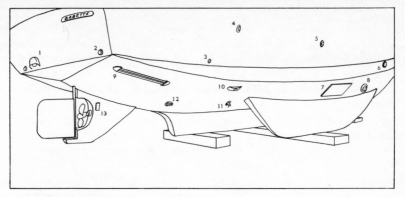

Drawing 7.   The skin fittings on a modern yacht:
1. *Engine exhaust outlet.*
2. *Cockpit drain.*
3. *Engine cooling water tell-tale outlet.*
4. *Bilge pump discharge.*
5. *Galley sink waste pipe.*
6. *Toilet soil discharge. Reach inside with antifouling paint.*
7. *Radio ground plate. Copper or sintered brass. Keep bright.*
8. *Toilet intake. Strainer easily clogged by paint.*
9. *Keel cooler for engine. Difficult to keep free of antifouling as the planking behind the tubes should be treated.*
10. *Transducer for depth sounder. Has a delicate surface which must not be scraped or painted.*
11. *Impeller for log/speed recorder. Is normally sited further forward. Should always be withdrawn when not needed.*
12. *Salt water intake for deck-wash pump. There may be a similar fitting for engine circulation water when a keel cooler is not used.*
13. *Zinc sacrificial anode. There may be others. Prevents corrosion of propeller and other metal fittings. Must not be painted and may need frequent renewal.*

extended handles of varying lengths can speed work tremendously, though they are not so convenient to load with paint from a sloping tray as rollers with normal length handles.

The main problems with roller technique are judging how much paint to take from the tray, making it cover the roller evenly, and how to roll the paint on to the surface with the correct pressure and number of traverses to ensure the requisite film thickness and evenness.

One is more likely to apply too much than too little and a watch must be kept for curtains as the enamel is laid off. Antifouling paint is too sticky to produce run marks and application can be as thick as possible. However, Hard Racing, graphite paints, and metallic copper antifoulings which can be burnished must be laid off with a brush as for enamel, to produce a smooth surface.

89

When correctly used a roller can apply paint more evenly than the average man with a brush and a roller can reduce the quantity of paint needed by as much as 10%. Do not forget to put a drop of oil on the roller bearings occasionally.

With rollers or brushes, in very cold weather, ordinary paint and varnish will work more quickly and more economically when kept warm during use. The final two coats should never be thinned to improve the workability. The best way to keep paint warm is to have two pots in use, each having only about $\frac{1}{2}$ in (12 mm) of paint inside. While one pot is in use the other one is kept just resting in hot water. If a proper wide paint kettle is used this will float on water when only containing $\frac{1}{2}$ in (12 mm) of paint so a large container of water may be used which, after once being heated with a blow-torch should remain hot for nearly an hour.

Antifouling

A not unfamiliar sight in winter is the yacht hauled out ashore with her bottom still covered with dried weed and barnacles. A tremendous amount of work can be saved later on if all fouling is scrubbed or scraped off immediately a craft is hauled out for laying-up. At this time barnacles will come off using a scraper made from plywood while a household scrubbing brush will make short work of all types of weed.

Class (c) boats invariably have a rough finish below the waterline but Class (a) finish is worth striving for as it makes a big difference to performance under sail or power. Any good paint maker will recommend a full specification for use under their antifoulings. Where a hull has been stripped off the chosen treatment should be given and this maker's products adhered to in the future. Unfortunately, paint makers or their various products, tend to come and go sometimes so there is always an element of luck.

Work below the waterline should always be left until last at fitting-out time, especially on a planked wooden hull for not only should work proceed from high level to low level (the way the paint drips!) but any seams that are opening up will be partly sealed with antifouling paint just before launching.

For a Class (a) finish chocks under the keel must be shifted to enable antifouling to be applied along the whole underside of the keel. Caution is required to avoid applying paint to a radio earth (ground), log impeller, cathodic protection plates or echo

Picture 25. The use of a grid enables underwater scrubbing and painting between tides to be tackled without having to lie prostrate on a wet beach.

Picture 26. A comfortable working position is necessary to make a good job of boot-top painting without masking tape. Will he get away with a single coat?

sounder transducer. An engine cooler is best painted, and so is the inside of a toilet soil pipe outlet (to avoid constriction of the orifice by barnacles) but the strainer holes for WC and engine water intakes should be reamed after painting if they appear clogged.

For a Class (a) job, the maker's underwater specification must be adhered to from bare wood to antifouling coat. Class (c) owners invariably apply two or three coats of black varnish as an undercoating to the antifouling. Each Spring, any powdery antifouling is rubbed away and one coat of black varnish applied, preceded by additional coats where any bare wood shows through.

Some Class (b) owners use the (a) method and some the (c). Numerous variations are possible. For instance, old craft which tend to leak when under way may use Black Rubber Sheathing (see Chapter 3) in place of black varnish and some old vessels may have copper sheathing.

Hulls sheathed with glass fibre need the same treatment as all-plastics craft. Cascover nylon sheathing needs its special vinyl undercoating. Copper sheathing needs no antifouling paint; it requires only annual scrubbing and cleaning, plus careful checking for loose nails, damage, and corrosion.

Black varnish is a poor undercoat for most makes of anti-fouling as it causes *alligatoring* of the surface about half-way through the season, the black varnish showing through like the joints in crazy paving. The system lends itself to a cheap antifouling where a second coat is applied mid-season.

Cast iron ballast keels are remarkably resistant to rust and can normally be given the same treatment as the rest of the hull. Steel bilge keels, whether galvanized or not, should receive the appropriate steelwork paint specification. Lead keels do not corrode and are normally treated with the chosen antifouling and its undercoat. Should a concrete keel be encountered, this can well be primed with one of the special preparations used for painting swimming pools.

Antifoulings containing metallic copper have always been popular as they can be applied at any time prior to launching and can be burnished for a racing finish. Beware, however, not to use them on or close to steel, zinc or aluminium, as serious electrolytic action may be set up in salt water. Copper paints will cover about 500 sq ft per gallon (10 m² per litre) whereas Kobe and similar thick paints cover about 320 sq ft (7 m²), but two coats are best for copper.

Hard Racing Copper (International Paints Ltd) is a quick-drying cellulose base material which can be scrubbed every two to three months without needing renewal, and may be left high and dry for six weeks without harm. It can be matted with fine abrasive paper for a racing finish. Spraying (with 10% thinners) is ideal, but if brushed on, one must never work back over the part already coated.

The antifoulings containing poisonous chemicals which are allowed to leach out slowly in water are normally applied a few hours before launching. When the intention is to launch on a morning tide, the best time for antifouling is during the evening before. As long as the paint does not become rock hard before submersion (and this depends largely upon the weather) the paint should last well.

As most weed grows just below the waterline, many owners apply a second coat of antifouling over this region and over the rudder just prior to launching.

When antifouling between tides do not put her up too high in case the next high water is lower and she gets beneaped! As the tide recedes, scrub her with fresh water, working in waders or a rubber suit if necessary. Fresh water dries off more quickly than sea water.

In order to paint on the dried surface it may be necessary to start at the waterline, transferring to the keel as soon as that has dried off and continue upwards in case the tide starts to rise.

Some owners carry a can of antifouling on board. Should they happen to run aground accidently on a falling tide, they then proceed to apply some antifouling as though they had beached the boat especially for this purpose!

Deck Painting

Decks on dinghies, runabouts, and launches are frequently varnished while many larger boats with laid teak decks have varnished covering boards and king planks. Although fine sand can be sprinkled on wet varnish to produce a non-slip surface, working decks are invariably painted unless made of scrubbed teak.

Decks covered with grp sheathing or Trakmark should have an integral anti-slip surface, but painting becomes necessary as the appearance deteriorates over the years. The big paint makers produce a full range of deck coatings including non-slip varieties for use on wood and canvas, epoxy resins for grp, and PVC paint for Trakmark.

Where the thick plastics sealing compositions such as Dekaplex are used over wood, canvas, or metal, no other coating need be used as these materials are available in the usual range of deck colours.

Special fine grit is available from the makers to sprinkle on to any material (including epoxy resin) to produce a non-slip surface. Grit or fine silver sand can be mixed with the paint before application or sprinkled on the surface while wet. Normally, the latter process is to be preferred.

Name Boards

Many yachtsmen use the standard transfers, Letraset, or stick-on metallic letters for name boards, though the Class (a) owner invariably has his in carved wood or gold leaf. New name boards can make a lot of difference to the appearance of a craft and many an owner could, with advantage, spend a few winter evenings carving or lettering.

Those not artistically minded may be able to enlist the help of a draftsman or sign-writer to rough out the name on a piece of paper which can then be pricked through lightly on to the teak boards.

Real gold leaf makes an attractive and lasting job. Two varieties are available in the form of small books, thus preventing loss of leaves in a strong wind. Real gold which has been beaten into microscopically thin leaves is the most expensive form, but the cheaper type where the gold has been sprayed on to a paper backing is quite satisfactory and is the more frequently used.

To fix gold leaf, a thin coating of goldsize or varnish is applied accurately to the area to be covered. A page of leaf is torn from the book and the gold surface is pressed on to the adhesive. The paper is peeled away and the process repeated until the whole of the leaf has been used up. The surface beneath the gold leaf should be prepared with all except the final coat of varnish. A well rubbed matt surface is essential for applying the goldsize accurately and although only one full coat of varnish is usual to permit the gold to show at maximum brilliance, care should be taken that this varnish is replaced immediately should it tend to flake.

Down Below

On a dinghy the interior paint and varnish often need more frequent attention than the outside if a smart appearance is to be maintained. For cabin boats the wise owner works out a program so that only a limited amount needs to be done each year. Bilges and internal ballast can sometimes be made to last as long as three years without painting although some cleaning work may be necessary to keep things smelling sweetly.

Most Class (c) boats, as well as many Class (b), will have black varnished bilges. This is quite satisfactory, but one should not attempt to change from paint to black varnish or vice versa.

Although an admirable procedure, only Class (a) owners normally rub down beneath the cabin sole prior to repainting! The others rely on a scrub (see Chapter 12) with one of the special bilge cleaning detergents followed by a good hosing with fresh water. If two coats are given every two or three years, the paint build up will be so gradual that the need for stripping can be almost forgotten.

Where white paint is used in cabins a modern good quality brilliant white is essential to avoid the yellowing that used to occur long before the paint film had lost its gloss. Catalyst materials are ideal below decks as they do not suffer from lack of adhesion there, and they may be burnished if necessary to retain a high gloss. Teak oil makes a good finish for bare hardwood.

If the cabin table can be brought home and sprayed with catalyst lacquer a superb finish similar to French polishing can be achieved. Catalyst wood lacquers are extremely tough, some being resistant to cigarette burns.

For the cold internal surfaces of metal and plastics hulls anti-condensation paints (some of which contain granulated cork) are an advantage where the surfaces are not lined with expanded or foamed material. Although most anti-condensation preparations may be overpainted with ordinary gloss finishes, a matt or eggshell finish is superior from the moisture collecting point of view. Household emulsion paints should not be used as explained earlier.

Special paints can be obtained for resisting the heat of an engine. No marine engine looks right, or ever seems to work right, unless kept neatly painted. Green or gray always looks workmanlike though metallic finishes in bright colours are found on new engines. If the makers' correct enamel can be kept in stock so much the better.

Few owners ever use the special paint made for the inside of water tanks and treatment is often left too late until the galley pump spews out rust coloured water. This means the tank had better go ashore, for the treatment described in Chapter 9.

Other peculiar painting jobs may crop up. One worrying problem is what to do with the inside of a centreboard case. On a dinghy the case is often made from solid mahogany which receives no preservative treatment whatever when new, or afterwards. Some careful owners plug the slot through the keel and fill the case with linseed oil for a week every few years and some do the same thing with *pentachlorophenol* timber preservative. Paint or varnish does not survive very well inside the case with chafe from the centreboard or plate.

On a cruising yacht the position is somewhat different. The case is likely to be accessible only upwards through the keel slot or through the hole below decks where the hoisting chain feeds through.

It helps to know what treatment the inside has received over the years, for there is little purpose in using a rot preservative on top of paint, or paint on top of black varnish. A steel case should have been galvanized originally and if an inspection from beneath reveals no rust it may be prudent to leave well alone.

As the centreplate or board must be dropped right out to make an inspection, it pays to apply some sort of preservative while the opportunity avails. Fortunately, the slot on a cruising boat is normally wide enough to enable an improvised long-handled brush to be inserted, but should the slot be very narrow (accommodating a metal centreplate) it may be necessary to plug the keel slot and fill the trunk with preservative poured in through the chain aperture. If this keel slot stopper is made neatly with a drain cock incorporated it should be possible to run off the preservative which can then be stored for future use.

As dropping a centreboard means chocking up the keel or digging a trench underneath it, this is an opportunity to draw a few keel bolts for inspection. At the same time all necessary work must be done on the centreboard, including its through fastenings, hoisting gear, pivot pin, ballast weights, friction pads, and edge protection bands.

When one buys a secondhand yacht or sailing dinghy it may prove difficult to discover whether the existing coatings were alkyd or catalyst. The best way to check this is to try burnishing the surface with metal polish. This action will improve the gloss on a catalyst finish but will cause any other type to go dull. However, there is no sure way to discover the difference between one-can and two-can polyurethanes.

Under ideal factory conditions superb results are possible by spraying all coats except for priming, while spray is ideal for the attractive speckle finishes used inside some plastics cruisers.

Considerable experience and the best equipment are necessary before the amateur attempts spraying. Precise masking of all extraneous parts is essential, plus sheeting over adjacent yachts. Paint makers' data sheets should be consulted beforehand to ensure that the correct type of apparatus is chosen, with correct nozzle, spraying distance, air pressure, and paint dilution. Some paints are intended only for use in airless spray guns.

96

CHAPTER 5

DECKWORK AND SHEATHING

On all craft except small launches, proper deck maintenance is extremely important. Even on a racing dinghy the plywood decking is an important structural member and being so readily visible its appearance is, to most people, an immediate indication of the condition of the rest of the boat. On cruising yachts deck leakage can be disastrous, rain water percolating through to the shelf, beams, and frames, causing rot much more readily than salt water. A cruising boat deck must also be safe to move about on (even when wet) while its good appearance is an asset.

Types of Decking

The upperworks and decks of modern grp yachts are frequently single mouldings having a glossy surface except for certain areas with anti-slip surfacing. Here you have a perfect watertightness and smart appearance, but a snare for the unwary crewman who slips on a glossy part during an emergency when the decks are wet.

Most motor cruisers and sailing yachts over 30 ft (9 m) in length and of Class (a) construction have teak decks, perhaps at more than one level. The older craft have *laid* teak, the planks being almost as thick as they are wide, caulked, and payed with marine glue. Class (a) craft built since 1950 are more likely to have marine plywood sheathed over with thin teak strips to give an appearance identical to laid decking. With both types of teak deck the planks may be either *swept* to follow much the same curvature as the sides of the ship when viewed from above, or they may all be laid straight fore-and-aft.

Teak decks should need very little maintenance. Frequent hosing down and occasional scrubbing keeps the timber and the seams in ideal condition but few yachtsmen are ever able to attend to this properly. To keep the wood smart a preparation such as *Teakbrite* can be used to minimize the time required for deck cleaning.

Most well built steel yachts have teak clad main decks while the coachroof and its coamings may be entirely of timber.

Commercial steel craft may have decks in painted chequerplate but more often a rubber/cement composition such as *Semtex* is spread over the surface to a depth of about $\frac{3}{4}$ in (18 mm) with self-colour or painted surface. Ordinary non-slip deck paints do not adhere very well to Semtex and it pays to use the special coatings made by Dunlop. If damage occurs to Semtex it may be chipped away and a new mix floated on.

Renewing Canvas

Canvas decks have always been widely used on small craft. Although highly satisfactory when well maintained the common fault is that on new craft the canvas used is often too thin, similar to calico weighing about 6 oz per sq yd (200 g per m²) whereas twice this weight produces a much longer lasting job. Recanvasing with untreated white cotton or flax canvas still produces the cheapest covering for old canvased decks, although *Trakmark,* grp, *Cascover,* or *Samcolastic* may be used as alternatives.

Marine plywood is usually used for the foundation underneath canvas nowadays although tongued-and-grooved boarding is still the cheapest way. As most boatyards lay the canvas on wet paint to act as an adhesive, the canvas tends to crack along T & G seams after a few years and leaks are inevitable, sometimes leading to rot.

When relaying canvas the results are more satisfactory and work is simpler if the paint is allowed to dry on the wood before fitting the canvas. The job is tricky enough without having to keep wet paint where it belongs. Special adhesives are produced for this purpose, some of which, being of a rubbery nature, are less likely than paint to produce cracking.

Where cracks and minor damage appear on old canvas decks, these should be sealed with a mastic such as Jeffery's *Seamflex* or Detel *Spreading Paste* before any new deck paint is applied. Where the cracking is general, it might pay to cover the whole deck with one of the liquid plastics sheathings such as *Dekaplex.*

Picture 27. Paying short lengths of seam in a leaky deck. Scrapers made from bent files are lying on deck plus a small brush to dust out each seam before pouring the marine glue.

Picture 28. Using a cartridge type sealer gun to lay bedding composition underneath a guardrail stanchion bracket.

This material cannot be brushed out like paint and except for the edges it may be found easier to apply it with a wide stripping knife. The adhesion, sealing, and wearing qualities are good provided two coats are applied, with one additional coat each successive year. Such materials are not cheap, but they will prolong the life of worn canvased, laid, or plywood decks for many years. The colour range available is not great but covers the most popular shades.

When new canvas must be fitted the opportunity should be taken to eliminate the causes of failure which may have been overlooked by the builders or previous repairers. Two faults have already been mentioned; using too thin a canvas and sticking this down with paint. Two other faults often need to be rectified.

Firstly, the edge of the deck is often left sharp with a half round beading fixed to the topsides and flush with the deck, the canvas being secured beneath the beading. The beading shrinks slightly after building, and the canvas soon gets chafed through on the sharp edge of the deck. When renovating, round off the deck edge generously and fit the beading about $\frac{1}{2}$ in (12 mm) lower down the sheer plank.

99

The second fault is that the quarter-round beadings used to secure the canvas along all coamings, around hatches, etc, are not shaped to fit the angle formed by the camber of the deck. These beadings come from the sawmill with the back angle a true 90°, but this angle may need altering to about 100° by planing. When fitted, the beading edges then seal tight along the deck and coaming with a pocket of mastic sealer trapped in the corner.

The third fault concerns lack of care in planing the T & G decking perfectly smooth before laying the canvas over it. Unless this is done a few joints are sure to be slightly proud and these show through the canvas, causing unsightly ridges which soon wear unfairly. Planing the boarding will also produce a fair camber throughout instead of a series of flats. Proud joints are not always the builder's fault as pine timber tends to shrink unevenly after planing flush.

Before commencing a recanvasing job one must remove all toe-rails, deck fittings, and edge beadings, so this is not a job to be undertaken lightly. The re-use of old beadings is never wise and as some yards nail these on they may have to be split during removal. When replacing them the use of brass (or preferably bronze) wood screws is well worth the extra cost, avoiding hammer marks, splits, and ensuring better water-tightness.

This may also be an excellent opportunity to renew old and battered toe-rails or handrails with smart new ones of teak or mahogany, to renew any faulty deck fittings, to get chainplates regalvanized, and to renew fastenings.

If the old canvas was stuck down with paint it may be necessary to burn it off. Frequently some areas come away easily while others prove obstinate and a Stanley *Surform Plane* is useful to rasp down to bare wood. Any copper tacks must be pulled out and all other nail heads punched well down before planing or sanding is started. After priming, at least two coats of paint should be applied and although an old fashioned white lead exterior paint is ideal for this many people use a mixture of all the oddments of undercoat and gloss paint they can find!

To minimize the number of joints, canvas up to 3 yds (3 m) wide may be obtained, but if only the more common 1 yd (1 m) canvas is available as many seams as possible should be sewn (by a sailmaker or awning maker), after cutting out but before fixing. All other joints made during fixing should be sealed

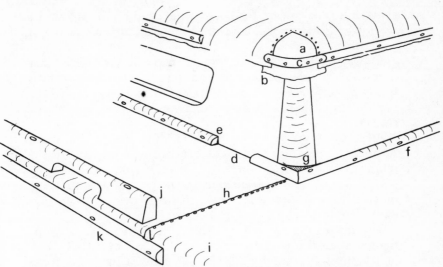

Drawing 8. Recanvasing the most awkard type of decks and cabin top.
(a)Separate patch to cover rounded corner. (b) Canvas to be trimmed after fitting beadings. (c) Beading here made of lead to take radius neatly. (d) Canvas not turned up coaming in this case as efficient sealer to be used. (e) Quadrant beading shaped to permit a pocket of sealer to lodge behind. (f) Screws into coaming give better seal than if vertical into deck. (g) Quadrants mitred with filler inserted to meet rounded corner post. (h) Canvas joint fixed with close tacking instead of sewing. (i) Deck edge well rounded. (j) Footrail refitted and through-bolted. Note scupper. (k) Canvas bedded under half-round beading. (l) Small notch in back of beading to house double canvas thickness at joint.

with impact adhesive or mastic and secured with a row of closely spaced copper tacks near to the exposed edge. The canvas along these edges is usually turned under for about $\frac{1}{2}$ in (12 mm). This creates a hump and in practice it proves quite satisfactory to leave a raw cut edge (or preferably a selvedge) as this is soon sealed over with deck paint.

On wide expanses of deck such as big fore decks and coachroof and wheelhouse tops a central fore-and-aft seam is convenient when using narrow canvas as it simplifies the marking out and fitting of the canvas around the usual centre-line obstructions such as hatches; ventilators; mooring post; anchor windlass, or masts.

On decks which are so wide that several pieces would be necessary, running the canvas athwartships is usually to be preferred. Where edge beadings have to jump over either a sewn or a tacked seam the back of the beading should always be notched out accordingly with fastenings arranged close at either side.

Canvas seams should be lapped in the direction of water flow like the tiles or shingles on a roof. Therefore, canvas laying should start at the lowest part of the decking, usually the narrow side decks on most dinghies, sailing and motor cruisers.

A few tricks will be learned while tackling these simple areas. Although as mentioned above, laying canvas dry is generally more satisfactory than sticking it down, in places where the deck is slightly hollow, resin glue may be used. It used to be the practice to soak the deck canvas in water before fitting into place, but this is rarely done nowadays.

The main essential when laying is to stretch the canvas as tightly as possible in all directions. Along the narrow side deck of a cruising yacht, the edge along the coachroof coaming should be fixed first. Borrow a sealing gun which holds packs of mastic, and run a bead of this along the corner before offering up the canvas. Secure the canvas around the middle of the length with one or two copper tacks into the deck close to the coaming, leaving enough canvas running vertically to allow a little to be trimmed off after the quarter-round beading has been fitted.

Stretch the canvas towards the bows and continue tacking into the deck at intervals of about 4 in (100 mm) right to the end. Then pull out towards the stern and do likewise. Now run another bead of sealer along, press the new beading into this and screw it into place. If the correct amount of sealer has been used it should ooze out slightly along the beading edges.

Starting in the centre, stretch the canvas athwartships and tack to the topsides. Stretch the canvas towards the bows and continue tacking from the centre pulling the canvas tightly athwartships before each tack is driven. Then the half-round sheer beading is screwed into place and the excess canvas is trimmed off with a sharp knife.

Although there is no likelihood of rain leaking underneath the canvas on the deck edge, some types of sailing craft can have the gunwale submerged for considerable periods when under way and on this type of vessel it pays to use the sealer underneath the canvas and under the beading.

Suitable sealers are available at hardware stores *Seelastic, Dow Corning,* and *Evomastic,* are the most readily available.

 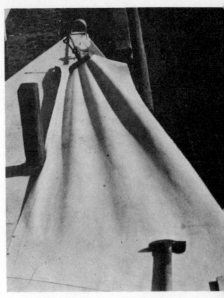

Picture 29. Applying bedding composition to the toe rail before bolting down on completion of recanvasing a deck.

Picture 30. To ensure that deck canvas remains free from wrinkles, thorough stretching is advisable. In this instance the canvas has been pinched with a G-cramp and two blocks of wood, a cord attached to this being bowsed down overboard.

Each maker supplies his own size of gun which holds a big cartridge of sealer. On squeezing the trigger, the sealer is ejected from a nozzle rather like toothpaste from a tube and a continuous ribbon may be laid rapidly just where required without getting the sticky material on one's hands. Aerosol type sealer packs are also made (e.g. *Handiseal* and *Secomastic*) which exude the contents at the press of a button.

Some of the sealer is sure to ooze out when the beadings are fitted. Most of this can be scraped off with a small piece of plywood or with a well rounded stripper knife. A rag soaked in turps will do the rest. Each deck fitting or its mounting chock must be set in mastic to prevent water seepage. The above sealers will do this, but special bedding compounds (some being of the synthetic rubber variety) are produced by the leading paint makers.

Make sure all quadrant (quarter-round) beadings are shaped to fit the angle between deck and coamings, as mentioned above. This is an essential point which is often overlooked.

It may not be possible to make the quadrant mouldings in single lengths on the longest runs and in any case long lengths of moulding are difficult to handle and are easily broken. Simple butt joints are quite commonly used, with a screw fastening close to each side of the joint.

When two pieces of quadrant meet at a coaming corner the mitred joint may not be a true 90°. Should the coamings have rounded corners a space will be left behind the mitre and this can be filled with epoxy resin.

Should the corner be of very large radius the correct procedure is to make a curved quadrant from solid wood to fit neatly around the corner post. When fitting the canvas to a curve, a series of cuts must be made to enable it to turn up without puckering. Much the same will be necessary where the quadrant mouldings are used around deck obstacles and fittings.

One sometimes sees metal cleats, eyebolts and similar fittings, attached direct to a canvas deck. A much sounder idea is to insert a pad of wood between the metal and the deck, and although teak is ideal for this a pad of $\frac{3}{8}$ in (9 mm) or $\frac{1}{2}$ in (12 mm) marine plywood is often quite suitable, especially if painted.

The quadrant mouldings generally fitted by yacht builders are frequently rather too small in section, $\frac{3}{8}$ in (9 mm) being quite common. When renewing these it pays to go to the next larger stock size. Bigger mouldings are easier to handle and less liable to break where the screw holes pass through. There is also another advantage. Many small craft have coachroof coamings which are too high for good appearance. This may be mitigated if the quadrant mouldings are painted the same colour as the deck (instead of being varnished), big mouldings helping this illusion.

Instead of making the screw holes to bisect exactly the angle at the back of the quadrant, try to get the screws nearer to the horizontal, but note some boats have coamings which sit on top of the deck so beading screws must then be driven nearly vertical.

Butt joints are not really suitable for the half-round sheer beading, a scarf joint being more resistant to the damage which may occur along this part. Each scarf should be made on similar lines to the scarf joint in the planking of a clinker boat, facing aft so that any collision while the yacht is moving forward tends to keep the scarf in place instead of tearing it off.

On small fragile mouldings the scarf should be resin glued. A scarf angle of about 6 to 1 is about right, preferably with a $\frac{1}{8}$ in (3 mm) lip at the exposed end to eliminate a fragile feather edge. Two screw fastenings through the scarf are sufficient. Prime the backs of all mouldings and also the butts and scarf surfaces.

Laying Trakmark

Embossed PVC materials such as *Trakmark* are tailored in a similar manner to canvas. A special impact adhesive is used to fix the material to the deck and all joints are overlapped about 1 in (25 mm) and sealed with this adhesive. As these joints create a hump and are liable to peel away when kicked, some people prefer to use butt joints covered by narrow half-round aluminium or brass strips fastened with small screws and laid on sealing compound. Exposed butts always shrink apart after laying.

As an impact adhesive is used, the material cannot be shifted once laid, so one or two helpers are almost essential to enable the sheeting to be held up until accurate positioning is certain. Small sheets are naturally easier to lay than large ones and working in small units invariably leads to greater economy when tailoring peculiarly shaped pieces from a roll.

Very few tacks should be necessary before everything is clamped down permanently with the beadings, and sealer is not essential under these.

Because adhesive is used to hold *Trakmark* in place the bare wooden decking requires no more than priming prior to gluing. The impact adhesive is applied to both surfaces and at any time after the glue feels dry the two parts may be brought together for a permanent bond.

A piece of thin plywood makes a good tool for applying the rubbery solution but a special toothed metal applicator is available.

New materials similar to *Trakmark* are constantly being introduced and as the makers provide full instructions for laying, the amateur should find no problem when using these in conjunction with the above notes.

Apart from glass fibre, Cascover, Samcolastic and other sheathing systems, house-boats and certain Class (c) vessels may adopt cheaper forms of covering such as linoleum, roofing felt, and painted hessian (burlap).

Deck Leaks

Covering a deck is by no means a simple job and should not be undertaken lightly. Deciding when it must be done is somewhat similar to working out when the outside of a yacht's hull should be completely stripped of paint. The evil day can be postponed repeatedly by curing leaks individually and repairing surface damage, while new materials are always appearing to enable the day to be postponed even further.

Leaks are sometimes extremely difficult to locate for not only does water often emerge inside at a point quite remote from the external leakage point, but rainwater leaks may appear in different places from leaks due to shipping green seas and spray, while the right conditions of wetness rarely occur when one is ready to explore for leaks.

When a certain spot along a quadrant moulding or at a deck fitting is suspected one can quite easily fabricate a small embankment with *plasticene* or window putty so that a pool of water can be retained at the likely spot and a watch kept below to observe the results. A larger well can be created by using strips of plywood in conjunction with plasticene.

It may not always be necessary to strip off mouldings and fittings to enable them to be properly bedded in mastic, as some excellent (though expensive) sealers, such as *Polyseamseal* (made by Darworth Inc., Simsbury, Connecticut) in large tubes are available from yacht chandlers and are ideal for curing this type of leak. These tubes have a fine nozzle attached enabling a thin ribbon of the white sealer to be run along a corner. They shrink to a neat fillet of hard rubber consistency on drying with excellent adhesion and lasting qualities.

There was a time when caulked teak decks were popular on small yachts, but to avoid excessive weight the planking had to be too thin to support caulking reliably. Most of these decks have now been sheathed with one process or the other to eliminate the persistent leaks, but where a caulked deck will not stay tight due to slight movement of the seamed planking, the trouble can usually be cured permanently by recaulking with *PRC* or *Calfa* as described later in this chapter.

When seams have been caulked and payed with marine glue in the conventional manner a leak can sometimes be cured by remelting the glue, using a short piece of steel (shaped to the width of the seam) which is first heated in a flame. The metal should not be too hot as overheating causes the glue to lose its

106

elasticity. This job is rather tedious when required on long lengths though by using two tools one of them can always be kept hot.

If electricity is available a big electric soldering iron can be shaped to do the job. Remember that although teak is quite resistant to scorching, this is not so in the case of a pine deck. Scorch marks can be avoided by keeping the temperature of the metal as low as possible and shaping it slightly narrower than the width of an average seam. The wood should not be moistened as this might vitiate the adhesion of the glue when molten.

If much of the paying appears loose and brittle it may all need renewal. If the paying was properly done originally the seam glue will have adhered to the caulking cotton or oakum and some of this will be pulled away when the paying is raked out. However, if the caulking is in good condition it pays to leave it in place and harden it down with the correct width caulking iron, using slightly more marine glue when paying the seams once more. Details of caulking are given in Chapter 3.

Another (though rather costly) method sometimes used for sealing the caulked pine decks on certain working craft which are converted to yachts consists of laying an entirely new surface with teak strips about $\frac{3}{8}$ in (9 mm) thick over the whole deck. These strips are normally 5 in (125 mm) wide with one false seam grooved up the centre.

After bedding on resorcinol glue and fastening with brass panel pins, the shallow seams are filled with PRC or a similiar synthetic rubber composition. Depressions worn in the old deck should first be filled up to level with Jeffery's *Mendex* and screeded off with a straightedge. Any protruding nail heads should be knocked down and if possible the whole of the old deck should be smoothed off with a belt sander.

For a similar appearance, especially on small decks, this sheathing may be carried out with *Plydek,* a form of plywood with the outer surface of thin teak strips with the caulking already in place. Full sheets are normally made 8 ft by 4 ft (2400 mm x 1200 mm), so unless athwartships joints can be covered in some way laying Plydek on areas longer than 8 ft (2400 mm) is difficult.

When improving a yacht of poor specification with pine boards or perhaps ordinary plywood for the cabin sole or cockpit flooring, Plydek can be used to great advantage. Unless there is little or no wastage it works out more expensive than

107

using thin teak strips, but Plydek saves a tremendous amount of labour and does not require so perfect a backing of solid wood.

Sheathing with Glass Fibre

No method of sheathing using resins should be undertaken when the old surface is painted or treated with preservative. These sheathing materials are expensive and unless perfect adhesion can be assured, the amateur is advised to try some other form of protection.

When used on perfectly dry new wood a successful job can be guaranteed, but getting rid of patches of old paint is difficult unless the surface is planed or power sanded to remove a film of wood. Even then there may be trouble due to the heads of fastenings close to the surface.

On new work the correct type of resin putty which is compatible with the sheathing resin will have been used. On old work, all seams may have to be repayed and all the stoppings over nail and screw heads replaced with the resin putty, as nothing must be allowed to vitiate the bonding of the sheathing to the wood.

These notes on sheathing are intended to apply to the outside of a hull as well as to decking, though it must be remembered that on a large hull which cannot be turned over, applying glass fibre beneath the waterline can be much more difficult and messy than dealing with the level and accessible surface of a deck.

Sheathing a deck is normally done for only two reasons on an old boat: curing leaks and minimizing future maintenance. The reasons for sheathing the outside of a hull may be slightly different because below the waterline it can be used instead of copper sheathing to exclude teredo worm and other marine borers, and it also reduces galvanic action. On a plywood planked hull it helps to protect the relatively thin skin against chafe and other damage on the topsides as well as the bottom.

Although polyester resin is normally used with glass fibre materials, two-can polyurethane paint or varnish will do almost the same job on any good surface, while the more expensive epoxy resin should always be used where good adhesion is suspect.

As so many variations in materials and surfaces are possible the amateur should obtain advice from one of the many suppliers of these materials who advertise in the practical

Yachting Journals. Advice from several sources is not a bad thing as some of the firms deal with only one type of resin and costs can be quite variable.

When working on a vertical surface the resin must contain (or have mixed into it) a *thixotropic agent* to prevent it from draining downwards along the surface. As this cannot be done with most polyurethane paints, if these materials are used with glass fibre they are only suitable for use on horizontal surfaces. To colour polyester resin a large quantity of special pigment must be added. This is not necessary with a polyurethane paint as the requisite colour can be chosen from the makers' chart.

For sheathing, woven glass cloth should always be used, as the cheaper chopped strand mat used for grp hull construction does not give a good enough surface for sheathing. Sometimes *scrim* (a very open weave cloth looking rather like small mesh netting) is used for the main reinforcement with a single layer of thin surface tissue cloth just below the surface to give a good finish.

Note, however, that for deck sheathing, where anti-slip properties are very important, a rough surface is a big advantage and scrim cloth throughout is the best way of producing this, coupled with a sprinkling of sand on the outer gel coat. Scrim produces an effect rather like treadplate whereas chopped strand mat produces a surface like marmalade spread on toast. Be careful to keep sanded resin clear of deck cleats.

Many yachtsmen expect sheathed topsides to have as good a surface as a plastics hull, but this is never possible and the surface is likely to be rougher and more wavy than the original timber.

Another thing that sheathing cannot be expected to do is to strengthen a weak hull that works when under way. In a hull that works, there must be some movement between the timber and the glass fibre, or a certain amount of bending along seams. Such movement will eventually cause the sheathing to part from the hull; water will get behind it, rotting the wood or perhaps freezing and causing delamination.

Where grp sheathing is used on a carvel or clinker hull its thickness must be sufficient to resist the inevitable slight movements along the seams as the planking dries out and takes up again from season to season and extra care should be taken with such a boat to see that she is not left out of the water any longer than is necessary.

The following table shows approximate details of the weight, weave, and number of thicknesses of glass cloth required for sheathing yachts of various sizes both on deck and for topsides and bottom.

TABLE 4
GRP Sheathing Specifications

Specification		Light Cloth	Medium Cloth	Scrim	Surface Tissue
Weight of material	oz. per sq. yd.	7	12	9	2
	gr. per sq. m.	237	407	304	68
Thickness of material thou.		9	15	15	3
	microns	220	380	380	762
Total resin for one layer	lb. per sq. yd.	1·4	2	2·4	included
	gr. per sq. m.	48	68	81	included
Total resin for two layers	lb. per sq. yd.	2·1	2·7	3·6	included
	gr. per sq. m.	71	92	122	included

Boat length in feet and metres	Sheathing Job	Light Cloth	Medium Cloth	Scrim	Surface Tissue
Under 14 ft (4·3)	Exterior of hull	1 layer	—	—	—
14–20 ft (4·3–6)	Topsides	1 layer	—	—	—
condition good	Bottom	1 layer	—	—	—
	Deck	—	1 layer	—	—
14–20 ft (4·3–6)	Topsides	1 layer	—	—	—
condition doubtful	Bottom	2 layers	—	—	—
	Deck	—	—	1 layer	—
20–30 ft (6–9·2)	Topsides	1 layer	—	—	1 layer
condition good	Bottom	2 layers	—	—	—
	Deck	—	—	1 layer	—
20–30 ft (6–9·2)	Topsides	—	1 layer	—	1 layer
condition doubtful	Bottom	—	2 layers	—	—
	Deck	—	—	2 layers	—
30–50 ft (9·2–15)	Topsides	—	1 layer	—	1 layer
condition good	Bottom	—	2 layers	—	1 layer
	Deck	—	—	1 layer	—
30–50 ft (9·2–15)	Topsides	—	2 layers	—	1 layer
condition doubtful	Bottom	—	3 layers	—	1 layer
	Deck	—	—	2 layers	—

Glass sheathing is frequently a messy job. Having good helpers makes things easier for not only does this speed up the work, but it also enables one to clean sticky fingers with acetone and hot soapy water occasionally without holding up the job.

The first operation is normally the application of thinned resin (or a special type of resin) to prime the bare wood. This resin is mixed with a *hardener* (and perhaps also an *accelerator*) but does not normally require the addition of a thixotropic agent or a pigment.

Only the area intended to be sheathed during the next few hours should be primed as in general grp work should proceed almost continuously without allowing any layer to cure completely before applying the next. Follow the maker's instructions explicitly when mixing resins and use a mixing paddle on an electric drill when large quantities are involved.

As soon as the priming coat has gelled, a thick coat of the moulding resin is brushed on quickly and a previously tailored sheet of the glass cloth is pressed into the resin by means of a washer or a vane type roller or by stippling with a stiff brush. This rolling operation must be carefully undertaken from the centre of a panel towards the edges so that all air bubbles are squeezed out.

On cruising boats the glass cloth is normally hung vertically like wallpaper, while on boats which can be turned over (such as dinghies, launches, and runabouts) laying fore-and-aft is simpler, especially if one roll width will cover one side of the hull.

Where cloths are joined there should be an overlap of about 1 in (25 mm) and the joints should be staggered where two or more layers of cloth are used. The cloth is flexible and can be pulled in any direction during moulding to conform to the curvature of a hull.

Subsequent layers of cloth should preferably be applied within one day of the last layer to prevent the resin from curing completely. However, one must not forget to run over the hardened surface with a Stanley *Surform* to remove any stiff threads of glass or curtains of resin as these can affect subsequent layers.

When a planked hull is to be sheathed from the boot-top to the keel only, a shallow rebate can be planed along the boot-top line to house the sheathing and make it flush with the topsides. Where this is not done (as on plywood boats) the sheathing may be ground off to a feather edge on completion, but remember to assist this when using two layers of cloth by ending the inner one 1 in (25 mm) below the outer one.

For deck sheathing the cloth may be tailored in a similar manner to deck canvas. The beadings should be fitted before the resin hardens completely or trimming off the protruding excess sheathing will be most difficult. If the sheathing turns up the coamings behind the quadrant beading, any varnish or paint on the coamings in this vicinity must, of course, be scraped clean to secure a good bond with the resin.

111

As soon as the last layer of glass has been placed and the resin set, pigmented gel coats of special resin may be brushed on to produce the final surface. These coats should not be built up to a great thickness or they become brittle and are liable to craze in time or with local damage.

On decks, only one layer of pigmented resin should be brushed on or the intended roughness of the scrim cloth will be hidden. As the gel coat wears with use additional ones will be painted on over the years. This layer must not build up into too great a thickness on the areas which are little worn.

By repeatedly rubbing down heavily on topsides and applying extra gel coats of resin (or preferably two-can polyurethane paint) it may be possible to attain a fine surface which can be burnished to a mirror finish, though this takes much time. Costs can be reduced by adding 25% by weight of *filler* (such as powdered titanium oxide or chalk) to polyester finishing coats in addition to the pigment.

Sheathing with Cascover

The *Cascover Process* is exclusive to Borden Chemicals Ltd, North Baddesley, Southampton. Information and kits should be obtained direct from them. Although slightly more expensive than grp the process has certain advantages, being generally less messy, more convenient to use on overhead surfaces or under the turn of the bilge, and more practicable than grp on clinker boats.

The process consists of sticking a layer of finely woven nylon cloth on to the bare wood with resorcinol glue and finally coating the nylon with from three to five layers of *Cascote* eggshell finish vinyl paint which may be overcoated with deck paint, antifouling or topside enamel.

Although two grades of nylon cloth are available, the lighter 7 oz per sq yd (240 g. per m²) cloth is only used for sheathing dinghies and similar size craft while the heavier $12\frac{1}{2}$ oz per sq yd (430 g. per m²) cloth is used in a single layer for all sheathing work on larger vessels. Both are made in widths of 38 in (1 m) and 54 in (1370 mm).

As the glue does not soak right through the cloth one's hands do not become contaminated during laying, but to ensure close contact of the nylon to the glue thin strips of pine must be stapled on top of the cloth until the glue has hardened.

112

Picture 31. Sheathing a dinghy with the lightest weight Cascover nylon. The operator is applying glue before folding the cloth over the keel. The cloth will be cut and glued into the centreboard slot at a later stage.

Picture 32. Heavy Cascover nylon being fitted to the bottom of a round bilged motor launch. Note the spacing of the temporary laths stapled to the hull as gluing and stretching proceeds.

The strips of pine are normally made about $\frac{7}{8}$ in (22 mm) wide and a bare $\frac{1}{8}$ in (3 mm) thick, close sawn in lengths to suit the girth of the hull. The staples used have $\frac{3}{8}$ in (9 mm) prongs and are inserted with an industrial trigger tacker, one of which can be hired from Borden if not available locally.

The battens are normally fixed fore-and-aft at intervals of about 18 in (450 mm) on flat and convex surfaces and as close as 2 in (50 mm) on sharp concave curves. Vertical strips are stapled over the full height of the work at intervals of about 30 in (750 mm) according to the system of cloth laying.

These strips may appear to be rather troublesome but in practice they enable the nylon to be stretched perfectly in all directions, and as work proceeds along the hull or deck, there is no need to keep interrupting work to look back for sagging or wrinkled cloth on the earlier sections.

With Cascover (as with grp and most other sheathing processes) all skin fittings should be removed and the recesses enlarged by about $\frac{1}{32}$ in (0·5 mm) all around and deeper to allow the sheathing to turn underneath. When gluing the nylon into these recesses, bare staples are used to hold the cloth firmly in place, or, alternatively, the actual fitting is replaced temporarily to act as a clamp.

Such staples are easily prized out on completion without causing too much damage to the cloth, and all staple holes are in any case completely filled with the vinyl coatings.

Should it prove impossible to remove certain skin fittings (such as a rudder strap) the sheathing should not cover this but should end neatly around it secured with bare staples. Sheathing should run continuously over wooden bilge keels, but should not cover iron or lead ballast keels.

Any metal stem band or keel band must be completely removed to allow the sheathing to run underneath it and this is an excellent opportunity to renew these strips which so frequently become corroded or damaged.

Having prepared the wooden surface for sheathing and completed all stopping with the correct resin putty, the next move is to sheath all the awkward small areas such as propeller shaft blisters, wooden keel, stem and forefoot.

To do the after face of the sternpost may necessitate removing the rudder; an excellent opportunity to check over the gudgeons, pintles, stock, and trunk. Sheath the rudder last with offcuts of cloth.

On dinghies, launches, and all light craft under about 25 ft (8 m) in length, Cascover nylon is normally laid fore-and-aft. If the 38 in (1 m) cloth width will not reach from waterline to keel (or whatever part is to be sheathed) the selvedge is run along the waterline or boot-top (preferably into a recess as explained above) and a joint overlapping about 2 in (50 mm) is made towards the keel, the full width cloth being fitted first.

The nylon is first tailored to fit with some overlap at the stem and sternpost by holding it roughly in position by means of drawing pins (thumb tacks) and before removing it the centre is secured to the hull with a pine strip and staples, the cloth being stretched sideways during this process. All the cloth from this strip to the stem is then rolled up.

Glue is brushed on to the surface for a distance of about 30 in (750 mm) from the centre strip and the cloth is then stretched over this and secured with strips and staples. For stretching the cloth a small piece of hardboard, held and used like a cabinet scraper is ideal.

114

The next similar panel towards the stem is then started and the process continued to that end of the boat.

Having completed that, the centre pine strip is pulled off, the cloth is rolled up from aft and gluing procedure is continued from the first panel that was completed. The next day all wooden battens can be prized off and any additional strips of cloth glued into position.

It pays to give at least two coats of the vinyl dope before skin fittings, keel bands etc. are replaced. No rubbing down of the vinyl coating should be undertaken until the weave of the cloth has been almost completely obliterated.

For all craft longer than about 25 ft (8 m) the cloths are normally laid vertically downwards from sheer to keel, working from aft so that the joints overlap in the direction of water flow. The joints will always show slightly where the finished surface is glossy and to overcome the problem there is no reason why the topsides should not be laid with a single fore-and-aft sheet of Cascover with vertical cloths overlapping this from boot-top to keel.

A useful trick ensures that where sheathing ends along the boot-top an accurate clean cut line can be formed with no glue starvation right at the edge and no glue deposited on the topside paint.

To accomplish this a planed pine batten 2 in (50 mm) wide and $\frac{1}{4}$ in (6 mm) thick is tacked to the hull with its lower edge exactly where the sheathing is to end. A pencil line is marked along the hull at top and bottom of the batten and the batten is then pulled off.

A roll of 2 in (50 mm) Sellotape is obtained and a strip of this is stuck to the hull between the two pencil lines.

Glue and cloth are allowed to run on to the tape for, say, half its width, and when the glue has set and all the temporary pine strips have been removed, the batten is tacked back into its original position and a sharp trimming knife is passed along the lower edge, severing the sheathing in exactly the right place.

On removing the batten the *Sellotape* may be stripped away, taking the 1 in (25 mm) or so of sheathing with it, leaving perfectly clean topsides and a fine sheathing edge which is firmly glued. Do not let the glue get too hard before cutting.

Using Cascover on decks involves the same procedure as for hulls together with the system of tailoring suggested for canvas and grp deck sheathing. A team of three people is ideal – one applying resin and cleaning brushes, one stretching cloth into place, and one fitting the strips.

Other Sheathing Systems
Copper sheathing under the waterline is rarely used nowadays owing to the high cost, but it has the enormous advantage of never needing to be antifouled, the metal acting as a permanent layer of metallic antifouling paint. This is a great advantage for long distance cruising where facilities for slipping may not always exist.

Unfortunately, the finest sheathing system for hulls ever devised is not at present available. Under a patent held by Camper & Nicholson Ltd, Gosport, prefabricated glossy sheets of grp were manufactured by Morgan Giles Ltd, Teignmouth, by laying up the sheets on polished steel tables.

These sheets arrived on site with cellophane covering the glossy surfaces and brown paper backing over the rougher surfaces of partly-cured resin. With the sheets glued to a hull with polyester resin, a superb transparent finish could be obtained, eliminating the problems experienced in fitting cloth to overhead surfaces.

Another popular modern sheathing material for decks and hulls is *Samcolastic*. This material comes in rolls like thin roofing felt, which is tailored to fit in the usual manner. After each sheet has been positioned and pinned, the material is soaked with a special liquid which causes it to adhere and also to cure, leaving a rock hard sheathing of reinforced plastics.

All sheathing materials can be obtained through yacht chandlers and this is normally the correct procedure for the amateur to adopt. Some of the newer materials such as Samcolastic are advertised by the makers, agents or importers and may be ordered direct.

Amongst the liquid sheathings available, those for decks have already been mentioned and Black Rubber Sheathing for use below the waterline was described in Chapter 4. *Limpetite* is a catalyst hardening synthetic rubber compound produced by Protective Rubber Coatings Ltd, Paynes Shipyard, Bristol, which sticks fast to timber or steel hulls producing a leakproof hard rubber sheathing of almost indefinite life.

Deciding what form of sheathing to adopt is made easier if the approximate relative costs are known. The following table

116

TABLE 5
Costs of Sheathing Processes

Material	Amateur Cost per sq. yd. (m.)		Boatyard Cost per sq. yd. (m.)	
	£ in U.K.	$ in U.S.A.	£ in U.K.	$ in U.S.A.
Polyester resin and one layer cloth	1·80	5·50	3·90	15·00
Polyester resin and two layers cloth	2·50	7·60	5·50	22·00
Epoxy resin and one layer cloth	2·40	7·70	4·50	17·50
Epoxy resin and two layers cloth	3·00	9·40	6·20	24·20
Cascover 7 oz.	2·70	7·50	4·80	17·00
Cascover 12½ oz.	3·60	10·00	5·70	19·50
Samcolastic (painted)	2·30	7·00	4·80	17·50
Limpetite (3 thou.)	3·40	9·80	5·00	16·00
Dekaplex (2 layers)	1·40	4·00	2·60	10·50
Black Rubber Sheathing (two coats)	0·50	1·40	1·10	4·20

NOTE: Materials not normally available in U.S.A. are costed as shipment direct from U.K.

attempts to summarize these for all the materials mentioned, to cover both amateur and professional work.

Sundry Deckwork Jobs
Although the owner of a modern grp boat need not be concerned with much of the above maintenance, his decks could well be more dangerous to work from than wooden ones, so it pays to watch this aspect of safety closely. Self-adhesive strips of nonslip material, such as *Safety-Walk* (made by the Minnesota Mining & Manufacturing Co) can be fixed to grp hatch tops and in other strategic places without looking unsightly.

Ventilation is most important, especially on metal, ferro-cement, and grp craft which are not so well insulated against condensation as wooden vessels. Few yachts have adequate ventilation when unoccupied and as owners should always be looking for ways and means of improving their boats it may not be a bad idea to add extra ventilators and louvres through the panels of cabin doors if books and mattresses are inclined to feel damp.

Some care is necessary in the choice of ventilators. The common screw-down mushroom vent is cheap and neat but is

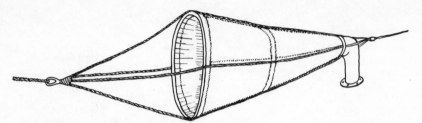

Drawing 9. An improvised tropical windsail. Drogue or sea anchor fitted over cowl vent and directed into wind.

by no means sprayproof and is a snare for trapping ropes. The screw threads have a habit of seizing and should thus always be well lubricated.

The traditional ship's cowl vent is neither spray nor rain proof but directs an enormous quantity of air below (or extracts it, according to which way the cowl is facing) and looks rather attractive on certain types of vessel. Cowls are especially useful for supplying air to engine spaces where a little wetness getting below may be of no importance and half cowl or shell

Drawing 10. Left – sectional drawing of a Revon sprayproof ventilator. (a) Air and spray entering. (b) Air only going below decks. (c) Baffle. (d) Water only descending to trapped scuppers.
Right – An ideal type of windscoop. These are fitted through open portlights from the inside and turned into wind in hot weather. Can be moulded by the amateur in glass fibre.

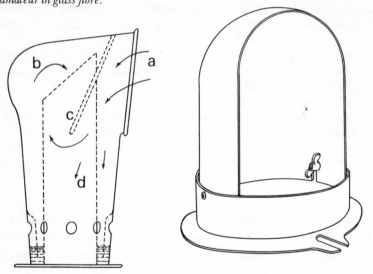

vents screwed to the sides of a wheelhouse or cabin top (and piped to the engine room) are particularly neat.

Cowl vents that are not essential under way should be equipped with waterproof covers having shockcord sewn into the hems. Cowls that might obstruct deck ropes should be of the rubber variety which collapse immediately when fouled.

For all other uses some form of sprayproof ventilator is necessary. The Tannoy *Ventair* is a neat and readily available mushroom type ventilator (made in either stainless steel or plastics) having a spray trap built in, with drain holes on to the deck. The similar *Ventilite* has a circular decklight in the centre making it particularly useful over dark compartments such as forepeaks, after lockers, and toilets.

The other makes of sprayproof ventilator such as the *Afco* and the *Revon* stocked by the big yacht chandlers are usually of the cowl type which can be oriented into or away from the wind. The simple venturi extractor vent also stands above deck and is only sprayproof when pointing in the correct direction.

Excellent *Dorade* type sprayproof ventilators can be built-in below deck at the stemhead of a yacht, or at the corners of the coachroof. Tubular steel or alloy samson posts, mooring bitts, and bollards, can be made into ventilators on big craft.

Holes should not be cut through the walls of a hollow alloy mast to pass air below decks without consulting the spar makers but on certain motor cruisers with hollow masts it may be possible to incorporate a vent at the masthead or even to take the engine exhaust up the mast. In the tropics, windsails should be made to fit into hatches and skylights (and perhaps metal windscoops to fit to portholes) for maximum through-draft in calm hot weather.

Skylights and hatches are frequent causes of leaks and considerable ingenuity may be required to cure these. For teak and mahogany fore hatches the Maurice Griffiths double coaming idea has been almost universally used for many years but to cure leaks in single coaming hatches and in hinged skylights the two simplest alternatives are either to install a synthetic rubber (Neoprene) seal all around the shutting edges, or to have waterproof canvas covers which are rigged either when the yacht is left at moorings or when under way in rough weather.

CHAPTER 6

SPARS, RIGGING AND GROUND TACKLE

Although the ropes and blocks associated with a modern Bermuda (Marconi) rig might appear simpler than the gear required for the older type of gaff rig, the Bermuda equipment (if the modern necessities such as spinnaker, halyard winches, sail track, adjustable sheet fairleads, and sheet winches are incorporated) is considerably more expensive and involved than the old-time counterpart.

Bermuda equipment is more fragile than gaff and extreme care is necessary when stepping and unstepping a Bermuda mast to avoid dents if of alloy; breakage when suspended centrally; bending spreaders or jumper struts; crushing electric wiring; or brushing against delicate masthead navigational equipment.

Stepping the Mast
For all sailing yachts shorter than about 25 ft (8 m) with the mast stepped in a tabernacle the amateur can raise and lower the mainmast reliably with the aid of two assistants, using a tackle (pronounced *tayckle* by seamen to differentiate from fishing tackle) from the lower eye of the disconnected forestay to the stemhead. The only problem arises when the mast is nearing its fully lowered position and the forestay ceases to have any lifting effect.

To overcome this, one can either rely on two strong men aft to manhandle the mast into an improvised crutch well above deck, or have some arrangement of moving struts to hold the forestay high above the tabernacle, thus keeping the mast fully under control throughout the movement.

Many ingenious devices have been propounded for mounting a strut, some utilizing the ship's legs, a spinnaker boom, or a launching trolley. However, the enthusiastic owner is recommended to make up a special pair of legs to form an inverted 'V' with the lower ends pivoted through the chain plates and the apex having a notch to take the forestay. Standard steel water piping is ideal for such legs with ends flattened to allow bolt holes to be made.

For an average hollow mast 25 ft (8 m) in length with the apex of the 'V' at least 4 ft (1200 mm) above the tabernacle pivot $\frac{3}{4}$ in (18 mm) bore steel water pipe is adequate and for a 35 ft (11 m) solid mast 1 in (25 mm) pipe would be necessary. The legs must always be kept perfectly straight.

It pays to make a small drawing of the system to find out at what point the apex should be seized to the forestay so that the legs are more or less vertical when the mast is horizontal. Few large yachts have masts in tabernacles, but if a really big mast gets out of control when being either raised or lowered it could do tremendous harm, so the owner of such a vessel is advised to resort to a dockside crane when his mast needs moving.

If a single strut hinged to the tabernacle bolt is used instead of legs, guys from the tip of the strut to the sides of the vessel are essential to prevent the strut from collapsing sideways. It must be remembered that these guys will need to be slackened during lowering if they are made off below the level of the tabernacle pivot. Some owners like to carry equipment on board for mast lowering purposes when their cruising grounds include rivers with low bridges.

Masts stepped through the deck on to the keel are common in craft over 30 ft (9 m) in length and are still very numerous amongst the older vessels below this size. The amateur can deal with such a mast provided its weight is under about 300 lbs (160 kg).

This limit arises because although a heavier mast can be lifted free of the deck with a simple sheer leg device, it will probably have to be manhandled to get it from the horizontal position on deck over the side of the yacht and on to the ground, or on to a wharf.

To lift the mast heel clear of the deck a sling must be attached with its upper eye a little higher than the centre of gravity of the mast, so the length of the sheer legs chosen must be adequate to deal with this height when the mast heel is above deck plus an allowance for the sheave blocks and hook at the apex of the legs.

If the position of the centre of gravity is not known, half the

121

height of the mast will usually err on the safe side, ensuring that the mast does not tip over if no one is able to control the heel as it comes clear of the deck.

A suitable sling can probably be borrowed from a boatyard or the local harbourmaster. This can either be in the form of an endless hemp rope strop or a single length with a large thimbled eye at one end. A loop around the mast close to the eye is knotted in the rope (or a marling hitch is made) and when this loop has been pulled up the mast with the hoisting tackle to the correct position the tail end of the sling or rope is made fast below the gooseneck band. A long-handled boat-hook is useful to prevent the loop from jamming as it goes up the mast.

Once the mast is suspended freely the heel may be swung between the sheer legs by hand while the mast is lowered gently into prepared crutches or padding on the deck. The bases of the sheer legs should rest on pads at the sides of the foredeck, lashed to ensure that spreading and fore- and aft movement is impossible. A guy from the apex may be led to the stemhead while another guy aft is necessary if the legs are almost vertical.

At the correct stage of the tide a mast can be transferred from the deck to a wharf by sliding it across on two planks but when it has to be raised or lowered a considerable distance the matter is far from simple without a dockside crane.

The local Scout Troop may like to have a go at this. Rigging a derrick with swinging leg is good fun, but it takes quite a time. Sometimes the same sheer legs which were used on deck can be utilized by rigging them on shore. Set them to swing athwartships with a tackle on the back guy. With the sheer legs leaning outwards over the boat the mast is raised to the necessary height, controlled with a light rope at each end. The sheer legs are then swung nearly vertical by hauling on the back guy tackle and the mast is lowered gently on to trestles.

Much the same procedure can be used for stepping a mast as when unstepping it. Needless to say an extra careful check is advisable before stepping to ensure that all electrical wiring and lights are in order; that all shackles, clevis pins and bolts are moused with seizing wire or lock-nutted; that all blocks are rove the correct way, and that no one has forgotten to reeve the signal halyards.

With the mast correctly dressed, all standing and running rigging should be frapped to the mast with stops of twine

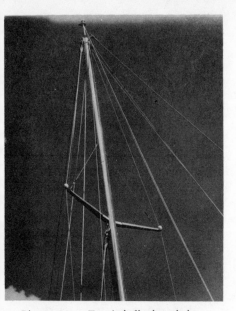

Picture 33. Tennis balls threaded on to topmast shrouds to prevent chafe on spreader ends. These can be taped or sewn to keep them in place. Alternatively, they can be cut to cap the spreader ends completely.

Picture 34. Baggywrinkle adds character to deep sea cruisers as well as effectively preventing chafe. On this gaff cutter it has been fixed to the after shrouds to protect the mainsail when running and also to the twin topping lifts.

which can be broken by pulling the rigging, or by codline running-bowlines with their falls led to the spider band cleats.

Such work is much simpler with light dinghy masts, but to avoid accidents when trying to manhandle one of these vertically into position it may pay to careen the dinghy over on her side so that the mast can be stepped horizontally.

Deck Wedges

The strength of some cruising and racing boat masts is calculated on a rigid fixing at deck level so that the mast wedges may be structurally important as well as for sealing the deck aperture. The wooden masts of large yachts were often made octagonal at deck level, simplifying the making of wedges considerably. Most modern alloy masts of all sizes are circular or pear-shaped.

Mast wedges should be of teak or iroko to avoid swelling. A slight taper prevents them falling right through but they should not be driven too hard and they should protrude below deck slightly to enable them to be driven out.

If new mast wedges have to be made, twelve or more narrow straight ones may be used to eliminate the necessity to carve out six curved ones. Some masts are leathered or coppered to prevent bruising by the wedges. Hard rubber mast wedges are used where the deck aperture is lined with a smooth metal (or grp) sleeve.

No system of readily removable wedges can be watertight so a flexible waterproof coat is normally fitted tightly around the mast down to a seal on deck. The traditional form of mast coat was sewn up from canvas and sometimes painted. It was lashed tightly around the mast while turned inside out and was folded downwards to the deck (thus concealing the lashing) as soon as the mast had been stepped.

The seal on deck was usually obtained by bedding the canvas in glazier's putty and securing it in place with a metal ring (or two half rings) secured with wood screws. When a complete ring is used in this position one must remember to place the ring on deck before the mast is stepped!

When renewing an old type mast coat, PVC/nylon material (as used for heavy boat covers) is preferable to canvas or Terylene (Dacron) sailcloth (see Chapter 7).

Modern craft with alloy masts may have a special metal bush at the deck aperture with a Neoprene gaiter between a water stop on the mast and a shaped spigot on the bush. With this type of fitting the wedges may be of Tufnol (or other plastics) moulded to shape and with an eye at the top to facilitate removal.

Examinations and Repairs

With a mast stripped for laying-up (see Chapter 12), thorough examination for defects is easy. Boxed sheaves may have been removed to get the internal halyards out, revealing any wear in pins or sheave sides.

The eyes, welds, rivets, and fastenings of mast fittings and tangs should receive scrutiny for cracks, wear, corrosion and other defects.

Mast track fastenings are notoriously troublesome and loose ones can cause jammed slides. If not possible to use longer or thicker screws, wooden plugs should be shaped and glued into loose screw holes to enable fresh holes to be bored. Driving the screws in varnish may help to keep them tight. The rims of external tracks are more likely to get buckled than the internal variety. Where action is needed one can usually fabricate (from ordinary mild steel bar) a small anvil to fit under the track so that the rim may be peened straight with a hammer.

By shifting a length of track slightly, damage can be cut out, or new screw holes bored. Tracks with nylon slides are best left dry. Some owners with metal slides like to grease or oil the track, though this does tend to harbour dirt. A slide with a piece of felt attached (and perhaps with an oil cup also) can be made to enable the track to be oiled frequently on a standing mast.

Luff grooves in alloy masts do not normally need any attention, but on a hollow spruce spar an examination of the glued joint inside the groove is advisable. At the same time any other glued joints can be checked and if a one thou (25 micron) feeler gauge can be pushed into the joint over a length of more than about 3 in (75 mm) it may be advisable to insert some resin glue, with or without additional fastenings.

A disposable hypodermic syringe is useful for this job. By driving very small holes at intervals or pressing the needle direct into the seam a One-Shot resin glue such as *Cascamite* can be introduced. Do not expect a very sound bond, as cleaning the joint may be impossible. A few thin screw fastenings will no doubt be expedient.

Fittings on spars should never be allowed to work loose as this would put tremendous stresses on the fastenings. Cleats are notorious for this as they are often fixed with woodscrews instead of through-bolts. Oversized screws should be fitted before the old ones sheer off at a critical moment.

Eyebolts through solid spars may work loose in time due to crushing of the wood, but the trouble is easily mastered by sinking a short length of *Tufnol* tube into the mast to act as a bush. The tube should not run right through the mast for fear of weakening the spar and a large diameter bush recessed for a distance of one-quarter the bolt length, close to the eye, should result in a permanent repair. To countersink the hole for the bush with an ordinary wood bit a temporary softwood plug should be driven into the old bolt hole.

Where cleats and mast bands have worked loose and chafed away the wood of a spar it may be possible to rebuild this with epoxy resin (such as *Araldite*), but this will not replace any lost strength in the spar.

Mast Sheathing

Lost strength can be replaced nowadays by sheathing part (or the whole) of a spar with grp. The results are often unsightly on a varnished surface so it may be wise to pigment the resin. This procedure follows the same lines as hull sheathing (see Chapter 5) using woven glass cloth.

Where a great increase in strength is necessary on a large mast ten or more layers of cloth may have to be used, but on a dinghy mast two layers may suffice. If a mast is sheathed for its entire length glass tape is convenient, wound on spirally. This method is not practicable where there is a luff groove, and all fittings, including track, must be removed to ensure a successful job.

There is no way of calculating just how much sheathing a defective mast requires and sheathing is best looked upon as a makeshift method which may last indefinitely but which could fail at any time.

Solid Spar Defects

Solid spars frequently have longitudinal cracks following the grain of the wood, but as solid spars are normally made with a big safety factor, limited cracks of this type are not too detrimental. A spar with cracks at right angles to the grain may be liable to break without warning and should be condemned. Any sort of cracking in a hollow spar should be treated with great suspicion.

Various recipes abound for soft putties to fill the harmless cracks in a solid spar, from the old-time mixture used by Claud Worth to *Seamflex* and the modern catalyst synthetic rubber compounds. Whatever is used, it must never harden like glazier's putty or knifing stopper. It should match the wood and must take varnish satisfactorily for use on a conventional varnished spar.

Unsightly scars (perhaps where a fitting has been removed) on a spar are traditionally repaired by a *graving piece*. This is a thin vertical diamond of matching wood inlaid flush and secured only with glue. Some people glue strips of balsa wood into wide cracks and this can be stained to a good match before varnishing.

Hollow spruce masts with modern fittings are highly resistant to rot, but the older type of gaff mast may eventually become rotten at the *hounds* (where additional cheeks called *bolsters* are used to support the crosstrees and shrouds) and at other places where rainwater is liable to lodge, such as mast bands and eyebolt holes.

Another moisture trap is the timber batten sometimes used to support the mast track, allowing it to remain straight past circular mast bands. These are all points to watch when purchasing or surveying an old boat. So is the heel tenon of a mast which fits into a mortice in the mast step. Where a mast has not been unstepped for years it might be wise to raise the mast sufficiently to inspect the step.

If one suspects that the heart of a large solid mast has rotted invisibly from the heel to deck level (through hearing a dull sound when tapping the mast with a hammer) it may be possible to borrow one of the tools (used for testing telephone poles, etc) which bore a minute hole into the spar and removed a complete core sample. Seal the hole with a glued dowel on completion.

Spars with protruding knots may have had much wood scraped away during previous refitting operations which could lead to loss of strength. Signs of this may also be seen on hollow spars where the diameter is reduced on either side of metal fittings. Protruding knots can be planed down flush but it may be prudent to keep one's eyes open for a replacement spar in case renewal becomes a matter of urgency.

Metal Fittings
Galvanized mast fittings with any sign of rust should be stripped off for regalvanizing. Stainless steel fittings need careful inspection for cracks and must be condemned or rebuilt where there is any suspicion of this. Cadmium plated steel fittings are occasionally used on alloy spars as well as on wooden ones and although these can be replated a change to new stainless steel fittings may be wise.

Any boatyard or ship's chandler can arrange to send mast fittings and chainplates away for regalvanizing but many local firms can now undertake zinc or aluminium metallizing which, if correctly done, has the same life as galvanizing.

It often pays to renew all the fastenings when a fitting is replaced and stainless steel screws and bolts are worth adopting, especially in the smaller sizes. Avoid zinc plated or sheradized fastenings where galvanized ones are not available and if the intention is to have ordinary black steel bolts galvanized or metallized, remember to cut the threads down with an adjustable die (so that the nuts run on very loosely) to allow for the thickness of the zinc coating.

Needless to say brass bolts should not be used in conjunction with galvanized fittings for fear of electrolytic action in contact with salt air and water. Brass bolts and fittings are also best avoided adjacent to glass fibre.

When there is trouble with fittings on an alloy mast it may be advisable to return the whole thing to the original makers. Fittings may be attached by means of pop rivets but the usual handyman tool using $\frac{1}{8}$ in (3 mm) pop rivets is rarely suitable, $\frac{3}{16}$ in (4 mm) rivets being the smallest normally used for spars.

In some instances it may be possible to use stainless steel nuts and bolts instead of rivets. To do this, a long piece of copper wire is passed through each hole, the tip of a bolt is soldered to the end of the wire and the wire is pulled back, feeding the bolt into its hole. Leaving a short piece of the wire to hold with the fingers, the remainder is clipped off and a nut is run on to the thread. Final tightening is accomplished by holding the tip of the bolt with pliers or grips, then the surplus length of thread is cut off. The nut may be secured by means of *Loctite* or by riveting over.

Before a mast is stepped any metal sheaves which have not been overhauled during the winter should be oiled to prevent squeaking and undue wear. Tufnol and Nylon (Delrin) sheaves must *not* be oiled. The threads of galvanized shackle pins and rigging screws must all be coated with graphite grease after cleaning. If this is not available white waterproof grease as used for propeller shaft bearings is suitable.

Tuning Up

With the mast in its step, make off the forestay and a pair of shrouds, then set the remaining rigging screws (often called *bottle screws* or *turnbuckles*) correctly at leisure, making sure they are the right way up with the lefthand thread at the bottom. If you forgot to make notes of the rigging screw adjustments (or to mark the threads with tape) at laying-up time, set the mast vertical athwartships by checking an equal dimension with a free halyard to the sheer, port and starboard. Sight up the track and get this dead straight unless you have a racing mast with a curved top section.

On Bermuda masts the upper shrouds are normally the

Drawing 11. Don't neglect the seizing wire. After tuning up, secure all rigging screws.

1. Shows additional security for a turnbuckle with knurled locknuts top and bottom. These can work loose and cause the loss of a mast.

2. Same applies to a bottle screw. Remember to tape over the sharp ends of seizing wire and all split pins.

3. Mousing the anchor shackle. Also essential on all rigging shackles, especially aloft.

4. Mousing a hook. Normally a temporary procedure, so marline will suffice. Mostly needed when using slings with a crane, lifting the engine, or stepping and unstepping the mast.

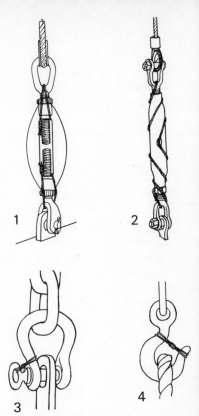

tightest while the forestay is tighter than the backstay or lower shrouds. After a trial sail (during which all equipment and sails should be used to check them) the rigging screws can be secured with their locknuts or with seizing wire, and parcelled with vinyl tape if necessary to prevent corrosion and to hide sharp split pins or ends of wire.

Remember to check radio antenna insulators for cracks and other damage. Tape over any clamps or Jubilee clips used to connect the antenna lead to a stay, and make sure no strands of wire are exposed which could by-pass the insulator.

Although setting up the lanyards through lignum vitae deadeyes (instead of rigging screws) on a gaff rigged craft takes a considerable time, there is very little tuning to do as such shrouds are normally left relatively slack.

Certain sailing dinghies and other small craft use lanyards formed from many turns of codline between a thimbled eye on the shroud and the chainplate instead of rigging screws. For further details of lanyards refer to Chapter 7.

One frequently sees chainplate eyes which are not in line

with the rigging screws. This may not matter where a shackle or toggle is used between the two but where the rigging screw has a fork end attached direct to the chainplate with a clevis pin or bolt, any misalignment of the eye can put a great strain on the two parts. In any case, unless there is plenty of play between the fork and the plate, flexing of the rigging when rubbed against a quay may bend the rigging screw and eventually lead to failure.

Similar things can happen aloft with the tangs of mast bands and the shackle between a block and an eye bolt (such as on the peak halyard of a gaff boat) may be of the wrong size or shape so that as the block swivels athwartships the shackle becomes jammed between the two eyes.

There are several ways of overcoming problems like this. Changing a D-shackle to a bow shackle or choosing one with a wider mouth may do the trick. To gain more play at the eyebolt, a heavy galvanized shackle can be replaced by a lighter stainless steel one of equivalent strength.

Amateurs frequently fit two shackles together where extra freedom is required or where a block should be turned at right angles, but this is not a very seamanlike improvisation. Less chafe with neater appearance is likely if a single twisted shackle or a straight one of better shape and size is substituted.

Some stainless steel shackles have a screwdriver slot at the end of the pin so there is no eye to mouse through. The same fitment is used on modern rigging screw forks and guardrail fittings. Especially where such screws are aloft, Loctite fluid should always be used on the threads to prevent them working loose.

Standing Rigging

For Class (a) sailing yachts stainless steel standing rigging of 1 x 19 construction or stainless steel rod rigging is almost universally used. Classes (b) and (c) usually adopt galvanized wire at about 30% of the stainless steel cost.

If not properly cared for galvanized wire may rust after two seasons though with proper preservation treatment its life span can be trebled.

As the lower ends always rust first it pays to make shrouds with an equal eye each end so that they may be reversed at the first signs of corrosion. The useful life of wire rope may continue for a few seasons after the first signs of rust though

Picture 35. Up the pole! A comfortable working position has been attained on this bosun's chair. Note the use of a canvas bucket to hold tools.

frequent examination for broken wires (especially at an eye splice or a swaged terminal) must be undertaken to ensure safety. Plastics coated galvanized wire rope (see Chapter 7) has a much longer life and may well be worth its additional cost.

Most owners manage to renew their standing rigging gradually over the years to spread the cost, as deterioration is rarely equal on all the stays in unison.

Spliced eyes are still used, especially for the larger ropes, and mainly on gaff boats. *Talurit* ferrules are popular for swaging wire rope around a thimble and many chandlery shops and boatyards possess the equipment for doing this.

As it may not always be possible to measure the exact length of a shroud, conventional splicing on the job is still sometimes the best method, though *Norseman Terminals* (see Chapter 7) can be fitted reliably by the amateur to 1 x 19 rope in any position. Note that these terminals cannot be used at present on flexible wire ropes of 6 x 19 construction used for halyards and other running rigging.

Although stainless steel does not corrode, failures are not uncommon due to fatigue, so it pays to examine such wire at least once a year (especially close to swaged fittings and other rigid attachments) in case there are any broken wires. As soon as one broken strand is found in a stainless steel shroud or forestay, the faulty rope should be renewed without delay.

Many a gaff boat looks incomplete without the traditional

131

sheer pole (to prevent the deadeyes twisting) and *ratlines* up the shrouds. Ratlines of cordage (see Chapter 7) look better than those made from wooden battens and they are less likely to cause chafe. Ratlines make a useful ladder for attaining a high lookout position, though the shrouds are too close together near the hounds to enable a man's foot to fit between.

In practice, with the mainsail hoisted, the mast hoops create a rather more convenient ladder for getting aloft than most ratlines. To enable the hoops to be used when the throat halyard breaks or runs aloft, the topping lift can be adapted to get the sail up. To emulate gaff rig, some alloy Bermudan masts are now equipped with permanent step irons each side similar to those used on telephone poles.

In its most rugged and simple form the gaff mast requires no bands and tangs to secure the standing rigging aloft, each stay having a simple soft eye spliced at the end which slips over the top of the mast to rest upon the bolsters at the hounds or upon special thumb cleats or ridges higher up. Although the throat halyard block is normally fitted to a crane or bracket through-bolted to the mast, the peak halyard and topping lift blocks may be equipped with strops around the mast to avoid the necessity for eyebolts.

Stainless steel rigging requires no protection, but careful attention is needed with galvanized steel wire to avoid premature corrosion. At one time soaking in boiled linseed oil (or painting this on) was used for standing rigging, sometimes followed later by two coats of yacht varnish. For running rigging soaking in a mixture of engine oil and petrol (gasoline) was popular, but with the advent of *anhydrous lanoline* (stocked by many druggists) all other methods have become obsolete.

This looks like petroleum jelly (Vaseline) and when smeared on to any type of wire rope it creates a long-lasting water-repellant surface which will not leave dirty marks on sails. Application is simplest by using the bare hands or a small piece of rag, exercising caution in case any broken strands of wire are protruding.

Details of parcelling, serving, splicing, and stropping blocks are given in the next chapter.

Beware Chafe!
Modern rigs include overlapping masthead jibs which, when sheeted in hard can chafe on shrouds and spreaders. Split tube

shroud rollers can be fitted to existing stays quite easily and may save an enormous amount of wear on the foot of a genoa. Shroud rollers used to be made of split cane or rubber hose, but the modern counterparts in Tufnol or PVC are superior.

Riding on a special bearing attached to the stay (with another stop at the top) these rollers rotate readily and will not lift to permit a sail or rope to slip underneath. A length of 4 ft (1200 mm) may be adequate for all except the largest yachts and although only the foremost pair of shrouds normally need antichafe rollers some owners fit them to each shroud as an extra precaution and to attain uniform appearance.

The best time to fit these rollers is when new rigging is being made up as the tubing then used need not be split and is therefore cheaper.

When squared off, most mainsails tend to press against the spreader shrouds and although this may merely lead to a dirty mark on a white sail for the weekend yachtsman, it can mean expensive sail repairs for the deep sea cruising man.

The tips of the spreaders can be even more injurious though protection is simple. A good binding with PVC tape may be adequate, or an old tennis ball may be cut to fit as an overall cap tied into position. Norseman Ropes Ltd produce small moulded plastics wheels to be threaded on to new stays so that they fit on top of the spreaders and rotate when chafed.

Many racing dinghies have swinging spreaders which, with the slackness in the lee rigging, tend to push away from the mainsail and lessen the amount of chafe. The intelligent use of runner levers or tackles can minimize sail chafe on a yacht so equipped and on a long tack it may pay to pull the lee running stay towards the shrouds with a lashing or shockcord to prevent it flogging about against the mainsail.

Much damage can be done to the clew of a jib when this is permitted to flog against the mast fittings while tacking and this can often be mitigated (and the jib sheets prevented from snarling up around the halyard cleats) if a temporary preventer rope is rove from the mast above the spider band to a ventilator or other fixing on deck a few feet forward of the mast.

Deep sea yachts still use *baggywrinkle* on the after shrouds, runners, and topping lifts, to prevent the mainsail from rubbing.

Baggywrinkle looks like coconut matting and is made up by

simply knotting short lengths of old rope through the lay of a length of sound cordage. This is then wound around the stay and seized to it at each end to form wads about 1 ft (300 mm) long with an equal distance between them. This not only gives a deep sea air to a vessel, but is extremely effective in preventing chafe.

Do not forget to tape over all sharp fittings aloft, remembering that a spinnaker could collapse against the jumper struts or other protrusions on the foreside of the mast.

A radar reflector fixed permanently to a spreader or between the jumper struts is quite common but can cause disastrous chafe. Above the mast truck may appear the only place for a radar reflector with freedom from chafe, but even here a conventional burgee staff would probably foul it. When a reflector is hoisted on a signal or spinnaker halyard, its position may have to be changed with each alteration to the setting of the sails to avoid risk of chafe.

The chafing of ropes, spars, and fittings, may need watching almost as much as sails. Gaff, lugsail, and Gunter rigs are more prone to chafe troubles than Bermudan. No parts should be allowed to chafe together unless one part is protected with leather, renewable copper sheeting, or perhaps a pad of Tufnol.

Leathering is a job that any amateur can do and as well as the essential places such as gaff jaws and around oars, leather has many other uses such as for a boom crutch, over strops and soft rope eyes; on legs; and at the ends of a ridge pole to fit underneath the cockpit cover.

The life of anti-chafe leather is remarkably long when properly maintained. The best treatment is regular painting with *neatsfoot oil* which keeps the leather supple and slippery. *Tallow* used to be used on leather but is messy and smelly, having no advantages over neatsfoot oil.

The leather used around oars is usually about $\frac{1}{8}$ in (3 mm) thick and can sometimes be obtained from boatyards, frequently from handicraft shops, but only occasionally from shoe repairers. The same hide is quite suitable for covering big gaff jaws. For strops; the ends of ridge poles; small gaff jaws; and for lining the chocks used to support a dinghy on deck or to hold a boat hook or spinnaker pole, leather from an old pair of shoes, an old brief case, or travelling bag, can often be utilized with complete success.

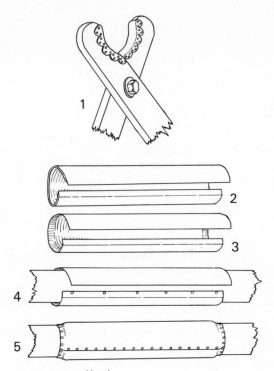

Drawing 12.   Some uses of leather:
1. Anti-chafe lining for the boom scissors. The castellations avoid puckering when leathering a curve and keep the tacks away from the working surface. Clearance between scissors created by large brass washers of suitable thickness.
2. Cutting out leather for oars. The scarf joint is made by skiving the outside of the overlapping piece and the outside of the underneath piece.
3. Skive from the inside around each end for a neat tapered finish.
4. After soaking secure to the oar with widely spaced copper tacks.
5. Stretch the piece around the oar and tack the long seam, then tack down the ends.

When leathering gaff jaws and similar curved chocks, there must be no tacks on the wearing surfaces so the leather must be cut out to provide radiating segments or castellations which can be tacked to the surrounding wood. Steel gaff jaws are usually leathered all over, the two pieces being sewn together around the edges. Soaking leather in warm water makes it shrink on tightly when dry. All wood beneath the leather should be well varnished or painted beforehand.

Sheet copper is used in a similar manner around masts and

spars, where strops or rigging eyes fit over. The tips of oar blades are also sometimes sheathed with copper, or a copper strip about ¾ in (18 mm) wide is tacked around the blade near to the tip to prevent the wood from splitting.

Coppering is not always suitable for chafe protection on spars and other equipment as the edges of the metal are liable to get bent outwards and cause injury. For oar tips 26 gauge (0·5 mm) copper is usual, while for taking mast shrouds and deck wedges 22 gauge (0·75 mm) is suitable for craft up to 40 ft (12 m) in length, and 18 gauge (1 mm) for most larger boats. Thick tarred paper (or Kraft paper) should be used under all coppering around spars.

Running Gear

Although synthetic fibre ropes such as Terylene (Dacron), nylon, and polypropylene, are now almost universally used (in conjunction with flexible wire rope) for running rigging, natural fibre hemp ropes (especially lightly tarred sisal) serve well for the large Class (c) yachts and work out cheaper with reasonable care.

Although synthetic fibres are more expensive than most types of hemp, their useful life is much longer, provided chafe can be avoided. For most yacht work synthetics should prove cheaper in the long run.

Being stronger for a given size, synthetic rope may be of smaller diameter than hemp, which helps to reduce the cost. However, it should not be forgotten that where tackles are used in place of winches for halyards, *davits* (pronounced *dayvits* by seamen), and sheets, rope sizes less than about 1¾ in (44 mm) circumference are uncomfortable to handle where a man's full strength must be applied to them. Therefore, although 1 in (25 mm) Terylene rope might be strong enough for the topping lift on a 40 ft (12 m) ketch, 1½ in (38 mm) hemp might be more suitable.

Prestretched Terylene rope is ideal for halyards (see next chapter) on both racing dinghies and cruising yachts. With all Terylene halyards regular inspections for chafe at the upper block must be made to avert a failure and if the position of the nip is close to the thimbled eye (as it normally is for a Bermudan mainsail) sufficient rope length should be provided to allow the eye splice to be remade occasionally thus shifting the nip.

136

Where a Terylene fall is attached to a wire halyard, very little wear affects the wire (provided the sheave is of the correct diameter and there is no chafe) but the nip of the Terylene comes at the lower sheave with an internal halyard, or at the block on the end of the wire in the case of an external halyard with a whip purchase. At the first signs of wear at the nip, these ropes should be turned end-for-end.

The life of other cordage (including main and jib sheets) can be prolonged by turning end-for-end though this must be done before too much wear has taken place. Many yachtsmen make their jib sheets in a continuous length knotted to the clew of the jib. This avoids the extra weight of thimbles and shackle flogging about and perhaps injuring an unwary crewman, but it also means that wet sheets may have to be stowed with the sail and the sheets cannot be turned end-for-end with any advantage.

Sailing dinghies do not normally require topping lifts as the boom is so light in weight and can be pulled from the gooseneck readily for stowage. To eliminate the extra gear aloft, some small cruising yachts could manage without a topping lift but this makes reefing under way difficult and the boom cannot be topped up when in harbour or when used for rigging a cockpit awning at night.

To avoid the need for boom gallows or scissors some modern cruisers use a short pendant (pronounced *pennant* by seamen) which attaches to a thimble on the standing backstay with a spring carbine clip or snap shackle when required.

Other yachts have a fixed length topping lift from the boom end to a point about half-way up the mast. Its length is adjusted so that it remains slack when under way but keeps the boom at a convenient height when the sails are stowed. At moorings, the mainsheet is tightened against the pull of a fixed topping lift.

In practice a conventional topping lift belayed at the foot of the mast is the best system. The need for a tackle or winch is eliminated except for large vessels as the fall can be swigged up (pulled away from the mast with one hand while the other hand controls a turn around the cleat) to obtain a purchase.

A topping lift rigged in this way may also prove invaluable one day as an emergency halyard or a jury shroud. Some yachtsmen prefer a topping lift tackle along the boom, but although this keeps the base of the mast clear it cannot be used with roller reefing.

137

Stainless steel flexible wire is liable to failure without warning, especially when running over sheaves which are too small, or where the unforgivable crime is committed of belaying flexible wire rope on a cleat. If a cordage tail cannot be fitted, have an eye splice in the fall end of the wire which slips over a hook or pin of suitable diameter.

Individual broken strands in a flexible wire rope may not indicate urgent renewal from a strength point of view but protruding strands can lead to painful injuries when handled by an unsuspecting person.

Even on modern craft one sometimes sees a single topping lift with its sheave some distance below the mast head, thus creating a likely snarl-up with the headboard as soon as the sail is hoisted. Similarly, on a gaff boat one may have to shift a single topping lift sheave above the uppermost peak halyard block to avoid trouble when hoisting sail. Large gaff craft usually have twin topping lifts and these can be positioned anywhere. Hanging the blocks under the crosstrees, away from the mast, is an advantage. Few rigs are incapable of some improvement and such work should always be looked upon as a part of yacht maintenance.

A broken parrel line may lead to damage on a gaff boat as well as causing some of the balls to get lost. Wire rope is often used on big craft, but where cordage is used, Terylene is advisable.

Few newcomers to yachting manage to escape from loosing the end of a halyard up aloft while sail changing at some time or other. This necessitates the use of a bosun's chair when one is not of the athletic type capable of shinning up a mast with legs wrapped around it and hands grasping a halyard!

Halyards with a whip purchase on the fall are the most prone to this, while, unless the bitter end of a fall is made fast to a hole through the centre of the cleat or secured in some other way, that too is liable to disappear aloft at a difficult moment.

Learn from an experienced friend how to belay a rope correctly on a cleat, and unless rapid release is imperative make it secure with a half-hitch aiming in the right direction. Learn how to coil down ropes correctly in a clockwise direction; how to fit tiers around coiled warps so they are always ready and untangled; how to capsize a coiled mainsheet or halyard to permit free running; how to suspend a coiled

Picture 36. Anchor chain ranged out for marking the length code. Coloured car enamels being sprayed on from Aerosol cans.

Picture 37. A stockless anchor. Chiefly used on big craft for stowing inside an external hawsepipe.

halyard from its cleat, and how to divide the coil of a heaving line prior to throwing.

The Bosun's Chair

Yachtsmen on extended cruises frequently carry a bosun's chair, but the average weekend yachtsman is unlikely to need such equipment at sea and will probably prefer to do masthead work in harbour by heeling his boat over when afloat alongside a quay or staging so that the required part of the mast can be brought within working reach.

A reliable bosun's chair is essential for safe working aloft but one does see people improvising with loops of rope to make a seat.

A suitable chair can be made from a piece of 7 in (180 mm) x 1¼ in (30 mm) teak or mahogany with the edges rounded off and all surfaces smoothed. A hole is drilled near to each corner to take suspension ropes, usually of 2 in (50 mm) circumference or $\frac{5}{8}$ in (16 mm) diameter 3-strand Terylene rope. Rounded edges to the holes lessen chafe of the ropes, and as a precaution against a possible breakage of the seat, the ropes are normally taken in criss-cross fashion underneath it.

139

The four rope ends may have thimbled eyes joined to a bow shackle about 2 ft (600 mm) above the seat. Alternatively, a single length can be used, spliced under the seat, and seized into an eye at the top without a thimble. A heavy man is not normally chosen to go aloft and the ideal length for the seat from one pair of ropes to the other is about 15 in (380 mm).

With a single part rope halyard made fast to the bow shackle a man can easily pull himself aloft single-handed on a bosun's chair, but in practice there should always be an assistant at deck level to keep the fall belayed at all times and to surge the rope around the cleat when lowering.

An all-wire halyard can be used with a reel winch though the wire cannot be handled by the man on the chair. As a preventer rope a spinnaker halyard or topping lift can be attached to a safety harness around the man's chest and kept taut in stages by the deckhand.

A rope made fast around the man's waist is useful to tie around the mast and prevent the man from swinging away from the location of work. This waist rope can be used in place of any other safety rope by lashing it tightly around the mast after each move of the chair, so that it would jam into position if it suddenly came under load.

Try to keep a record book listing the sizes, materials, and lengths of all running rigging parts on your boat.

Ground Tackle

Fortunately, the anchors, chains, and windlass on a well-found yacht need little maintenance. Whether of the Fisherman, Plough, or Danforth type, all anchors stowed on deck should rest in proper chocks with eyebolts provided to secure them with lashings. Stockless anchors (as used on large motor vessels) are normally self-stowing in the exposed end of the hawsepipe.

Anchors which are slightly rusty will continue to serve for many years if given two coats of aluminium paint each year, but any anchor showing distortion or any other damage should be renewed.

The shackle joining the chain cable to the anchor ring or eye should have its pin greased occasionally to make sure it can be released readily when the chain needs to be used for mooring up to a large buoy.

Check that the safety chain securing the stock pin on a Fisherman anchor is in sound condition and that the pin has a

Picture 38. Plough (or CQR) anchor on standard galvanized deck chocks. The queer object on the right is the ratchet windlass handle lashed down into wooden supports.

Picture 39. Danforth anchor stowed on the foredeck of a g.r.p. cruiser. A more substantial lashing might be advisable.

lanyard or wire attached to it ready for mousing when in use.

All chain should be unshipped from the cable locker each year and ranged out ashore for examination. When an old chain appears rusty throughout its length it can be re-galvanized and retested. As this proves quite expensive it may be expedient to buy a new length of chain and sell the original one for use on a light mooring.

Anchor cables are rarely long enough, so if rust appears only towards one end, this part can be cut off and a longer length of new chain attached with a tested split link. Note that if the chain feeds over a gipsy wheel on the windlass any new chain or split link must be of the exact size to fit the gipsy.

The bitter end of the cable must be shackled to an eyebolt in the cable locker to prevent the loss of both anchor and cable over-board, but many owners prefer to use a Terylene rope lashing for this (hemp rope might rot) to facilitate cutting the cable adrift with a marker buoy attached should an emergency departure prove necessary in a sudden storm or with a fouled anchor.

With any type of yacht larger than a cruising dinghy the inventory must include a kedge anchor and an ample supply of nylon warps to use with it. The popular polypropylene ropes are quite unsuitable for this purpose as they float and tend to trip the anchor. More secure holding is likely if the kedge has a few metres of chain attached to it with a ring at the bitter end to take the fisherman's bend of the kedge warp.

Some sort of length code painted on to a chain cable is essential on a big vessel to ensure that the correct amount has

141

been veered for the depth of water. When the cable is ranged out for yearly examination, this code can be added or re-painted, Aerosol cans of coloured cellulose paint are handy for this. A mark every two fathoms (4 m) is close enough, but do not forget to keep a note of your code system especially if this is somewhat complicated!

Many cruising yachts lack some of the useful ancillary equipment for ground tackle and it often pays the newcomer to take note of any useful gear being used by more experienced yachtsmen.

High powered motor craft careering through an anchorage are so common nowadays that chains can be snapped by the enormous surge loads imparted due to the artificial waves. A proper spring buffer with *claw hook* to fit between the chain links is ideal, but the amateur can improvise quite well without this by keeping an *angel* on board, consisting of a large bow shackle (or a span shackle) with a heavy weight attached.

When this is lowered down the cable under the surface of the water by means of a strong rope belayed to the samson post it creates a spring-loaded action on the cable and relieves the surge loads.

To avoid the complication of this, a springy coir or nylon warp may be rolling-hitched to the chain at water level and belayed taut to the mast, after which the anchor chain can be slackened away at the bitts or windlass so that the cable load is taken by the springy warp.

Naturally, a watch for chafe is essential with any of this equipment and it pays to check occasionally that the roller fairlead is properly lubricated and running free. On small craft with no windlass, a chain pawl mounted over the roller fairlead simplifies the task of weighing anchor considerably. The pawl prevents the chain from slipping back as one's hands are moved along the chain for the next pull.

Unless certain that an anchorage is not foul with old chains or rocks the anchor should always be buoyed. Attach the buoy rope to the crown of a Fisherman anchor or to the gravity ring of a CQR (Plough) anchor.

As some unsuspecting type might pick up your buoy believing it to be a vacant mooring, the anchor tripping rope can be brought back on board, but remember that a floating rope might foul someone's propeller. If a buoy is not carried on board, one can improvise by using an empty water breaker or fuel can.

CHAPTER 7

ALL ABOUT ROPES

Fortunately perhaps, most of us learn seamanship the hard way, starting boat ownership with an old sailing dinghy or motor boat which offers constant opportunities for repair and maintenance jobs.

Those who enter the sport by purchasing a brand new speedboat or a plastics dinghy after visiting a Boat Show may have no reason to read these pages at first, but even if professional help is used for all maintenance work, the time is sure to come when, through ignorance of rope splicing or sail repairing, an important race may be missed, or an afternoon's cruise for the family postponed.

Choice of Cordage

One must practise making the ever useful boat knots such as sheet bend; bowline; clove hitch; reef knot; fisherman's bend; rolling hitch, and slippery hitch, until these can be made even if one is blindfolded. An accomplished Boy Scout may be of assistance here, as demonstration is better than puzzling through a book of knots. When it comes to fancy rope work, including the monkey's fist for the end of a heaving line, a Turk's head for the tiller, or the Matthew Walker knot for gaff shroud lanyards, a suitable book may be easier to locate than an aged seaman!

It may be a good idea to keep a few lengths of scrap rope around the house to encourage one to practise knots or splices occasionally.

Some notes on the types of rope available and their uses were given in the previous chapter. The following table gives a cost comparison for a one yard (1 m) length of $\frac{7}{16}$ in (10 mm) diameter (1$\frac{1}{4}$ in (30 mm) circumference) rope in each of the materials normally available, together with details of some of the uses for each type of rope.

TABLE 6
Synthetic and Natural Fibre Ropes

Type of Rope	Approx. cost per yd. (m.)		Main uses
	£ in U.K.	$ in U.S.A.	
Nylon	0·15	0·45	anchor cable, warps
Terylene (Dacron)			
braided	0·14	0·77	sheets, signal halyards
prestretched	0·14	0·77	halyards, lacings
Polypropylene			
silky (e.g. Ulstron)	0·11	0·60	spinnaker sheets
hairy (e.g. Nelson)	0·07	0·40	warps, fendering
stiff (e.g. Sturdee)	0·05	0·30	ski lines, buoy ropes
Sisal	0·04	0·18	warps, halyards, fendering
Manila	0·06	0·26	warps, halyards, fendering
Italian hemp	0·09	0·54	halyards, deadeye lanyards, codline
Coir	0·03	0·15	fendering, warps
Cotton	0·07	0·36	sheets, lacings, manropes

To find the weight in lbs per fathom of a dry hemp, Terylene, or nylon rope, multiply the circumference by itself, and divide by six. To obtain the weight in kilograms per metre again square the circumference (in millimetres) and divide this by twelve.

In similar fashion it may be useful to know the safe working load of cordage in good condition. To get an approximate idea in lbs, square the circumference (in inches) then multiply this number by 300 for nylon or Terylene, 250 for polypropylene, 150 for Italian hemp, 120 for sisal, and 80 for coir. For the load in kilograms, take the diameter in millimetres and multiply by the numbers 43, 28, 17, 14 and 9 respectively.

Synthetic Fibres
Although many synthetic fibre ropes are known to deteriorate in strong sunlight they will not rot and should have a much longer life than any of the natural fibres.

Nylon ropes are white when new and turn gray with use. They are normally conventional *hawser-laid* three strand ropes, though the largest sizes may be *cable-laid,* i.e. three ordinary ropes laid up or plaited together. Nylon sinks in water and has good elasticity, making it suitable for warps and anchor cables.

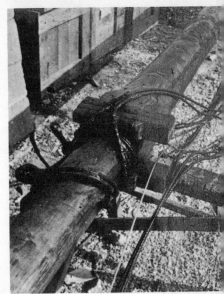

Picture 40. Deadeyes and lanyards for old gaff rigged boats are used only when the mast is left standing continuously. Italian hemp is still the most suitable cordage for the lanyards.

Picture 41. Splicing the shrouds is avoided on gaff masts by seizing the shrouds in pairs at the hounds. Note bolsters to which the cross trees are bolted.

White *Terylene* (Dacron) rope can be obtained prestretched and three-stranded for halyards while braided Terylene (with outward appearance like window sash cord) is free from kinking and ideal for sheets and other running ropes. Heavy Terylene mooring warps are made from three laid ropes plaited together, as in Marlow *Multiplait*.

Polypropylene rope is made in a hard shiny form for maximum strength, cable-laid in the larger sizes, and as a hairy three strand supple rope for frequently handled warps. Polypropylene is very sensitive to chafe (by internal friction as well as by rubbing) and although normally used for mooring warps, any loop on the end should be protected by sewn leather or a piece of polythene tubing. It comes in a variety of colours.

The stiff and shiny *polythene* ropes are extensively used for fishing nets and are the cheapest synthetics, though very durable. Other types of synthetic fibre come and go, so one may have to depend on makers' advertisements and literature to keep abreast of developments.

Natural Fibres
Sisal hemp is the most frequently used and the cheapest natural

145

rope fibre for a given strength. When new it has an off-white colour which darkens on exposure to light but all sisal rope used for boat work should be lightly tarred during manufacture and it then has a light brown appearance. Sisal is rough to handle and swells and stiffens when wet.

Untreated Italian hemp is light straw coloured and smooth. It has great strength and is the most expensive hemp rope, though traditionally used at least for the shroud lanyards on gaff rigged craft.

Manila rope, smoother than sisal, dark straw coloured and mid-way in strength and cost between sisal and Italian hemp, has always been the most widely used natural fibre for yacht ropes before the introduction of synthetics, but is nowadays used mainly in America. Indian and European hemp is the most popular fibre for making tarred marline and codline, while flax is used for seaming twine.

Cotton rope is pure white, soft except when wet, and was formerly used for main and jib sheets.

Coir rope, (made from coconut fibre) is the only traditional rope that floats on water and is almost rot-free. Being cheap and having great elasticity, it was favoured for mooring warps but has to be of large diameter to compensate for its low strength.

Cotton and linen, waxed and unwaxed, are still used sometimes for sewing threads.

The majority of natural fibre ropes are of three strand hawser-laid form, though four strand *shroud-laid* ropes are still made in Italian hemp. Very large ropes are frequently cable-laid while cotton and Indian hemp are used for making braided ropes such as window sash cord.

When laying-up, natural fibre ropes need washing in fresh water, drying thoroughly, and storing in a well aired manner. Rot is the bugbear of these materials and dry storage even on board is essential to avoid serious loss of strength. They all shrink considerably when wetted, necessitating adjustment in length with the advent of rain or spray while under way, together with ample slackness when unattended.

New hemp rope tends to kink easily and stretch considerably during the first few weeks of use. To obviate these annoyances, a new rope should be stretched tightly between two posts (or other fixtures) in the open air, for a few days prior to use.

New untreated sisal rope can be proofed by submerging in a mixture of one part *Cuprinol* to two parts kerosene.

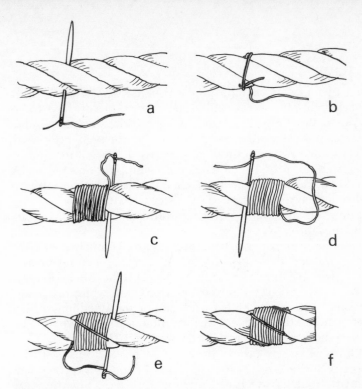

Drawing 13. A sewn whipping gives the most security to a rope end. (a) Thrust threaded needle through rope strand. (b) Start winding tight turns towards rope end, trapping end of twine under turns. (c) Thrust needle through rope to emerge between two strands. (d) Follow the grooves to other end of whipping and feed needle under one strand, pulling twine tight. (e) Follow this groove back again and feed needle under remaining strand. (f) Repeat to other end producing the appearance shown. Sew twine twice through a strand and cut off. Trim off rope end.

Drawing 14. The plain or common whipping. (a) Start well back from the rope end, winding against the lay in either direction. (b) Halfway, form a loop as shown and continue winding. (c) Pass the end through the loop and draw both loop and end under the turns. (d) Cut off the surplus twine and then trim off the rope end, but not too close.

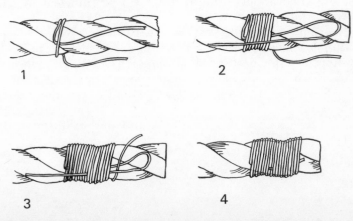

Rope Ends

Unless each end of a length of new rope is *whipped* or sealed in some way, the strands will unlay and may eventually have to be cut off. An unwhipped end on a lacing or other rope in regular use causes wasted time when threading through eyelets or fairleads and may even prove dangerous. It takes a maximum of two minutes to put on a temporary whipping or a few turns of vinyl tape and the practical yachtsman should never hesitate to do this. Braided ropes last longer than laid without a whipping but the outer covering gradually unravels and becomes unsightly.

Synthetic fibre ropes need whipping just as much as natural ones. Although the ends of synthetic cordage can be melted with a naked flame, this method can only be used for each individual strand on a large rope, an overall whipping being necessary for security. Melted ends can be moulded into a firm shape between the fingers. The heat lingers and to avoid burns it pays to lick one's fingers before attempting this.

Whipping large synthetic ropes is easy if one keeps in stock a supply of special sleeves for each size of rope. On coils of new rope, the makers use push-on rubber sleeves, but these are easily pulled off when a rope is in use. Superior sleeves in thin plastics are available which shrink tightly on to the rope when heated, making a permanent whipping.

Sewn or served whippings of thread or twine are ideal for either natural fibre or synthetic ropes and very little skill or equipment is needed to make them. Waxed Terylene whipping twine is the most commonly used nowadays, and is available on spools from any chandler in a range of thicknesses.

The thickness is not important but neater and longer lasting whippings are ensured if the thinnest twine is used for codline lacings and lanyards, while thicker twine and then marline is used for increasing sizes of rope. If the correct thickness of twine is used about fourteen turns will be sufficient for any normal whipping.

No whipping should be positioned too closely to the rope end or it may pull off during handling. The illustrations help to show how the most common whippings are formed, though many variations exist. The palm-and-needle or *sailmaker's whipping* is the most secure method and also has the neatest appearance.

A needle is loaded with thread and pushed through the

centre of a strand some distance back from the rope end. An old cork is pressed on to the needle point for safety, then all the whipping turns are wound on as tightly as possible against the lay working towards the rope end and burying the free end of thread underneath the turns. With point bared the needle is then pushed through a strand to emerge in the groove of the lay.

Following the direction of this groove the thread is pulled tightly across the turns, under the adjacent strand at the end, and back over the turns, following the lay to the other end. Using the needle again, the thread is transferred from that groove to the remaining one, pulled back over the turns following that lay to be sewn through the rope twice and then cut off. Details of needles and palms are given in Chapter 8.

A similar but less secure whipping can be made without a needle by unlaying the rope to start with, terminating with a reef knot tucked into the rope-end. On a braided rope a sewn whipping is applied by passing the needle in three random turns through the rope to anchor the end of the thread, applying the turns as above, then terminating with three more stitches through the rope.

For a *plain* (or common) whipping no needle is necessary, and although many different methods are used, the following one is quick and sure. With the rope held in the left hand place the thread along the top of the rope with its end well beyond the rope end. Start winding towards the rope end, holding the first turn with the left thumb to keep it stable.

Having made about ten tight turns (whipped length about one rope diameter) pull on the buried strand to tighten the very first turn, then fold the buried strand back over the turns and hold it with the thumb, leaving a loop just beyond the rope end. Continue winding with the looped strands underneath the turns. After another ten turns, cut the thread off with plenty to spare and pass this end through the loop.

By pulling on the other end (which is now protruding from the centre of the whipping) the loop will be drawn underneath the turns, taking the bitter end of thread with it. As this is done, keep the final turn tight with the fingers of the right hand.

When the loop is mid-way under the last ten turns, stop pulling and cut off both protruding parts of thread.

To obtain very tight turns on a big rope a *serving mallet* (see under Serving) can be used, necessitating support for the bitter end of the rope in a vice (vise) or with an additional pair of hands. When making up a new halyard or warp from a coil of rope, it may pay to apply the whipping before cutting the rope so that the additional length can be used for support. Some people use two separate whippings on the ends of jib sheets, but this is unnecessary when palm-and-needle whippings are used.

At laying-up time all cordage should be carefully examined for defects. Try to resist the dangerous temptation to relegate faulty halyards to mooring rope duties. Synthetic fibre ropes mainly need watching for chafe and cutting but in addition to these defects rot may be found in natural fibre rope.

To inspect for rot, the strands should be parted by twisting the rope against the lay. If the colour of the rope is a dirty gray, rot should be suspected. If the fibres break away when probed with a screwdriver or marline spike the rope must be condemned. Servings over eye splices or strops can sometimes accelerate rot and it may be prudent to renew such servings before time, to enable an inspection to be made. Much the same procedure is also advisable with galvanized steel wire rope.

Serving

No eye splice or strop should be made in wire rope without a final serving with marline or covering with leather. Serving protects the hands from damage caused by protruding ends of wire; prevents chafe; imparts a neat appearance to the splice, and for a considerable time it keeps corrosion at bay.

In days gone by, serving was used far more extensively than today. The shrouds on gaff rigged craft were sometimes served from top to bottom and it was not unknown for the galvanized iron rope then used to last for over twenty years. Eye splices in hemp rope used to be served over much more frequently than they are today.

Forestays cannot be served if jib hanks have to run on them, but when the bottom forestay splice is to be served, a *parrel ball* should be slipped on before making the splice to prevent the hanks from jamming over the serving.

Serving is a simple operation and the secret of success is to get the turns as tight as possible. Unless the right grade of marline is chosen gaps may appear between the turns though this trouble can be mitigated largely by careful worming and parcelling.

Worming consists of winding a single strand of marline or codline spirally along each depression in the lay of hemp or wire rope. Parcelling consists of a spirally wound layer of tape mummifying the rope, holding the worming in place and creating a smooth surface to receive the serving.

Worming and parcelling is wound on in the same direction as the lay of the rope (clockwise when holding an eye splice away from you and looking along the rope) while serving is wound on in the opposite direction. However, note that for shrouds, parcelling should start at the bottom of a splice to shed water, as described for taping rigging screws in Chapter 6.

Ordinary electrical sticky black insulation tape (not PVC tape) is quite the best material to use for parcelling wire rope, using $\frac{1}{2}$ in (12 mm) tape for ropes up to $\frac{1}{4}$ in (6 mm) diameter and $\frac{3}{4}$ in (18 mm) tape for bigger ropes. For parcelling cordage, strips of thin canvas may be used instead of insulation tape. If anhydrous lanoline or underwater grease is worked into a galvanized wire rope splice before parcelling this will minimize rusting.

When serving an eye splice in a conventional right-hand lay rope, the marline is started as for a plain whipping just beyond the splice or beyond the parcelling, then all the turns are wound on as neatly and tightly as possible towards the thimble.

To terminate the serving, make the last six turns oversized, by winding them around a marline spike as well as the splice. Pass the end of the marline through the tunnel thus formed, withdraw the spike, then work along the turns pulling each one up tight (if necessary using a pair of pliers or the spike) until, on reaching the end-most turn, this one can be pulled up tight by drawing the protruding end of the marline along beneath the six turns. This method of termination can also be used for a whipping, especially when the whipping is a long way from the rope end.

With any rope larger than about $\frac{1}{4}$ in (6 mm) diameter, it pays to use a *serving mallet* to ensure that all the turns are pulled up tightly. This looks like a hammer with a semi-circular groove along the top of the head. Both handle and head are normally made of either elm or lignum vitae. A range of sizes can be supplied by chandlers with grooves to fit any rope, but the amateur can make a simple serving board quite easily from a chunk of any hardwood, perhaps with head and handle the same width. The handle can be made very short for serving in a confined space.

In use, one or two turns of the marline are taken around the handle of the mallet to form a friction device, enabling the serving to be applied swiftly and tightly as the mallet handle is rotated, while the groove rides on the parcelled rope.

To eliminate the necessity for passing a reel of marline continuously around the rope with the mallet, a *Patent Serving Board* is used. This has a small rotating drum fitted to the side of the handle and one loads the drum with sufficient marline from the main kop or hank before starting work. This drum has an adjustable friction mounting to provide correct tension to the marline.

The only sure way to determine the length of marline needed for a serving is to wind a few test turns into position, measure the length of the marline used and the length of rope covered by the turns then calculate the full length required. Although it may be annoying to have to join the marline towards the end of a serving, this takes no time if the ends are twisted together and sealed under the advancing turns.

Servings are likely to last much longer and also have a neater appearance if they are given two coats of varnish on completion. Varnish may take a long time to dry on tarred marline but untarred stuff tends to rot internally and should be avoided. White synthetic cord can be used but may look peculiar except on small eye splices.

Plain and Racking Seizings
Seizings are used extensively on gaff boats rigged in traditional manner. They have only a few uses on a modern craft, such as for making the eye in a set of jib sheets. Seizings are used in the place of splices to draw two parts of rope tightly and permanently together.

They are always used when attaching the strop to a wooden block. When shrouds are fitted over the mast instead of being shackled to tangs, the job is done more neatly by seizing the shrouds in pairs to form single eyes at the hounds.

Seizings on cordage are normally made with marline of stout gauge or with codline. For wire rope, whether on top of a serving or direct on to the rope special *seizing wire* (made from seven strands of soft iron galvanized wire) should be used. If this cannot be obtained, plain galvanized fencing wire is superior to flexible wire rope.

For all important and permanent fixings the *round seizing* is used. A bowline eye is knotted at the marline end which is noosed around one of the ropes. Very tight turns are wound on, the last of which is a half hitch, enabling a second row of *riding turns* to be wound over the first row (staggered between them).

Pass the end through the bowline, then finish off with cross turns parallel to the strop (or ropes) in the form of a clove hitch with one half hitch at one side of the seizing and the other half hitch on the reverse side.

A figure-eight knot will prevent the bitter end from getting loose, but this will not happen if enough varnish is applied.

A *racking seizing* is used where the tensions on the two rope parts are in opposite directions. To make this, start as for a round seizing, but keep the ropes slightly apart so that the first row of turns can be passed in figure-eight formation – around one rope, down underneath the other rope, back over the top of that rope, then down and under the other one. Keep the turns one marline thickness apart to enable a second row of ordinary round turns to go on between the first set. Finish off as for a round seizing.

Seizings should not be too long. About twelve turns is common for the first row, with eleven turns for the riders. The total length should be about equal to the circumference of one main rope part.

Note that as well as for splicing, *Talurit* swaged ferrule sleeves may be used in place of seizings for many duties, but they cannot be used on top of servings. Most servings and seizings benefit from a good bashing with a mallet or soft hammer (e.g. rawhide, rubber, or copper) prior to varnishing. Whippings can be bedded down by rolling the rope ends on the floor under one's foot.

Serving and seizing is always simpler if the work can be held rigidly and professionals often prefer to use their serving mallet over a wire rope splice after the shroud has been firmly installed on the ship. For seizings, it should be possible to use a vice and a lanyard.

Splicing Cordage

Every practical yachtsman should be able to make an *eye splice,* whether for a hard eye (with a metal thimble inserted) or a soft eye (as used for lanyards on tool handles or dinghy rowlocks; the inboard end of a dinghy painter; or the rope on a bucket handle) as this is by far the most common form of splice ever needed on a boat.

A *wire rope to cordage* splice is frequently needed on modern

153

yachts having wire halyards with rope tails. A *back splice* is very useful as an alternative to whipping on mooring warps and on other ropes where the end need not be left small to pass through a sheave or bullseye. *Short splices* are used for joining two ropes of equal size together but are not often used on small craft today. *The long splice* does this same job without increasing the rope diameter appreciably and is mainly used nowadays for repairing sail bolt ropes.

Eye splicing is extremely simple but as it becomes somewhat fiddley with codline and similar small cordage, the learner is advised to practise on rope of at least $\frac{5}{16}$ in (8 mm) diameter (1 in (25 mm) circumference).

As the strands of most sizes of rope can be parted by twisting against the lay and using one's thumb, the only tool normally needed is a really sharp knife. With ropes larger than about $\frac{5}{8}$ in (15 mm) diameter (2 in (50 mm) circumference) a steel marline spike or a lignum vitae fid is handy for making an opening between the strands. With codline, a 2 in (50 mm) wire nail is all one needs to keep the strands apart while making a tuck.

Marline spikes and fids have numerous other uses on board a boat, but if one is going to do much rope work, a *shell spike* is a tool worth acquiring. This is pressed from stainless steel in the form of an ice-cream cone with a tapered segment cut out of its wall for the full length and a round wooden handle riveted into the large end.

When this spike is thrust between the strands of a rope it can be left in place while the tuck is made and then withdrawn, avoiding the frustration which sometimes occurs when the lay closes up on removal of an ordinary fid before the strand can be tucked through.

Eye Splices

The simplicity of eye splicing cordage will be noted from the diagram. From the bitter end of the rope the strands are unlaid for a length equal to about six times the rope circumference and a couple of turns of twine are knotted around this position to prevent the rope from unlaying any further. The required size of eye is formed by bending a loop in the rope with two of the newly unlaid strands lying across the top of the rope and one passing beneath.

The spike is thrust beneath the strand immediately under No 2 part and No 2 is passed through the opening formed against

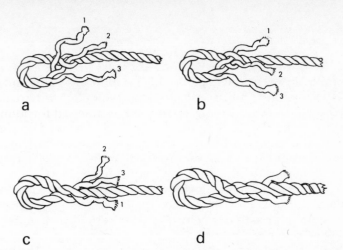

Drawing 15. *Eye-splices are widely used and so simple that every amateur sailor should have a go. (a) Tuck part 2 first, avoiding the temptation to commence with part 1. (b) Take part 1 over the strand just used to house part 2 and tuck part 1 under the next strand. (c) Turn the splice over. Tuck part 3 under the remaining strand in the direction shown. Pull all parts up tight. (d) Continue tucking over-one-under-one for at least three full tucks.*

Drawing 16. *Back splices can be used to whip a rope end in a minute or two but are too big to run through blocks. (a) Pass strand 1 over strand 2 and hold it there. Flip strand 2 over strand 1 and hold it to strand 3. (b) Fold strand 3 over 2 and tuck end under strand 1. (c) Draw up each strand gradually to form a neat and even crown knot. (e) Continue tucking over-one-under-one as for an eye splice.*

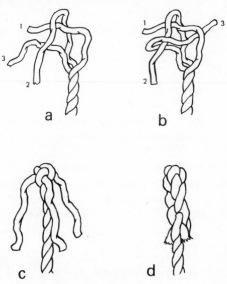

the direction of the lay. Rotating the rope slightly the strand beneath No 1 is opened up, and No 1 is tucked.

Now the rope is turned right over to allow No 3 to be tucked under the only remaining strand. No 3 must pass through *against* the lay as for the others, but do not worry about the awkward wriggle No 3 must take to do this – it will look neater as soon as all three strands have been pulled up tight to the rope and beaten with a mallet on completion.

To prove that you have made these first three tucks correctly, sight along the rope from either direction. If Nos 1, 2 and 3 stick out evenly with an angle of 120° between them you cannot be wrong. If two parts have been tucked under the same strand, or if No 3 has been tucked in the wrong direction, such errors will now show up.

Should you try to tuck No 2 or No 3 strand before the strand labelled No 1 in the diagram, a perfectly sound eye splice will be formed, but it will have a twist in it on completion. This might not matter where a thimble is inserted but it will spoil the appearance of a soft eye.

The remainder of the job is now plain sailing. In any order, taking each of the numbered parts in its natural direction against the lay, let it pass over the first strand lying beneath it, and tuck it under the second one.

When all three have been tucked, view along the rope once more to check that all three parts emerge evenly spaced. Having pulled each strand outwards and backwards until it beds down properly, repeat the process of over-one-under-one to form a splice with three full tucks.

To create a neater tapered splice in any rope larger than codline, once the three full tucks have been made one-third of the yarns may be cut out of each strand before making a fourth tuck. Then half of the remaining yarns may be cut out again, and a further tuck made. When splicing slippery plastics rope, one additional full tuck is advisable.

When cutting the yarns with a knife, do not cut too close to the main rope, but trim any protruding yarns with a pair of scissors or a lighted match after finally rolling the splice under one's foot on the floor or dressing it with a mallet.

Before starting the tucks in a splice, it usually pays to put a turn of *Sellotape* or a temporary whipping on the ends of strands Nos 1, 2 and 3 to prevent them from fraying or unwinding as they are tucked. With synthetic fibre ropes, this may be done by melting the ends with a match, though applying adhesive tape is quicker.

Splicing with four-stranded rope is similar to the above with Nos 1, 2 and 3 lying on top while No 4 rides beneath the rope at the start. Should a rope with left-hand lay be encountered the eye is merely formed in the opposite direction. The amateur rarely needs to make an eye in a cable laid or plaited rope, and normally uses a bowline instead of a splice!

The need to form an eye at the end of a braided rope can arise, and each rope maker has devised a special system to enable neat splices to be made. These ropes are normally formed with an outer braided sheath covering an inner core, so by slitting open the sheathing and withdrawing the inner core, the latter can be fed back into the hollow sheath to form an eye.

The *Dickinson* splice used by Marlow for their braided rope is formed in a slightly different manner by unravelling the strands of the sheath and core and tucking these back into the rope. The rope makers issue instruction leaflets and supply special awls and fids suitable for various sizes of rope. Instead of using these somewhat complicated splices, most amateurs prefer to sew the parts together and serve over, or use seizings, either method if done properly being as strong as a splice.

Most professional riggers insert thimbles *after* making their splices in hemp rope. When working with the less elastic synthetic ropes the thimble is best inserted as the first tucks are drawn up. The thimble is tied into position with temporary seizings of marline to ensure that a snug fit is retained on completion.

The amateur is advised to use this latter method with hard eyes in hemp also as to judge the exact size of eye which can be reamed open with a fid to allow a thimble to be sprung into place is difficult to achieve without a certain amount of trial and error. If the thimble seems loose, clap a seizing on the throat of the splice.

The Back Splice
Next to the eye splice the *back splice* is the most frequently needed type for the yachtsman. The rope end is unlaid for a distance of about six times the rope's circumference and no seizing is necessary at this point.

To start the splice a *crown knot* is formed as shown in the diagram. Sit down, clamp the rope vertically between the knees, hold strand No 2 out at right angles to the rope with the left hand, while flipping strand No 1 over it and at right angles to it with the right hand. While pinching the two together where they meet (using the left hand) flick No 2 strand back over the top of No 1 to rest on top of No 3. Now slip No 3 strand over the top of No 2 and poke its end downwards through the loop in No 1 strand originally formed when this was turned over to cross No 2. Draw all the strands up tight gradually working around and sight on the end of the rope to ensure that all three strands hang downwards with an angle of 120° between them.

Having achieved this, the rest is easy. Tuck each strand over one and under one, against the lay, for two or three complete tucks. A back splice is rarely tapered off though this can be done for extra neatness if required. When you see a rope end fraying, a crown knot can be formed with the loose strands in a few seconds, with a little practice, and this will prevent the rope from unravelling further for a considerable time. If just one tuck is taken after forming the crown knot a good temporary whipping may be formed.

Joining Ropes

For joining two lengths of equal rope together the *short splice* is normally used, but as this creates a swelling, a *long splice* must be used where the rope is intended to run though blocks.

A short splice is simple and quick to make. Each rope is unlaid as for an eye splice and the two are brought together so that the three strands of one rope intermesh evenly with the other three. A light seizing to one side of the joint holds things securely while the strands in the opposite direction are tucked three times full and twice tapering, over one under one all the way, against the lay. The seizing is then removed and the other three strands are tucked similarly.

The *long splice* is rarely used by yachtsmen nowadays. The start is made as for a short splice except that the unlaid strands should be about three times as long. Seize only two strands to the rope at one side of the start instead of all three as with a short splice. Now turn your attention to the other side of the starting point.

Gradually unlay the strand which was not seized and replace this as you go with the corresponding strand from the other side.

Proceed until only a few inches of this strand remain and put a temporary seizing around that point to keep it in position. Return to the start, release one more strand from the seizing and unlay this one gradually while replacing it with its opposite number from the other side, seizing the ends in place as before.

Cut off the remaining two strands a few inches from the starting point and you are now left with what appears to be a perfectly good length of rope with three pairs of short strands protruding. To house these ends, cut away one-third of the yarns in each strand, make an *overhand knot* (as for the first half of a reef knot) at each pair, then tuck the strands over one and under one. Halve the yarns again, and complete a further tuck to finish off. If preferred, this last tuck can be made around the same strand as the first tuck.

Splicing Wire Rope
One can imagine the newcomer to yachting, reading these words in the cabin of his plastics cruiser moored in a marina, wondering why, in this age of swaged rigging terminals anyone would wish to know how to splice wire!

However, there are still impecunious owners who can just afford to keep a big old-fashioned yacht which suits them perfectly, by doing all the maintenance work themselves – and most of them revel in doing it. Furthermore, this book is intended for owners living in remote areas of the world where the nearest rigger or ship's chandler may be a vast distance away.

Hard and soft eyes are quite the most frequent form of splice likely to be needed in wire rope nowadays. With new safety regulations or recommendations so much to the fore in all spheres, the repair of highly stressed ropes with short or long splices is frowned upon.

Eye splices in flexible wire rope up to $\frac{3}{8}$ in (9 mm) diameter are well within the ability of the intelligent amateur, though splicing the stiffer wire used for standing rigging may prove more troublesome. Remember that rope of 1 × 19 construction (so often used for standing rigging nowadays in both stainless steel and galvanized) is intended to have only swaged terminals, so the amateur wishing to splice his own standing rigging should be careful to order in 7 × 7 or similar construction.

Instead of using eye splices where gaff shrouds terminate in deadeyes, *seizings* are often used, with caps over the bitter ends.

This proves quite satisfactory if properly done with strong seizing wire used in four separate positions a few inches apart. This method of forming an eye can be used also for temporary repairs where no bulldog grips are available, or where it may be necessary to adjust the length of a rope at some future date. A thimble or solid heart must be used with this type of eye and the first seizing close to the throat must be especially secure. Where the rope is parcelled and served, the seizings may be positioned on top of the serving.

When splicing a hard eye in wire rope without a proper clamp the thimble or heart must be held in place with three seizings before the tucks are made, but any serving or leathering must be put on to the rope where the thimble comes before splicing commences. Where leather is used, this should be sewn on to the rope with the stitching on the inside of the eye and additional lengths of leather can be left trailing, later to be stitched over the splice.

Making an eye splice in wire rope is very similar to the hemp rope procedure, though it takes much longer due to the stiffness and greater number of strands. Although modern preformed rope does not fly apart when cut, each strand still needs whipping or taping to survive the tucks and to mitigate injuries. Riggers sometimes secure the tips by heating them to dull red and twisting tightly with two pairs of pliers. On small wire rope the ends can be twisted successfully without heat.

With six or seven strand rope, unlay a length of about thirty diameters and cut out the hemp, plastics, or wire heart strand to leave six free parts for tucking in.

Clamp the thimble end in a vice with the standing part of the rope leading away to the right horizontally, firmly tied to keep it taut. The six free strands should be uppermost in the vice. Divide them into two lots of three and bend the nearest three towards you around the outside of the standing part to be lashed out of the way beneath it.

Tuck the other three strands first. Thrust the spike horizontally through the central lay of the standing rope, attempting to avoid damage to the heart strand. All three of the free strands will enter this same aperture, but the spike must be manoeuvered so that the part nearest to you tucks under three strands while the next one in order passes under two strands and the furthest one from you goes under only one strand.

Having drawn these three tightly towards the eye, untie the

Picture 42. Test all mast screws for tightness at fitting-out time, and mouse all shackles. Spliced eyes are still used on the galvanized standing rigging of modestly priced sailing cruisers.

Picture 43. Wiring and taping the rigging screws after tuning the rigging. White boiler suit is ideal apparel when fitting-out, but the city shoes are not recommended!

remaining free parts. The lowest (and nearest to the vice) of these parts will be tucked after turning the splice over, just as described for cordage, but the other two parts can often be tucked without moving the rope in the vice.

Both these parts tuck underneath the next main rope strand below the aperture made to house the first three parts. Having pushed the spike under this strand, tuck the central one of the three parts against the direction of lay as before. Leaving the spike in position, tuck the topmost free part under the same strand but in the opposite direction so that the two parts cross each other under this strand.

To get rid of the last part, tuck this normally against the lay under the remaining strand, but note that the remaining strand is the second one beyond the strand used for the crossed (*locking*) tucks. The usual reverse wriggle will appear in this part to get it through against the lay. Although one part should emerge between each strand of the main rope the points of emergence may be some distance from each other up and down the rope, tending to make the splice look faulty. However, when the next row of conventional over-one-under-one

161

tucks have been made and the splice has been dressed with a soft hammer the appearance should not be too unsightly.

Use four full tucks in slippery stainless steel wire and three in galvanized. To taper for neatness, cut off two of the free strands and make a further tuck with the remaining four. Then cut off two more close to the lay, and make a further tuck with the two parts that are left.

Whether the thimble is loose or not, some riggers put a wire seizing around the throat, but this does not help to make the splice neater when overall parcelling and serving is applied.

Other methods of making wire eye splices can be used though the above is the most suitable for the amateur's small size ropes. Short splices in wire are made exactly as described for cordage.

Few tools are needed for splicing wire. Most people prefer an old screwdriver to a marline spike for opening up the lay, but work is far easier if the proper tool is used. The tip is shaped like a screwdriver while further along the tool is shaped like a marline spike having a groove cut along it to permit tucks to be passed when the tool is thrust well into the lay.

A pair of pliers should be kept handy. For cutting off strands there is no better way than using a sharp cold chisel and heavy hammer on an anvil made from a chunk of scrap iron. Special clamps are made to hold a thimble tightly in position without the need for temporary seizings and these clamps are supplied with separate temporary solid heart formers to enable soft eyes to be spliced.

Eyes subject to chafe may be served all over with seizing wire. Leathering or serving with marline is to be preferred for yacht work and these should always be given two or three coats of varnish on completion. Leather may become stained with oil during splicing and should therefore be scrubbed with petrol (gasoline) or other solvent before varnishing.

Making a Strop

A *strop* is a continuous length of rope (like a car fan belt) which can be any length and has many uses. Small strops are called *grommets* (pronounced *grummets*), a certain size forming the rings used for playing deck quoits! Smaller ones are sewn into the *cringles* (sewn eyes) on sails and these can be as small as 1 in (25 mm) in diameter. Large rope strops are useful for slings, anchor cable buffers and in ornamental rope work. Steel rope strops are universally used to form the eye and becket on blocks with plain wooden shells.

All strops longer than about 2 ft (600 mm) are invariably made by short splicing the ends of a length of cordage or wire rope, while small strops may be made up from a single strand of the rope like a grommet.

To make a grommet from three strand cordage, multiply the diameter of the proposed grommet (when laid out as a full circle) by about 4 and cut off a single strand unlaid from a piece of new rope to this length. Now proceed to lay up this strand to form a ring the size of the grommet going around twice so that a three stranded rope (looking exactly like the original rope) is formed.

If the grommet is to be served all over or sewn in as a cringle the ends can be cut off so that they butt closely together with a whipping to keep them in place. For other grommets under heavy stress the two ends must be tucked. Do this just as described for a long splice, cutting out one-third of the yarns, tying an overhand knot, then tucking over-one-under-one and hammering the joint to make it neat.

Although a wire grommet is formed in exactly the same way, it proves impossible to lay back all six strands by hand. The most one can normally lay up neatly is five and many people only manage to get four in. To make up for this loss of strength it may pay to use a strand from rope a size larger than originally envisaged.

A *selvagee strop* has the same appearance after serving as a spliced or grommet strop and is much quicker to make. Being stiffer, its main uses are for cringles made of cordage and for block strops in wire.

To make a selvagee strop, hammer a few nails into a plank in the form of a circle or ellipse representing the inside size of the finished strop and proceed to wind at least ten turns of marline, codline, seizing wire, or plain galvanized wire around the circle against the nails. Having put on seizings to secure the ends and at intervals around the strop to keep all the strands in position, withdraw the nails, parcel all over with insulation tape and serve with marline.

Small grommets or cringles can be made very quickly by winding marline around the tips of the fingers. When large selvagee strops are to have leather sewn on instead of serving, the strands are normally secured in position before leathering by the process called *marling*.

To do this a single length of strong thin cord is used making a half hitch at close intervals all the way. Marling is used for lacing the eyelets of sail covers together as well as for many other lacing jobs on yachts and it was the traditional method used in the Navy for making up a hammock into a neat bundle when stowed.

Stropping a wooden block is quite simple provided one judges the overall size of the strop correctly. It pays to check this by clamping the roughly made strop around the block and thimble to see if the neck is the correct length for a proper seizing. Should the strop be the wrong size, it may pay to keep it for another job and make a new one.

When a short-spliced strop is used around the block, the lumpy splice is normally housed out of sight in the deep score at the bottom of the block. For a block with a becket (and therefore an eye top and bottom) the splice should be placed at the side of the block.

Before stropping a block, remove the pin to grease both pin and sheave, varnishing the wooden shell inside and out while the sheave is removed. Give the strop serving one coat of varnish also, applying additional coats to the whole assembly after stropping.

Although cordage strops are simpler to fit, wire ones are essential to match the strength of a block. A primitive Spanish windlass may be rigged to pull the strop in close at the neck between the block and thimble, while the round seizing is wired on.

Not all wooden yacht blocks require strops as the more expensive ones are *internally bound,* i.e. the ash shell is assembled over a galvanized steel framework which takes the load from the sheave pin and has the eye and becket attached to it.

Rope to Wire Splicing
A form of long splice is used to mate the rope tail to a wire halyard, the system frequently used by sailing dinghies and small yachts without halyard reel winches. Unlay the wire rope for a distance of about 100 diameters, cut out the heart cord, then lay up again three alternate strands (to form a three stranded rope) for a distance of about 60 diameters, applying seizings where necessary to secure all strands. See Drawing 17.

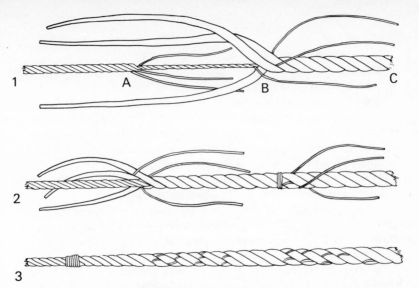

Drawing 17. A knowledge of tail splicing is essential as many yachts have wire halyards with cordage tails. The drawing is not to scale as an actual splice would be three times as long as shown.

1. Unlay the wire from A to C. Cut out hemp core. Rewind three strands from A to B. Cut off the other three strands near to B. Unlay the cordage as shown and taper the strands, especially towards the ends. Intermesh the three wire strands at B with the cordage strands and seize temporarily.

2. Lay up the cordage over the wire from B to A and seize at A. Start tucking the three wire strands from B to C into the cordage lay. Do likewise with the other three wire strands from A towards B.

3. Complete all tucking. Lay up the tapered cordage strands over the wire rope and seize the ends permanently. If necessary, sew any exposed wire rope ends under the cordage strands.

Now unlay the cordage for a distance 1½ times the length of the three stranded wire and taper each cordage strand so that the tips are only one-quarter of the full diameter. To taper, unlay all yarns and shave them down with a razor or cut them off clean at even intervals until only one or two are left at the tip. Grease the yarns and twist them back together into the required tapered strand.

Now mate the ends of the three stranded wire rope with the cordage, secure this point and lay up the tapered strands, housing the wire as a central heart. On reaching the end of the three stranded wire, mate the cordage strands with the remaining free wire strands and apply a temporary seizing.

Now tuck both sets of three wire strands into the cordage by winding each one round and around its adjacent cordage strand four times, in preference to the usual over-one-under-one routine.

Having cut off surplus lengths of the wire strands these should be sewn out of harm's way inside the rope lay. Parcelling and serving all over the splice makes a neat job where the bulkiness does not matter. To finish off the tapered cordage strands which are still hanging free, just continue laying them up over the top of the wire rope for a short distance and clap a whipping over their tips to keep them permanently in place.

The above splice is rather long, but being flexible, it will pass through a sheave satisfactorily when not under load.

When a new halyard must be rove inside a hollow mast, the new rope can be fitted end to end to the old and sewn in place with strong twine to create a joint that will pass reliably over the sheaves.

A broken halyard usually means the removal of the lower sheave box so that a cord with a small weight on the end can be fed down inside and retrieved at the bottom.

Splicing and seizing is not the only way by which amateurs can make eyes in wire rope. *Norseman* terminals (*Mate* in the USA) are screw-on fork or eye fittings which the amateur can attach to certain constructions of standing rigging wire very reliably if the maker's instructions are followed. Most big chandlery firms stock these terminals, but remember to ensure that the correct cones to suit the rope are ordered, and that only stainless steel terminals are used on stainless steel rope, or zinc plated fittings for galvanized rope. Some *Loctite* fluid may be necessary for securing the nuts and, especially with galvanized rope, it may be advisable to use *Thermofit* shrink-on plastic sleeves to seal the terminals against sea water corrosion.

Galvanized *bulldog grips* (wire rope clips) can be used in place of seizings to form hard or soft eyes. It pays to keep a range of sizes on board in case of emergencies leading to the improvisation of a jury rig. For the most secure job, three grips should be used, one as close to the thimble as possible with the other two spaced at about ten rope diameters apart.

Bulldog grips are made in the form of a small U-bolt with a cast block under the nuts, grooved to fit snugly around the rope. The block should be set against the standing part of the rope with the U-bolt over the shorter part.

The neatest wire rope terminals are called *swaged* fittings and can be used only by specialist firms. They are most frequently used on expensively built racing yachts where streamlined rigging is important. As with the Norseman fittings swaged terminals are normally made with fork, eye, or with a threaded stem for direct attachment to a rigging screw.

Similar fittings are used for rod rigging on big vessels. Single strand stays called *piano wire* are used on some sailing dinghies. This wire is normally in stainless steel and an eye splice is formed by making a ferrule from a short length of $\frac{3}{16}$ in (4 mm) copper tubing slightly flattened in the vice, and threading the wire through it. An eye is then bent around a stainless steel thimble and the end of the wire is passed again through the ferrule. Having drawn everything up tightly with the ferrule close to the thimble, the free end of wire is bent over the lip of the ferrule, which is then dressed with a hammer. A few turns of vinyl tape prevent sails getting torn.

Perhaps the most popular method of making eyes in wire rope nowadays is the *Talurit* (pronounced Taylor-it) method, as the equipment is available at most chandlery stores.

For galvanized rope aluminium alloy Talurit ferrules are used, while for stainless steel rope the ferrules are of copper. Having reeved both parts of the rope through the ferrule the eye is adjusted to the requisite size with the ferrule close up to the neck and the bitter end of the wire flush with the top of the ferrule. Specially shaped dies in a powerful press are used to swage the ferrule permanently on to the rope.

This method has the advantage of universal application to all types of wire rope and special ferrules are available for fitting to plastics-coated wire ropes without need to strip the coating.

Choosing Wire Rope
The table on page 168 lists the sizes and constructions of wire ropes suitable for yacht work produced by Norseman Ropes Ltd, showing also the approximate cost of a 100 ft (30 m) reel. Note that there is little difference in strength between stainless steel and galvanized wire ropes.

It has been found that the plastics-coated galvanized wire ropes may be as durable as stainless steel when correctly used. Although the slightly increased diameter offers more wind resistance, at around one-third the price they offer attractive possibilities. Examination of the wire for defects or fractures is difficult, of course, but galvanized steel is less prone to hidden breakages than stainless steel when completely coated against corrosion.

TABLE 7

Norseman Wire Yacht Ropes – popular range

SPECIFICATION	ROPE SIZE										
Diameter in mm.	2	2·5	3	4	5	6	7	8	9	10	12
Diameter in in.	5/64	3/32	1/8	5/32	3/16	1/4	9/32	5/16	3/8	7/16	1/2
Circumference in in.	1/4	5/16	3/8	1/2	5/8	3/4	7/8	1	1 1/8	1 1/4	1 1/2
1 × 19 stainless steel Breaking load	—	1165	1680	3000	4650	6700	9150	11950	14140	18600	26600
Cost	—	0·11	0·12	0·18	0·24	0·38	0·48	0·60	0·70	0·80	1·25
7 × 7 stainless steel Breaking load	650	900	1470	2150	3700	5200	—	—	—	—	—
Cost	0·12	0·14	0·16	0·20	—	—	—	—	—	—	—
7 × 12 or 7 × 19 Flexible stainless steel Breaking load	600	900	1400	2140	3350	4800	6550	8550	—	—	—
Cost	0·09	0·14	0·25	0·30	0·36	0·45	0·53	0·68	—	—	—
1 × 19 galvanized steel Breaking load	—	1165	1680	3000	4650	6700	9150	11950	—	18600	26800
Cost	0·04	0·04	0·05	0·06	0·06	0·07	0·09	0·13	—	0·18	0·23
7 × 7 galvanized steel Breaking load	490	705	1160	2500	3950	5650	7700	10100	—	15700	22600
Cost	0·04	0·04	0·05	0·06	0·06	0·07	0·09	0·13	—	0·18	0·23
7 × 12 or 7 × 19 Flexible galvanized steel Breaking load	—	750	1160	1940	2510	4890	6280	7560	—	10900	—
Cost	—	0·08	0·09	0·09	0·10	0·11	0·12	0·15	—	0·20	—
1 × 19 Seaprufe plastics coated galvanized steel Breaking load	—	1165	1680	3000	4650	6700	9150	11950	—	18600	26800
Cost	—	0·06	0·08	0·10	0·13	0·17	0·23	0·28	—	0·36	0·48
7 × 12 or 7 × 19 Norflex coated galvanized steel Breaking load	—	705	1160	2500	3950	4890	6280	7560	—	10900	—
Cost	0·05	0·08	0·08	0·11	0·13	0·17	0·21	0·25	—	0·40	—

NOTE: Costs are in £ (U.K.) per yd. (m.). For costs in $ (U.S.A.) multiply by 6.
Breaking loads are in lbs. For kg. multiply by 0·3732

CHAPTER 8

SAILS AND CANVASWORK

Although Terylene (Dacron) polyester fibre sails are almost universally used for yacht work nowadays some owners still find that cotton sails, especially for gaff rigged boats, require less maintenance.

Cotton sails tend to loose their shape with age and so were superseded by Terylene for racing long before the same change occurred for cruising. Cotton, and especially its stitching, is more resistant to chafe than the modern materials, but unless treated by proper rot-proofing and water-repellent chemicals, cotton sails must never be stowed when wet or unsightly mildew will set in, followed by eventual rotting. Mildew can occur on Terylene leaving similar marks, but this never affects the strength of the material.

New cotton sails require very gentle stretching in light airs before they are subjected to strong winds or reefing. Being less airtight than Terylene, they can never prove so efficient to windward and are thus more appropriate to gaff rig (or for the auxiliary sails on a motor vessel), where close windward sailing is not attempted.

A good suit of cotton or flax sails can be kept serviceable by the keen amateur for twelve seasons without recourse to the professional sailmaker, whereas with polyester fabric at least one sail is likely to require professional restitching or patching due to rips, chafe or cigarette burns every year during regular usage.

Synthetic fibres are prone to deterioration by strong sunlight, and although this mainly concerns owners in the tropics, a Terylene mainsail should never be left stowed along the boom without being covered by a sail coat.

Sail Bending

Cotton or flax sails are not suitable for the careless owner, for as well as the necessity for careful drying as mentioned above, vigilance is needed during use in the adjustment of the halyards, outhauls, and leech lines, to avoid girts and wrinkles forming when boltropes shrink due to moisture.

Gaff mainsails are especially prone to this trouble as incorrect adjustment of the peak halyard can create a girt from throat to clew which could damage the sail in time. The clew outhaul (and also the peak outhaul on a gaff sail) should be slacked off whenever the sail is stowed.

As long as headsails have the correct sheet fairlead position and the luffs are swigged up tight, they should look after themselves. However, a staysail set on a boom (or club) can form girts.

Spinnakers are invariably made from a flexible light-weight nylon material nowadays and great care is needed when raising or lowering these to avoid damage. Twin running staysails make a far more satisfactory down-wind rig for extended cruising than a spinnaker. With gaff rig twin staysails on booms equipped with tiller lines for self-steering you get more freedom from chafe than the traditional squaresail and raffee.

Bending the mainsail on a modern cruiser is usually a simple matter of sliding the foot along the boom track; screwing up the shackle at the tack cringle; reeving the clew outhaul lanyard and hauling this up tight (or shackling the clew to a screw outhaul fitting and winding this up); feeding the slides on to the mast track and then closing the gate at the bottom; attaching the halyard with D-shackle or snap shackle, then inserting all the battens.

A similar procedure is necessary for a sailing dinghy but instead of track along the boom and up the mast, there may be grooves to house the footrope and the luffrope. This simple system is not suitable for cruising vessels as the sail cannot be lowered with a run and the unsupported luff tends to blow away to leeward unless an extra hand is available to muzzle it.

Once bent and set, the only additional item of gear sometimes fitted to the small Bermuda (Marconi) cruiser mainsail is perhaps a kicking strap (boom vang) from the base of the mast to the underside of the boom. This is particularly useful when running, as it can be used to reduce the amount of belly in the sail, lessening chafe against the after shrouds

Picture 44. Useful items of canvas-work to occupy the yachtsman's winter evenings – a well fitted sailcoat; guard-rail dodgers; pram hood over hatchway; webbing gripes to secure dinghy. Note the liferaft in g.r.p. casing just abaft mast.

Picture 45. Motor launch pad fenders sewn up from oddments of canvas and filled with kapok or foam rubber. These are fixed permanently inside the gunwale and flipped out-board when required.

or spreaders. With bendy masts and booms, Cunningham holes and leech lines, racing dinghy sails can be adjusted to a variety of shapes while under way.

Tiers made from rope are not kind to a sail and proper ones of tape (or shockcord with toggles) must be made up.

Bending a gaff mainsail is more involved, and the same applies to most gunter and lugsail rigs. Although modernized gaff sails have been tried with tracks along mast, boom and gaff, this loses certain merits of the traditional easy-to-lower gaff mainsail with mast hoops, so most owners of these vessels still adhere to the old system with the sail laced permanently to the gaff, loose-footed along the boom when reef points are used, but laced to the boom for roller reefing.

Such sails must be left bent throughout the season, hence the reason why tanned rot-proofed sails are commonly seen on gaff rigged boats.

To bend a gaff mainsail, the tack and clew cringles are lashed to the eyes on the boom and any lacing securing the foot to the boom is rove. The same procedure is then applied to the gaff, enabling the sail to be hoisted a short way to facilitate lashing the mast hoops to the cringles or eyelets along the luff.

Although one often sees ordinary marled lacing along booms; gaffs; lugsail yards, and on the mast with a gunter sail, the single line of half hitches is not very secure and the whole lot may carry away should the line chafe through at any point.

171

Separate lacings at each eyelet are much more reliable. They should be knotted centrally to the eyelet, each end passed around the spar in opposite directions, through the eyelet then reef knotted at the other side of the spar, or under the bolt rope.

When a continuous lacing must be used, the end can go through each eyelet, between the bolt rope and spar, around the spar, then back between and through the eyelet again. The above method of lacing may be used where a roller reefing boom has a lacing batten fixed along it. Where such a boom has instead a semi-circular groove along the top for the boltrope to sit into, individual lacings prove best, knotted under the boom like reef points.

For the lacing used to keep a gunter luff to the mast, simple marling is again unsuitable and the method illustrated should be used.

Remember that the lowest gaff mast hoops must not be seized permanently to the sail eyelets or neat reefing will not be possible. Either lacing may be used in this vicinity, or the cordage securing the mast hoops may be tied with a slippery hitch. This problem rarely arises where slides and track are concerned as by opening the gate at the bottom of the track the required number of slides can be released when reefing.

Mast hoops remain permanently around the mast and are not normally covered with leather as the friction would cause them to jam on raising and lowering sails. Jamming sometimes occurs with small hoops of the conventional laminated ash or hickory variety, especially when lowering sails, but this trouble can be obviated by attaching a single length of codline to each hoop running down the forward face of the mast. A tug on this line will then free all the hoops in unison.

Renewing mast hoops is not difficult provided the mast can be lifted out of the boat. It may then be necessary to remove the gooseneck bands (frequently made in halves bolted together) to slip the hoops on and off. When the mast cannot be unstepped, laminated hoops in two halves can be glued up over a jig and copper riveted when *in situ*. For a very big mast the ash strips can be steamed and formed into hoops around the mast by cramping pegs inside two old hoops to create a jig.

The slides on a big Bermuda mainsail should be attached to the luff eyelets with shackles, but seizings of twine; marline; codline; nylon tape, or leather thongs, are commonly used (in

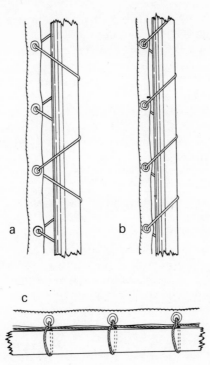

Drawing 18.   Lacing and marling appear frequently on boats. (a) This shows a special type of lacing used for the luff of a Gunter mainsail and is less liable to jam on lowering sail than other lacings. (b) Here is the most common form of lacing, often seen along booms and lugsail spars. (c) This is marling, with a half-hitch at each eyelet. Makes a very tight lacing.

that order) from dinghies to deep sea cruisers. As many strands as possible should be taken around when forming these seizings, ending with cross turns around the centre of the seizing between the slide or hoop and the bolt rope. When renewing these and for the hanks (snaps) on a jib luff, it may be best to match the cordage and method of seizing previously used if this looks sound.

Very small slides often have a circular thimble fixed to them for seizing to the luff eyelets, but it should be noted that the twine is intended to pass around the score of the thimble, not through the hole, and a sail needle threaded with the twine speeds up the job.

Bermuda mainsails should never be used without leech

battens of correct size. Incorrectly fitted battens may prove the cause of constant sail repairs especially if the ones affected are not removed when reefing. The absence of battens is one of the merits of a gaff mainsail.

Remember that a sail may be damaged more severely when left flogging than at any other time. This happens most frequently when racing dinghies are being launched or taken ashore, but one also sees it occurring on cruising yachts, especially when the owners are trying to motor to windward with the sails hoisted.

Sewing Canvas

Small stitching repairs to dinghy sails may seem similar to dressmaking and can be tackled in the normal household. Hand sewing through several thicknesses of the material used for large cruiser sails is a man's job. Every keen amateur seaman should know how to sew canvas, for unless an owner always takes a crew with him experienced in such practical work, that yacht will not be capable of meeting all the various types of emergency which can happen at sea.

Sewing Terylene sailcloth is nothing like as pleasant as working with cotton, and although vinyl coated nylon materials are now widely used for making waterproof covers and sail coats many firms still prefer to work in cotton for making such things as dodgers, awnings, fendoffs, and bunk flaps.

White cotton canvas is stocked by many chandlery stores, usually in 12 oz (400 g) or 15 oz (500 g) thicknesses, while some stores also keep green proofed canvas. Small articles made of the usual white cotton duck canvas are readily proofed by brushing on *Kuhls, Gnu, Cuprinol* or other rot proofers and redressing annually is advisable to keep articles constantly exposed in good condition.

When sewing cotton canvas, the sail needle will part the threads so that stitching does not weaken the cloth. With Terylene sailcloth, however, the needle pierces a hole as through paper, so a different technique is required to avoid weaknesses.

The smallest possible needle with the thinnest Terylene thread of adequate strength should be used. Avoid sewn eyelet rings or grommets with stitching radiating outwards all around. The circle of holes formed may so weaken the canvas that the eyelet pulls right out when under load.

174

The few tools needed for sewing canvas cost very little so it pays to get a complete range to suit all requirements. Sail needles have a triangular shaft to part the threads neatly and can be purchased singly or in packets of 25. The smallest ones are Size 18 and the largest likely to be needed by the yachtsman are Size 12.

Many chandlers do not keep needles smaller than Size 17 but No 18 is essential for sewing medium Terylene, while ordinary household needles are generally more satisfactory for use on dinghy sails. A range for average needs would consist of six No 18; four No 17; three No 16; two No 14; one No 12 and a packet of household darning needles.

The smallest needles break rather easily during heavy sewing hence a few spares should always be kept. If needles are stored by sticking them into a lump of cork, the points are sure to corrode in time and a better place is an old flat tobacco can with a little oil poured in.

Sailmakers use a palm instead of a thimble to force needles through thick canvas. A palm is in the form of a leather strap shaped to fit around the hand with an indented metal disc fixed in the centre to press on the eye end of the needle. Special palms are made for left-handed operators.

A small sail hook is another cheap and useful tool to keep. The hook is intended to fit through stitches or through canvas and an eye is attached (sometimes swivelled) to enable a lanyard to be made fast, thus holding a seam out straight and taut for stitching.

A sharp knife, some stainless steel pins, a marline spike, and a pair of scissors will be frequently in demand and a piece of rounded steel (or a proper sail rubber) is useful for creasing canvas along a seam line. A lump of beeswax is sure to be needed sometimes and any type of unwaxed twine sews more easily and beds down closer if the strands are pulled across the corner of a lump of soft wax two or three times after threading the needle.

When the amateur sailmaker becomes enthusiastic enough to start making covers, awnings, and sailbags during the winter, it will pay to get a few brass eyelets with the correct size tools for closing them.

Eyelets with a hole diameter of $\frac{5}{8}$ in (15 mm) are a good choice but if two sizes can be stocked one could choose $\frac{1}{2}$ in (12 mm) and $\frac{7}{8}$ in (21 mm). Although a knife can be used to make correct holes through the canvas for inserting eyelets, a proper wad punch makes a better and quicker job, and a small block of hardwood should be kept handy for use as an anvil under the punch.

For hand sewing one needs to learn how to make two types of stitch. The simplest one is the *round seam* stitch, which is normally used where only one side of the work is visible on completion. Items like sailbags and fendoffs are always stitched inside out, a single row of round seam stitches being used. The turned-back raw edges of canvas are then left inside on completion.

Where a tabling (hem) is made around the edges of an awning or at the top of a sailbag this may be visible on both sides with the raw canvas edge tucked under, and the *flat seam* stitch is used in these places, as well as for joining the long overlapped seams used when rolls of cloth are made up into wide awnings or sails.

Round seam stitching is quick and easy to do, but the secret of success with either method is to measure out the stitch spacings along the seam, perhaps with other ruled lines to ensure that all stitches are made equidistant from the canvas edge.

As seen from the diagram the stitches are normally made with folds of the two pieces of canvas held together, the needle being thrust through four layers of canvas, brought back over the top and then passed through four layers again. When the two pieces are parted into their correct positions and creased down a scarcely visible seam should result with short neat stitches crossing it.

For the neatest job, about ten stitches to the inch should be used. Where a rougher job will suffice or with thicker canvas, as few as six stitches to the inch can be used but the needle should then be passed through the seam at 30° to lessen the stitch angle across the inside of the seam.

The diagram explains the formation of a flat seam stitch along a section of tabling. As the stitching is visible on both sides the needle should always be angled in the direction of progress so that the slope on each stitch is approximately equal when viewed from either side. If not hurried too much at first, neat work can be done with very little practice.

The needle should enter downwards through the single layer of canvas close to the seam then, tilting the needle, the point must emerge in the correct place on top of the seam after a single thrust with the palm. In very heavy canvas it may be necessary to stitch in two movements, once down through the single layer and once with the hand beneath the work to push the needle up through the triple layer.

When joining two sheets of canvas together the work is turned over on completion of one flat seam so that the other one can be stitched in exactly the same way. Raw edges of canvas must be turned under to hide them. Where there is a selvedge turning under is not necessary.

A few other types of hand stitch may be necessary in sail repair work, and these are mentioned later in this chapter. For all other canvaswork, the two types of stitch described above are all that one needs to know.

For most work, needles should be loaded with a double length of twine, the two ends left free, and the total length no more than 2 ft (600 mm). The ends at the commencement of stitching should be laid along the seam and sewn under at least three stitches. When the twine runs out, twist the remaining ends with the new pieces and again sew under. At the end of a seam, back-sew two stitches and pass the needle under three further stitches before cutting off.

Sail Repairs

Restitching the machine sewn seams on a professionally made sail in material up to about 6 oz (170 g) can be tackled on a normal household sewing machine. Several sewing machine makers (such as *Singer*) have depots in big towns where the special large needles for sewing twine are stocked.

Although a zig-zag stitch is used by professionals for sail seams, a straight stitch of smaller pitch is almost as good and is certainly suitable for restitching sails which are too old to be worth the expense of a sailmaker's attention.

In addition to restitching, the most common sail repairs concern the darning or patching of torn areas, repairing eyelets and cringles, chafe at clews and headboards, and re-roping.

The *herringbone* stitch (or some variation of it) is generally best where the sail is torn in a straight or L-shaped manner. A round seam stitch can be used for a hurried emergency repair, but it tends to pull the two parts too closely together putting an unfair strain on the surrounding canvas.

177

The illustration of herringbone stitching shows the most popular way of doing this. A slight gap is left between the two torn parts and the locking turn between each stitch fills this space completely. With Terylene (Dacron), every alternate stitch should be longer than the remainder to prevent the weakness of single pierced rows of holes.

Turning the corner with a right-angled rip needs care. The stitches should radiate around the angle and should be longer than usual with alternating lengths, especially on the side where they tend to bunch up.

A much neater repair can be made to torn parts of nearly all sizes by means of patching. The most important thing about patching is to use a piece of material almost identical to the weave of the original cloth.

For dinghy sails and nylon spinnakers, patches are best stitched with a household sewing machine, finishing off with diagonal rows to pin the two layers of material closely together.

Whether machine or hand stitching is used, the cutting procedure is the same. Additional scissor cuts are made so that the cloth can be folded back to leave a neat rectangular aperture.

Having creased these hems to hold them in position, the patch should be prepared to the same general shape as the aperture but allowing a generous overlap all around after turning under and creasing the outer edges of the patch. Note that the corners should be cut off to enable the edges to be turned back neatly, meeting as mitres.

Hold the patch in position by means of pins, glue, or adhesive tape, and then sew around the outer edge first with a fine flat seam stitch, (or by machine) turning the sail over to complete similar stitching around the aperture hem. Repairs on cotton sails may be creased down with a steam iron but any form of heat treatment on synthetic fibres should be avoided.

The self-adhesive film with tear-off backing used for sail numbers and the rolls of adhesive linen tape stocked by chandlers are quite useful for emergency sail repairs and can last a considerable time on sails used in light airs.

The repair of chafe on sail corners is difficult for the amateur to do neatly as it may involve re-roping and re-eyeleting. Much useful work can be done, however, by stitching an additional layer of cloth on either side of the sail, ending close to the eyelet or cringle and the roping. On an unroped sail the

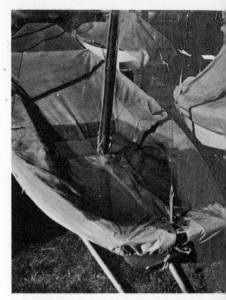

Picture 46.   Hatch covers are easy to make and protect brightwork as well as preventing leaks. Shockcord inside the hem makes for quick fitting.

Picture 47.   Dinghy covers without ridge poles soon fill with rainwater. The extra weight tears the eyelets out and makes removal a troublesome task.

Drawing 19.   The two commonest types of canvas stitching.
1. Round seam stitching. The two parts of canvas are shown parted for clarity but would in practice be held together.
2. Flat seam stitching. Canvas edges are sewn under so appearance is equally neat on either side.

Drawing 20.   Repairing torn sails by hand stitching: (a and b) Two types of herringbone stitch for repairing short tears without puckering the cloth. Method (b) is generally used as the needle always enters the cloth from the same side. (c) The first step in patching. Use flat seam stitching to fix the patch to the sail. Turn patch edge under first. Use pins to position patch correctly. (d) On the reverse side, cut out a rectangle well clear of the rip, turn the edges under as shown dotted and fix with flat seam stitching.

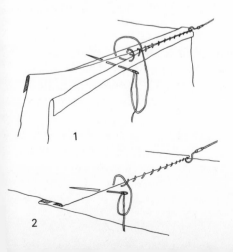

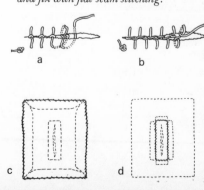

tabling can be parted to allow the patch to pass underneath it. This will help to mask the repair.

The patch on one side should be slightly larger than the other so that flat seam stitches (or machine stitching) can be completed on the turned-in edges of the smaller patch first. Having sewn all edges, some further rows of straight stitches (perhaps radiating from the cringle for neatness) should be run right through all layers. A simple *running stitch* can be used for this purpose, following along ruled lines, pushing the needle straight down through, along and up through, then along and down again, all stitches being of equal length.

Sail Bolt Ropes

If the roping around the corner of a heavy sail seems prone to chafe, it might be expedient to cover this with sewn leather. Where wooden or metal headboards are sewn into the reinforcement at the top of a mainsail, holes or gaps are provided to enable stitches to be taken right through.

It may be necessary to unpick the stitching so that when new reinforcing pieces are put on, the criss-cross stitching between the holes can be replaced much as before. The holes can usually be located by feel but may show up when creased over with the sail-rubber.

The most frequent re-roping operation is the replacement of galvanized wire luff ropes on jibs. The additional cost of stainless steel wire rope may not be worth while when re-roping an old jib, but special finned sheath plastics coated galvanized steel wire ropes are made by *Norseman Ropes Ltd,* especially for this purpose. If ordinary galvanized rope is used, the tack end (which always rusts first) should be treated with anhydrous lanoline bound over with vinyl tape. The whole length of the rope can be taped over as this helps the rope to grip the tabling of the sail, but avoid the use of black insulation tape as this might discolour the sail.

First remove the old rope by unpicking the single row of running stitching usually placed hard up to the rope to keep it from moving inside the tabling. On a dinghy jib, the eye splice on the tack or head end can be cut off and the wire rope pulled out through the tabling, with a gantline attached to enable the new rope to be drawn in.

If the new rope eyes cannot be spliced *in situ*, the tabling must be unpicked and this is necessary anyway on big jibs where the luff rope is taken right around proper thimbled cringles at the tack and head. As this will entail cutting out the hank eyelets, new ones of larger size must be inserted later.

Some jibs have separate tablings (sometimes made from wide Terylene tape lapped right around both sides), so if this is renewed, hank eyelets of the original size can be used, then all stitching and extra reinforcement at head and tack can be made good.

When boltropes need renewing, a sail is normally nearing the end of its life, but these ropes may become chafed locally necessitating the splicing-in of a short length or a new strand as mentioned in the last chapter.

The method of sewing a boltrope on to the tabling of a sail will be obvious after examining one. With the rope stretched horizontally in front of you, the sail behind the rope and hanging downwards from it, work from left to right pushing the needle between the strands against the lay.

The sail tabling should be stitched around about one third of the circumference of the rope, each stitch nestling the canvas down into the lay of the rope. Most workers draw a straight pencil line along the rope to prevent this getting twisted when lined up with the edge of the tabling.

Using prestretched Terylene three-strand rope, no additional stretching is required when Terylene cloth is sewn to this. When roping a cotton or flax sail with Italian hemp rope, however, prestretch the rope (see Chapter 7), then fix the rope bar taut while sewing the tabling pulled free of all wrinkles.

The renewal of reef points and lacings is purely a matter of examining the previous method and replacing in the same way. Reef points usually consist of a single length of cordage the centre of which passes through an eyelet or cringle with both parts sewn through the sail just below this. Where there is no eyelet, three loops may be formed in the rope on either side, sewn through the sail in a crowsfoot formation. The ends of reef points must be well secured with palm-and-needle whippings (see chapter 7).

Note that the equipment for points reefing should be checked over periodically and carefully stowed in a cockpit locker or inside the main hatch. You may need three pendants (pronounced *pennants*) to lead from the leech earrings to the bee-block on the boom; some tiers to secure the luff earrings, and, sometimes, a set of reef lacings.

Useful Canvas Parts

Much money can be saved by making up the many pieces of canvas equipment to be found on board a successful cruising boat, and such work can be tackled during winter evenings.

Ordinary cork-filled fenders on a rope lanyard make a good example to start with. Granulated cork may often be obtained from fruit stores (being used for packing grapes) and sometimes from wine stores, while at modest cost chunks of foam rubber suitable for making soft fenders may be bought from upholsterers. Kapok is occasionally used for this purpose, while although lumps of expanded polystyrene can be obtained gratis from firms that manufacture this material, it may break up into tiny pieces under pressure and need repacking.

Remember that most yachts use fenders which are too small so choose a generous size. The vertical cylindrical type with a single rope is generally the kindest to topsides; anything square shaped should be avoided at all costs.

Before cutting out each top and bottom panel, draw a circle in pencil showing the seam line (using a saucepan as template) and allow about 1 in (25 mm) of square canvas all around, outside this line. Insert an eyelet in the centre of each disc, gauged to fit the chosen rope.

Cut out a piece of canvas for the sides (adding 1 in (25 mm) spare top and bottom) of sufficient length to wrap around the pencilled circles plus the usual amount of spare each end, drawing straight lines for all seams.

Having creased along the seam lines, sew the top disc on to the wall piece first, with the work inside out, using the round seam stitch as previously described.

Now, to make the vertical seam meet exactly, one of the pencilled lines may need adjusting slightly. This is the reason why the vertical seam should not be sewn before fitting one or both of the discs.

Sew about 75% of the way around the bottom circle, complete the vertical seam, then turn the fendoff right-way-out by gradually pushing all the canvas out through the space.

Pass the rope lanyard through the eyelets at top and bottom, securing this with a fancy knot (or a plain figure-eight knot if preferred) then fill the fendoff with cork or other material using a funnel stapled up from cardboard. When full, the opening may be sewn up from the outside with round seam stitches.

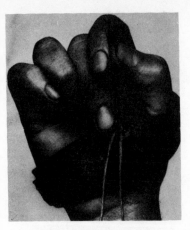

Picture 48. How to wear a palm and hold a sail needle. Special palms are made for left-handed people.

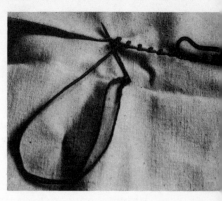

Picture 49. Making a flat seam stitch. See how the sail hook is used, and note dark thread woven into canvas along selvedge to guide the stitching.

Making a canvas bucket is similar to the above, except that the top rim should be turned over to form a tabling about $1\frac{1}{2}$ in (38 mm) wide, sewn along with flat seam stitching. The rim can then be roped for additional stiffness by making a grommet of the correct diameter and sewing this on as for roping a sail.

The bucket handle may be of rope, spliced into the grommet, or sewn from canvas in the form of a double thickness strap stitched to the walls of the bucket. These buckets are useful for carrying stores when shopping and are handy for holding tools, especially when working aloft. Alternatively, the bottom can be made from a disc of thick marine plywood.

Making a proper carpenter's tool bag with two handles is simple and this will be found most useful at fitting-out time. Other items made on similar lines include sail bags; a case for rolled charts; and covers for hatches, skylights and ventilators, some of which may have draw strings or shockcord sewn into the tabling.

Unlike fenders, the interior of some of these items may be visible, so the spare canvas along the seams can be trimmed off close to the stitching for neatness, while a superior job results if these edges are turned inwards and sewn along.

Most of the other canvaswork jobs that amateurs can do involve flat seaming, tabling, and eyeleting, to produce such things as dodgers, a cockpit cover, bunk flaps, the waterproof cover for a dinghy, or windsails to improve summer ventilation through hatches and skylights.

Bunk flaps may be triangular or trapezoidal in shape with the upper corners eyeleted for lanyards to the deckhead, the lower edge being secured to the bunk bottom with a screwed batten. This is generally a better device than a leeboard for keeping one in position while sleeping under way.

Cotton canvas is warmer to feel than Terylene for such a purpose but it may be advisable to allow for easy removal of the canvas for annual cleaning. In addition to the tabling, some reinforcement should be sewn in way of the eyelets.

Vinyl coated nylon fabrics make excellent long-lasting waterproof covers, though more expensive than canvas. Awning makers frequently use a water sealing adhesive along all the seams as well as stitching. This has the added advantage of securing the seams in position before sewing, eliminating the need for pins or sticky tape to locate the material.

A cockpit tent to fit over the boom is a useful fitting on a small yacht, adding extra space when in harbour, especially at night or in rainy weather. If clear PVC windows are inserted these should be machine sewn through to a reinforcing *surround* on the inside. To prevent wrinkles, do not cut out the opening in the tent until some stitching is complete.

Permanent cockpit covers and similar sheets must always be well secured with lanyards or shockcord and special single horned metal or nylon (Delrin) cleats are available to screw on to the planking just below the sheer beading for this purpose.

Remember that a short time spent making canvas covers for hatches and cockpit during the winter can reduce the amount of maintenance on varnish work to these parts enormously. Pram hood type dodgers can also be made by the amateur with a little care and patience.

Numerous brands of rot proofers exist but many yachtsmen prefer to paint all canvas covers white or perhaps a pale green. Special canvas paint (such as Ryland SP) must always be used for this purpose as the canvas can then be rolled up without fear of the paint film cracking.

Making canvas dodgers to fit on the guardrails alongside a cockpit (or right around a stern pulpit) is a simple job involving tabling and eyeleting. To put the ship's name on to these the letters may be cut from self-adhesive sail numbering material. This does not hold as well to cotton canvas or painted surfaces as it does to Terylene, though it will last several seasons if pressed back into position when starting to peel off.

Stowing Sails

The making of sail coats is linked closely with the manner in which a sail is stowed along a boom, as the neatness of stowing can make a big difference to the size of the sail coat.

Stowing a mainsail is normally a two man job as the leech needs to be pulled out as the folds of sail are flaked down or rolled. The neatest method of stowing a heavy mainsail, especially when gaff rigged, is to flake all the way, allowing even folds of sail to droop over alternate sides. To stow a jib fold the clew and leech parallel to the luff, then fold longways. Alternatively, coil the luff (making the sail look like an air-sock) before rolling up the canvas to meet the coiled luff rope.

When crewing, remember that many owners have their own pet method for stowing each sail and this applies especially to spinnakers where special folding with the corners exposed may be required to permit faultless hoisting direct from the sail bag.

Eyelets and Cringles

Although a *cringle* is strictly a heavy duty thimbled eye formed outside the boltrope by weaving a rope grommet (sometimes leathered) through two eyelets set in the tabling, the word cringle is nowadays frequently used for the thimbled eyelet inside the boltrope at the corner of a sail, or at the end of a wire luff rope.

Light duty brass eyelets are very easy to fit. Each eyelet is formed from two parts, a base with a spigot and a ring. If the correct size wad punch is not available, a rough hole can be cut by making two crossed incisions with a knife and then cutting off the corners with a pair of scissors.

The spigot is pushed through the hole from underneath and while the base rests upon the specially shaped anvil, the ring is dropped over the spigot and the spigot is then swaged neatly over the ring by hammering it with the specially shaped punch. The most important requirement for strength is to make the canvas hole a snug fit around the spigot so that no canvas gets trapped between the ring and the spigot.

To make a heavy-duty eyelet, sew a stainless steel or brass ring around a hole slightly smaller than the inside diameter of the ring and then swage a sailmaker's annealed circular thimble tightly and immovably into the hole. This is difficult for the amateur to do without the correct tools. With proper

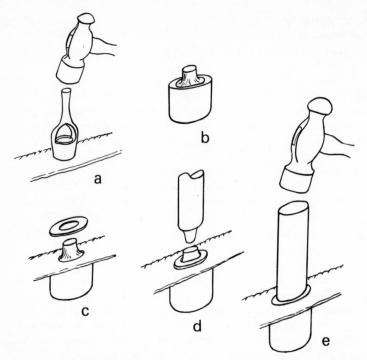

Drawing 21. How to insert a brass eyelet: (a) Cut hole through the tabling by means of a wad punch and hammer. Alternatively a trimming knife may be used by making two crossed incisions and cutting off the four tabs so formed. (b) Place spigoted part of eyelet on to the special die. (c) Feed spigot up through the prepared hole and place eyelet ring over spigot. d) With die still in place swage spigot over ring, using the specially shaped punch and a hammer.

grommet cringles a solid round thimble is used, the grommet being expanded with a fid, which is removed quickly as the thimble is forced in.

With all sail and canvas repairs the *stitch in time* motto is most appropriate. Natural fibre materials must be watched carefully for rot and synthetic materials for chafe. To check for rot, try piercing the material with a large needle (on the reinforced parts of a sail) and examine this afterwards with a magnifying glass. If any strands have broken probe further with the needle; easy severing of the threads means that they have been weakened by rot.

Wherever repair work is necessary unpick any stitching with care to note exactly how it was done originally. If you get really keen on this type of work it may be possible to scrounge an old sail found lying at a boatyard which can be unpicked and used for practice repairs at odd moments.

Sail Care

At laying-up time all sails should be stretched out on a floor or lawn, scrubbed both sides with hot water and detergent, rinsed with a hose, and hoisted to an upper floor window sill to dry. The thick corner patches may take several days to dry out completely. Small jibs and dinghy sails can be washed in a bath tub.

This is a good time to examine each sail for defects. The likeliest trouble spots are batten pockets; bolt ropes; all stitching; dirty areas where chafe has occurred; the leech tabling and headboard, plus the clew and foot on a jib. Mark all parts needing attention with a crayon.

Any stains are best tackled before washing. Mildew can be mitigated by a stiff brushing followed by scrubbing with a mild disinfectant/bleach solution. A 5% solution of *oxalic acid* (salts of lemon) washed thoroughly afterwards may remove rust stains.

Grease and tar can be obstinate. Start with hot turps substitute (white spirit) scrubbed on with a nail brush and dried off with rag. Then, if required, apply a molecular hand cleansing jelly (such as Swarfega or Dirty Paws) washing this off with detergent and hot water.

If this proves unsuccessful, consult the sailmaker or return the sail to him. When using the services of a sailmaker for cleaning, laundering, storing, or repairing sails, action must be taken in the autumn.

When storing your sails, leave them loosely flaked and refold them occasionally. Mice are said to nibble synthetic as well as cotton sails. A trap can be set in a loft, but if some paper and rags are left nearby the mice may prefer these to the sails!

CHAPTER 9

MECHANICAL EQUIPMENT

Even sailing dinghies have some items of mechanical equipment such as self-bailers, drum winches, shroud levers, or trailers, so it could be said that all yachtsmen need to be mechanically-minded to ensure that their equipment works reliably when demanded. When it comes to main propulsion engines (or to auxiliaries) the owner or crew unable to carry out essential running repairs could create danger if they ever put to sea.

Two-strokes and Outboards
To compensate for their lack of experience, amateur mechanics need to study handbooks and other maker's literature thoroughly, especially as soon as any different equipment is obtained. Where engines are concerned this usually means that one should buy the full workshop manual, a spare parts list, and perhaps two fault-finding charts, one of which can be sealed in cellophane and kept on board.

Outboard motors are made in such a huge range, from the delightfully simple single cylinder *Seagull* (which can be stripped down completely in less than one hour), to the huge multi-cylinder racing types which are considered by most yachtsmen to be far too complicated to touch.

As modern outboards are designed to function when exposed to all types of weather, they prove most reliable provided overhauls are carried out in good time. Although four-stroke outboards are available (and even a few diesel and kerosene models as well) the vast majority are two-stroke (two-cycle) petrol (gasoline) motors.

Two-stroke engines have the advantages of not requiring sump oil; simplicity of construction with no valve gear, and

Picture 50. Auxiliary motors are rarely so accessible as this one. Regular maintenance is a sound policy as adjustments at sea frequently lead to mal de mer!

Picture 51. Small auxiliary engines are readily taken ashore. Even if major repairs are not necessary, thorough cleaning, painting and replacement of suspect parts is far easier in the workshop.

Drawing 22. With a handyman welding set the keen amateur mechanic can fabricate a tilting stand on the above lines to suit his own engine. This simplifies major overhauls greatly. Without an elaborate tilt lock device the engine can be held in any position with a jack and prop. A similar stand can be made from wood.

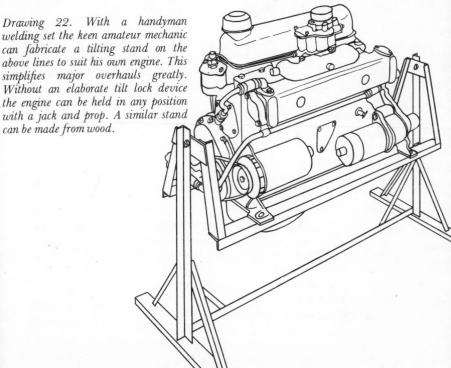

optimium power/weight ratio, but they are notoriously un-reliable as soon as compression weakens due to wear, and they drink more fuel than four-strokes.

According to the amount of use an engine has had, it may be wise to return it to the makers' agents for a check on the compression, perhaps every two years, even though the engine has been functioning perfectly. Running with a mixture of oil in the fuel, two strokes carbon up more quickly than four-strokes, and as the frequency of decarbonizing often corresponds exactly with the need to check for piston ring wear the two jobs can be done together. OMC (Johnson, Evinrude, etc) recommend 200 hours between de-cokes on their two-cycle outboards.

Some engines are made without detachable cylinder heads. As the complete block must be removed for decarbonizing, the pistons will be exposed, making renewal of rings or complete pistons a simple matter. The agents must be consulted to ensure that only the correct rings are used, the uppermost one having a rebated top edge if necessary to avoid hammering the lip sometimes worn at the top of the cylinder bore.

The amateur who feels competent to do his own decarbonizing (even though he may not intend to do more major work) should keep a set of replacement piston rings handy as he may find a ring broken on removing the block.

If one old ring can be removed, this may be checked against a new ring to find whether it has worn appreciably, and ring and bore wear can be checked quite effectively by inserting first an old ring and then a new one into the bore, measuring with feeler gauges the amount of opening at the ring gap in each case. The reading with a new ring will indicate the bore wear while the reading for an old ring will indicate the bore wear plus the ring wear.

Note that the opening is difficult to measure when the ring gap is of the diagonal or stepped variety but some idea may be gained by careful observation. The position of maximum bore wear normally occurs about one-third of the stroke from the top. To prevent a free ring from binding in the bore use a piston minus ring to push it in if possible. Take special care to remove the ring evenly from a blind bore (integral cylinder head), using two U-shaped stirrups bent from wire if your fingers are not long enough.

Two-stroke piston rings should fit over pegs in the grooves

to prevent the ends from catching in the ports. Therefore, do not rotate the block or piston when dismantling and do not try to assemble without using a piston ring clamp of correct size.

The exhaust systems on two-stroke engines foul up rather easily and this can affect the running in mysterious ways. Exhaust manifolds, silencers and piping can be boiled in a strong solution of caustic soda to remove soft carbon, but this treatment may harm aluminium blocks or heads.

Wire brush attachments of various shapes are available to fit the handyman's electric drill and these are invaluable for the rapid removal of carbon from pistons, ports, and cylinder heads. They may not get inside blind cylinder bores so that one may have to resort to patient hand scraping in such cases.

Stripping the crankcase may prove far more difficult than a top overhaul. The big end bearing may be enclosed between crank webs which are pressed on to a pin and the main bearings may be pressed into the halves of the crankcase.

The main bearing seals are most important for efficient crankcase compression and the ones between each compartment of a multicylinder two-stroke are just as important as the end two. Leakage through the seals is usually due to bearing wear, but simple renewal of the seals on a single cylinder motor may improve running for a considerable time.

A flywheel magneto or Dynastart should give little trouble with regular attention to points and lubrication. Spare coils and condenser can be kept handy, or fitted anyway to a secondhand engine if the magneto seems suspect. Any score marks on the flywheel mounting taper on the end of the crankshaft should be removed or lessened with fine grinding paste while rotating the flywheel by hand with the Woodruff key removed.

It may be advisable to borrow the special withdrawing tool to part an obstinate flywheel (without captive nut) from its taper, but when replacing the flywheel a good tap with a block of wood and a heavy hammer will ensure that the nut is wound on to completion, especially if no helper is available to hold the flywheel still, or if the crankshaft cannot be jammed in some way.

The gudgeon bearing at the little end of the connecting rod normally has a long life and may not need attention until new pistons are fitted. Many two-strokes have a shaped piston head. so the piston must be replaced the original way.

When excessive bore and piston wear occurs eventually, the makers' manual should be consulted to ascertain whether reboring with oversized pistons and rings is possible. If not, they may tell you that the customary procedure is to fit a new cylinder block, or to return the block to their agents only for suitable reboring.

Spark plug trouble is the curse of two-stroke engines, but this can be minimized by adhering to the recommended type of plug. Several spare plugs should always be carried on board (with the correct box spanner) and a misfiring plug should be changed immediately to prevent it and the cylinder from fouling rapidly. Fouled plugs and those of incorrect type can cause pre-ignition or running-on.

To find out which plug is at fault on a multicylinder engine pull off the caps one by one while the engine is running, the one which makes no difference to the behaviour of the engine being the faulty one.

By holding the internal contact of the cap a short distance from the plug (so that the crackling of the spark jumping across can be heard) this may boost the spark slightly and clear the fouled plug temporarily, but this operation may be difficult to carry out to an outboard motor when attached to the stern of a boat.

Correct fuel/oil mixture is most important for any two-stroke engine and the ratio recommended by some makers may be quite different from that sold ready-mixed at garages. Special oils are available for mixing with fuel, as ordinary sump oil tends to concentrate at the bottom of the tank when an engine is left standing. Shaking an outboard engine (or separate fuel tank) is advisable before starting, to prevent thick oil from entering the carburettor.

Carburettors vary in complexity from engine to engine, but the majority are of foolproof design with a taper needle controlled jet which is unlikely to block. Fuel flooding may be due to a damaged float or float valve, the usual cause being dirt on the valve seat. If this cannot be cured by tapping the carburettor, the float chamber may have to be opened to blow out the valve or wash it in clean fuel. Needless to say all fuel filters need checking for gauze damage if dirt is getting through, and for clogging if the flow of fuel is restricted.

Motors with integral fuel tanks can get water into the fuel through the air vent in rough weather so a motor with remote tank is advantageous for offshore work, while refuelling under way is then also much simpler. The streamlined cowlings now standard on all the larger motors are very effective in keeping spray from the carburettor and ignition system, but these casings can be a nuisance when any maintenance work is required.

If electric starting is not fitted, the simplest motors have a cord to wind around a pulley on top of the flywheel, while other motors have an enclosed recoil starter with captive cord and exposed rubber handle. The ratchet, pawls and spring of a recoil starter take quite a pounding in use, and although all spare parts should be available, most makers run an exchange unit service which is well worth using when trouble occurs.

Fitting a new clock-type recoil spring can be quite a dangerous job! The new spring must be wound several turns in an improvised jig. When of the correct diameter to fit into the housing, lash it around with strong cord. Once in place with the ends engaged in their correct notches the cord can be cut and removed. Fitting a new spiral-type recoil spring is a simpler job. A ratchet drum may be of die-cast whitemetal and is certain to wear out before the pawls. These parts are easy to replace.

Most outboards have a bevel gearbox under water which, if correctly lubricated should never require stripping. Individual makers' manuals and spare parts lists should cover the information likely to be needed concerning a reversing mechanism or clutch.

If one has the misfortune to drop an outboard motor overboard (and although a lanyard must be attached to it at all times it may still get wet) the best procedure generally is to remove the carburettor for cleaning, take out the spark plugs and rotate the engine rapidly to blow out any water, drain any parts of the fuel system which could become waterlogged then reassemble and give the engine a long run. Subsequently, an eye should be kept open for any visible corrosion and any mechanisms not completely sealed should be dismantled, cleaned and lubricated. Prolonged submerging in water normally warrants an immediate and complete strip down.

To prevent damage to the propeller and gearbox, most outboards have a shear pin, spring-loaded pawl, shock absorber, or friction drive, preventing the flywheel from stopping dead should the propeller strike hard ground. For a motor with a shear pin, spares must be carried and the same applies to spring pawls, as these sometimes break. Replacing pins or pawls takes only a few minutes but it may not be possible to do this without unshipping the engine from the transom mounting.

Most outboard engines are water-cooled, helping towards silent running. Although the circulation pumps used rarely give trouble it pays to ensure that the water intake holes are free (especially when in weedy water) by checking the tell-tale outlet frequently. Floating plastics wrappers sometimes cause blockages. The usual indication of overheating is a fall in engine speed followed by stoppage, the engine starting again and running normally for a further brief period after cooling off.

An engine may be run in the workshop for testing purposes for a few minutes without need for water, but a more prolonged though perhaps chaotic run may be effected by submerging the propeller in a tank of water! A firm mounting is necessary for safety reasons.

If an outboard motor must be left permanently clamped on board, an anti-thief lock is essential. This applies to motors of any size and it should be noted that many insurance companies will not accept loss by theft unless such a device is adopted.

An extra premium is usually charged for cover against dropping a motor overboard, but a rope lanyard always in place is an obvious precaution, with perhaps two lanyards in use when a motor is being transferred from a dinghy to the parent ship. Always tilt a motor to keep the propeller out of water when lying at moorings and have a large waterproof cover for the upper parts. When tilted, some outdrive (Z-drive) propeller units will not lift sufficiently to clear the water and the submerged parts become fouled rapidly. If the craft can be beached, a wash down with phenolic disinfectant will kill the weed growth instantly, enabling this to be scrubbed clean. Make sure there are no ropes in the water before starting the engine.

A wash down occasionally with fresh water and detergent is a good idea, plus protection with car body wax if you want the enamel to stay smart. See Chapter 12 for laying-up procedure.

Some attention to remote control cables and steering wires is advisable during the season as well as at fitting-out time. Where grease nipples are fitted into the outer sheathing of flexible cables a grease gun (preferably containing graphited cable grease) should be applied until grease emerges at the ends. When the grease tends to emerge at one end without showing at the other it may pay to bind the free end with tape (after removing surplus grease) and continue greasing. Outer sheaths without integral grease nipples usually lead to neglected maintenance with consequent wearing or corrosion of the inner cable causing failure.

Although cables with removable terminals can be withdrawn, the indentations formed by the clamps usually mean that the cable is too rough to feed in again and new wire must be used. However, if the clevis pin is removed from each end so that the terminal at one end can be moved up close to the sheath, a toy rubber balloon can be used to force grease inside the sheath.

The balloon is partly filled with grease, the neck is pushed over both terminal and sheath, and while this is sealed to the sheath by binding around it with cord, the balloon is squeezed to force the grease in. The pins and bearings of all linkages and steering wire sheaves must, of course, receive periodic oiling to maintain a smooth action.

Make sure that you carry a small box or bag on board containing the essential tools for running repairs, not forgetting a piece of rag, and keep at home at least one makers' set of gaskets to avoid unnecessary delays should you, or a local garage, need to strip down any part of the engine.

Diesels and Other Four-Strokes

As mentioned above, one should try to be a leap ahead of trouble as far as two-stroke engine performance is concerned but with diesels and other four-stroke engines, (except in the case of component failure) there is usually prolonged warning of piston ring and bore wear, bearing wear, valve leakage, and the need for decarbonization.

Cylinder wear is indicated by high oil consumption, accompanied by fuming from the oil filler cap or crankcase breather. Diesels must have perfect compression, but petrol (gasoline) engines will sometimes run with badly worn bores and rings.

Crankshaft main bearing wear is indicated by low oil pressure (although there may be other reasons for this); valve leakage is indicated by lack of compression on one or more cylinders, while the need for decoking is indicated by failure to reach peak engine revolutions accompanied by pinking on opening the throttle. Big end bearing wear shows as a metallic knocking while leaky oil seals and valve gear cover gaskets leave tell-tale weeps of oil.

Only a trained fitter can normally differentiate precisely between the noises made by wear in big ends, little ends, worn pistons, or valve tappets. A listening rod made from a length of light steel bar is useful for locating mysterious noises. While holding one end to various spots on the engine, keep your thumb over the other end with the thumb nail pressed to your ear.

Tappets are simple for the amateur to adjust by following the instructions in the workshop manual, but remember to fit a new gasket to the cover on completion or oil leaks are sure to ensue. Frequently only one tappet is noisy and this can be located by allowing the engine to idle with the tappet cover removed so that a feeler gauge can be inserted into the gaps while running, noting which one becomes silent.

It may not be possible to silence the tappets on a worn engine without decreasing the maker's recommended gap and such a procedure is not generally advisable.

Having removed the noise from the tappets, it may be assumed that any additional knocks are due to the other causes.

The majority of four-stroke engines used for marine duties on yachts nowadays are marinized versions of road vehicle engines. This ensures a high powered output for a given weight and size but it does create drawbacks. Engines designed for boat work have side covers on the crankcase so that the sump can be cleaned out without lifting the whole engine, while big end bearings can be checked readily and complete pistons and connecting rods withdrawn through the covers without disturbing the cylinder head or block.

Although such engines rarely need to be lifted out of the boat, there is so little working space in most modern engine compartments that the marinized car engine (which has to be raised off its bearers or taken completely out of the boat for overhaul) may be a quite satisfactory proposition for many yacht propulsion duties.

When the sump cannot be removed readily, it pays to change engine oil and filter elements more frequently than seems necessary. Note also that when an engine is fitted with a conventional pressed steel sump this must never be allowed to

Picture 52. Inboard/outboard, Z-drive, or outdrive propeller units should be tilted above water if possible when not in use to prevent marine growth and damage. Note the excellent launching slipway with wheeled cradle running on steel track.

Picture 53. An oilbath type anchor windlass deserves a good clean out ashore occasionally. Water leaking in can cause corrosion, and broken gear teeth may lead to a seizure.

come into contact with bilge water for any length of time or rapid corrosion could lead to a serious leak of oil when under way. If such a sump is zinc-sprayed for protection, this coating could cause galvanic action between any adjacent copper fastenings when bilge water is allowed to build up.

Top overhauls (decarbonization) can be carried out on most marinized engines with overhead valve gear without lifting out the whole engine, as the cylinder head (complete with valves) may be removed fairly easily and taken home for attention, leaving only the cleaning of the piston tops to be done on board. Always examine the cylinder bores carefully for score marks indicating a broken piston ring.

To break the cylinder head away from its gasket when all nuts have been removed some proper marine engines have lifting eyes which, when screwed downwards, act as jacks to force the head upwards. One must not forget to slacken these off completely before refitting the head.

Without these, the studs should be treated with penetrating oil and the head dressed sideways with a mallet (or a block of wood under a club hammer), then by turning the crankshaft smartly, the gasket seal may be broken.

Any form of tackle improvised from the cylinder head to sheerlegs (or other overhead support) is an enormous help, especially when dealing with a large engine. Be careful to work around lightly and evenly when using screwdrivers or other wedges driven into the joint, but special jacking recesses are provided for this purpose on some engines.

Once off, the head can, if preferred, be presented to a fitter to deal with, but provided the workshop manual is followed and one can lay hands on a suitable valve lifter, the work is not complicated.

You may not know whether new valves are required until the old ones have been stripped off, but note that hours of labour grinding-in valves by hand can be saved if usable old valves are first skimmed on a proper refacing machine. All essential spare parts such as valve stem seals, gaskets, etc should be obtained beforehand. Remember to have a supply of large and small containers to receive each part when dismantled. Precise labelling of these parts or the containers may save much time and worry later while a note pad is useful to make sketches and jot down data which might be needed when the time comes for reassembly. Have plenty of rag and keep a tank of kerosene (paraffin, TVO, or lamp oil) with a stiff paint brush and an old tooth brush for washing off parts.

Inspect each piece before dismantling. Make corresponding centre punch marks to avoid later confusion should a part fit more than one way. Even the flywheel should be pop-marked before disturbing it to avoid upsetting the balance. The valves may have numbers, but if not they may be kept in correct order by standing in holes bored in a block of wood. Workshop manuals do not normally mention such hints though they may warn you of such matters as draining the cylinder water jacket before removing the head!

Whenever an inboard engine is taken ashore for a repair job, it pays to do any additional work which could become necessary within the next few years. New big end shells do not cost much and as the sump should always be removed in these instances to clean it out, very little work is involved in fitting new shells. The first indication of serious bearing wear may be the appearance of minute specks of white metal in the sump or in the oil filter.

If the gauze screen between the crankshaft and the sump gets clogged with sludge, the oil circulation pump may become starved resulting in low oil pressure readings perhaps even when idling.

Before attacking big ends (inverting the engine for accessibility) it will probably be necessary to remove the oil gallery piping which feeds the main bearings. Make sure the pipes are free before replacing them.

Big end caps are normally numbered and marked for alignment and although care should be taken to replace the shells so that oil holes correspond, confusion is unlikely as each shell fits on to a peg or into a notch. Main bearing shells are not likely to need renewal so frequently as big ends, but the caps can be lifted to examine for scoring without needing to strip off the gearbox.

In assembling new shells a smear of graphited oil on the surfaces will eliminate any likelihood of a metal to metal contact before the oil pump starts to circulate on starting the engine.

Graphited oils are not very popular but several oil companies do produce graphited upper cylinder lubricant and running-in compound. Small amounts of the former added to the fuel can increase the life of valves and bores greatly.

A major overhaul at home can be done more quickly and safely if an *engine stand* can be made from timber or welded steel to support the engine at a convenient working height, preferably also enabling it to be rotated without assistance.

Try not to bodge the work through lack of any special tools (such as pullers; circlip pliers; piston ring clamps; thin-walled or extra large box spanners; a torque wrench, or perhaps an extra thin open-ended spanner) as it should nearly always be possible to borrow or hire these briefly.

This may cause delays but one can invariably find some other jobs to get on with one weekend while arranging to obtain the tools found to be necessary ready for the following weekend. You may need a nut breaker to split off nuts which are rusted solid and if one is unfortunate enough to break off a stud, the loan of a set of stud extractors will certainly be necessary. Always be careful to clean all parts before re-assembly, including all joints where traces of gasket may remain.

Few amateurs are qualified to carry out such work as reboring; fitting dry cylinder liners; crankshaft regrinding; gear box repairs; checking a diesel injection pump; renewing timing chain sprockets, or dealing with a turbo-blower, but the main essential in cutting costs is to do all the dismantling and assembling work, which is so costly in manhours, and then despatch the components to specialist firms for expert attention.

199

TABLE 8
Engine Maintenance Costs

Type of Engine	Change Filters and oils		Treat plugs, contacts, carburettor or injectors		Decarbonize engine and exhaust system		Fit new piston rings		Rebore or Renew liners Fit new bearings	
	Amateur	Boat-yard	Amateur	Boat-yard	Amateur	Boat-yard	Amateur	Boat-yard	Amateur	Boat-yard
4hp single cylinder outboard	Top up gear oil only		1	3	1	4	2	6	6	15
8hp 2-cyl. gasoline inboard	2	5	1	5	1	7	3	10	13	25
10hp 2-cyl. diesel inboard	3	7	2	6	2	12	5	15	14	35
20hp 4-cyl. outboard	Top up gear oil only		3	8	2	9	9	16	15	28
25hp 4-cyl gasoline inboard	3	6	3	7	2	17	9	22	21	51
30hp 4-cyl. diesel inboard	3	7	4	7	2	18	10	26	24	55
60hp 6-cyl. diesel inboard	4	8	6	13	3	24	15	40	42	69
100hp 6-cyl. outboard	Top up gear oil only		4	12	4	15	15	38	80	120
100hp 6-cyl. diesel inboard	5	9	6	15	5	27	17	48	64	98
250hp 8-cyl. diesel inboard	6	10	12	20	6	38	30	75	105	180

Costs shown in £(U.K.). For $ (U.S.A.) multiply by 5
Including removal and replacement of engine where applicable

By keeping a bottle of whisky in the workshop you may be able to persuade an expert to come and have a look at any real problems!

When reassembling an engine, coat all threads with graphite grease (to keep rust away and facilitate later removal), including sparking plug threads. Discard all rusty nuts and bolts and fit new ones. To clean up other corroded steel parts use fine emery tape with plenty of oil. Never use emery dry on steel and keep its dust well away from any bearings.

Do not neglect engine painting if this seems necessary. A smartly finished engine seems more reliable in a boat, and is certainly likely to receive better maintenance than an apparent heap of junk which is red with rust on top and slimy with dirt and oil at the bottom! Meticulous owners sometimes prefer a white painted engine so that the slightest weep of oil can be spotted instantly and cured.

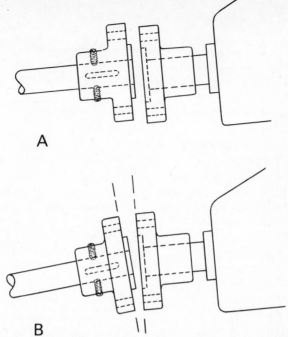

A

B

Drawing 23. Two types of error likely to be found when a shaft coupling is unbolted. Such errors must be corrected by inserting metal shims under the engine mounting feet.
A – The engine bearers have shrunk. Equal shimming required under all feet. If shaft is long and thin it may drop slightly under its own weight, so make allowance for this.
B – Forward feet have sunk more than after feet and need additional shimming. An error less than 3 thou. (76 microns) at outside of flange can usually be tolerated without harm.

Drawing 24. A small fuel tank for gravity supply: (a) Filler cap. (b) Vent pipe with fine gauze across orifice. (c) Sump with drain cock. (d) Outlet cock. A filter close to the outlet, is generally advisable. (e) Calibrated dip stick.

Drawing 25. A big diesel oil tank for pumped fuel supply: (a) Deck filler plate. (b) Vent pipe with swan neck above decks. (c) Fuel gauge with transparent plastics pipe. (d) Outlet union. (e) Injector and fuel pump relief spillage pipe. (f) Internal baffles. (g) Drain cock. Tank mounted with a slight fall towards this end.

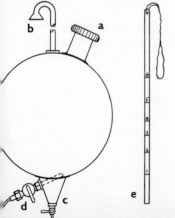

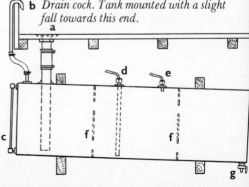

Care of Components

Over a period of years, one may find that more work is required to maintain an engine's components (such as the electrical system; sterngear; waste heat evaporator; pumps, and the exhaust, cooling, and fuel systems) than for the basic power unit.

The failure of one of these items at sea could be serious, and vigilance is needed to keep a leap ahead of trouble with ancillary equipment.

One safeguard against trouble is a gradual build-up of spare parts to be carried on board. The list starts with such obvious essentials as spare belts and continues through items such as spark plugs; contacts; injector nozzles; brushes; complete fuel pump (or repair kit); cartridge fuses; filter elements, and enough spare sump oil to take care of an emergency leak, perhaps due to a fractured oil pressure gauge pipe.

Engine makers supply boxes of spare parts for owners living in remote areas to keep in stock. It may be possible to ascertain the contents of these kits from the makers, but it should not be forgotten that spare parts lists may not include parts for all the ancillary equipment to be found on one particular yacht.

An incorrectly installed fuel system can cause lasting trouble and may need improving. A tank for diesel fuel (and the piping) must be of steel or grp. If of steel, the inside should not be galvanized or treated. The best materials for petrol (gasoline) or kerosene (TVO) tanks is tinned steel or grp. Brass and copper may cause the fuel to gum and are not considered good materials.

Although copper piping is commonly used, transparent plastics fuel pipe is generally superior except where there is much heat, and steel pipe is used for diesel fuel. Where long lengths of copper piping are used, horizontal anti-vibration coils are needed. The tubing should be annealed every three years (by heating to redness with a blow torch slowly passed along the pipe) to ensure that the copper is soft and unlikely to fracture. All unions must, of course, be brazed and not soft soldered. Before annealing, all fuel gum must be removed from the inside of pipes. Cellulose thinners is the best solvent, also for cleaning carburettors. Fill the pipe with thinners, plugging one end. Leave for one hour, drain, and blow through with an air line.

Whether copper or steel is used, a short length of flexible

fuel pipe is essential at the engine end. All piping should have a gradual fall from the fuel tank to a filter with transparent bowl and the piping may then rise gradually to the engine. There should be a stopcock at the tank, but note that this should normally be left open for a diesel installation (to prevent air lock) thus vigilance is necessary to ensure that the system always remains free from leakage. Note that with pumped fuel systems the outlet union may be at the top of the tank, with an extension pipe inside leading down to the bottom.

Air locks in petrol piping should clear themselves automatically with a gravity fed system, or, with a pumped fuel system, by operating the pump priming device. Failure to start a diesel may well be due to an air lock. The engine manual will describe the procedure to get rid of air, opening the bleed cocks systematically on the filters, fuel pump, injection pump, and nozzles while the throttle is kept fully open.

The fuel level in a tank must not be allowed to run too low in case air is drawn into the pipe. Big yachts have several fuel tanks (sometimes including a pump-fed gravity header tank) with elaborate systems for changing over or balancing tank levels, while there may be duplicate filters with change-over cocks so that a filter can be cleaned while the engine is running. An engine running on kerosene (TVO) has a change-over valve close to the carburettor to enable the engine to be warmed up on petrol (gasoline) supplied from a separate small tank.

Dirty fuel for diesels can cause injection pump wear and drooling injector nozzles which produce smoky exhaust. If a proper injector test rig is not available to test the pressure and spray pattern, some idea of nozzle behaviour can be obtained by removing each injector in turn and observing the spray while cranking the engine by hand with the union nuts or by-pass valves of the other injectors left open. Keep the hands and skin clear of the dangerous sprays.

Any blow-back through the nozzles can be found by easing the union nuts or by-pass valves one by one while the engine is running. Keep a supply of new annealed copper injector washers handy.

Cooling
Air cooled engines can be noisy and may take up much space by virtue of the air ducting required, but the elimination of any

form of water circulation system saves much maintenance work and likely causes of breakdown.

When sea water cooling is used a single rotary or plunger pump is used to draw water through the hull via a strainer often sending it first to the gearbox and engine oil coolers, then to the water jacketted exhaust manifold and up through the cylinder block to the head. The discharge may be into the exhaust pipe (perhaps via a water injection silencer) or direct overboard. With the former method there may be a small telltale outlet to show whether water is circulating without having to lean overboard to examine an awkwardly placed exhaust fitting.

The chief maintenance tasks consist of checks for weed or other debris on the intake strainer, greasing and packing of the pump and perhaps descaling the water jacket if encrusted with salt.

The intake strainer should have a seacock with a long tube rising from it having a removable perforated metal filter inside and a screw cap on the top. If the tube is correctly positioned it should be possible to check the strainer without needing to turn off the seacock. A probe can be inserted to ensure that the skin fitting grille is clear. Where the cap is below water level some water must be allowed to flood into the bilges when doing this.

Note that a three-way cock may be fitted to enable the engine cooling water pump to act as a bilge pump, so always ensure that the seacock is in the correct position for running and shut right off or directed to bilge when the ship is left unoccupied.

If rubber hose is used between the intake and the engine make sure that this is in good condition with stainless steel clips in preference to the sheradized ones used in automobile practice.

Closed circuit water systems may appear more complicated but are not subject to scaling and may have no sea water intake at all. Where a keel cooler is used one should keep in mind some alternative method of cooling, as a fracture of one of the external pipes could lead to engine failure.

It might be possible to connect an engine-driven or electric bilge pump to supply the engine with cooling water. Where an inboard heat exchanger is used there may be two circulation pumps, one for fresh water through the engine, and another for sea water to the heat exchanger.

Adequate water jacket temperature is important for long engine life, but if the temperature is too high with raw sea water cooling, excessive scaling may occur. If no thermometer is fitted, a capillary tube (or electrical thermo-couple) type can be wired to the outlet pipe close to the engine and lagged around with asbestos tape. Should the temperature remain consistently lower than the maker's recommendation, it may be necessary to install a by-pass with thermostat or cock to lessen the flow of water through the jacket, or an existing thermostat may have failed-safe.

Exhaust Piping
Except for fractures and joint leaks, diesel and other four-stroke exhaust systems need little maintenance, but it may pay to dismantle a section every few years to inspect for internal fouling and corrosion of the piping. Careful owners may like to keep some pieces of jointing material on board, with a few spare bolts, so that emergency repairs can be carried out if required. Although brass bolts are frequently used for exhaust pipe flanges, they do tend to work loose under heat and need checking periodically. Steel bolts liberally coated with graphite grease are generally better.

Water injection silencers keep the system cool and quiet, but may lead to rapid pipe corrosion. Although armoured rubber piping can be used (with Neoprene silencers) such materials demand a never-failing supply of water.

Some small craft need a seacock at the exhaust outlet when there is insufficient space to provide adequate fall to the pipe. If there is any risk of sea water driving into the pipe or if the craft might become heavily laden with rain water the seacock should always be closed when the ship is left unattended.

Ignition
Moisture on magneto and coil ignition HT leads is more critical on the water than on land, and trouble may occur if the cables are taken through a duct along the top of the engine. Occasional treatment with one of the well-known Aerosol water repellant sprays is a good precaution against trouble.

A spare distributor cap may be useful, as almost invisible hair cracks can cause an engine to misbehave. It pays to label cylinder numbers in Roman numerals on top of the distributor cap as incorrectly placed leads can cause a carburettor flare-up.

Contacts and spark plugs, must, of course, always be in perfect condition. Get a magneto checked professionally every few years. It may have an impulse mechanism to give a strong spark at low speeds, and failure of this can cause difficult starting.

Whenever a magneto or coil ignition distributor is removed (an operation which is nearly always necessary during overhaul and sometimes for laying-up) great care is necessary when replacing these parts to make sure that the timing is exactly right.

The workshop manual will explain the simplest method, for many engines have marks on the fly-wheel (sometimes visible through an inspection port in the bell housing) which show the exact engine position when the contacts should be breaking for No 1 cylinder.

Much the same applies to the timing of the injection pump on a diesel engine. One possible pitfall on a four-stroke engine is the fact that the flywheel marks are correct only on one revolution in two. As you require a firing stroke, place your thumb over the open injector or spark plug hole to feel when compression occurs, or hold a lighted match there and watch the flame.

Starting Gear

Little trouble is caused by electric, inertia, Handraulic, or compressed air starters on marine engines as most of them get relatively little use. Electrical troubles are perhaps the most frequent on craft that are neglected for months on end, or in open launches where moisture may be more penetrating.

For such installations, a diesel engine with no electrics at all proves very reliable. Engines up to about 30 hp with decompressors can have simple hand starting gear, but larger engines normally need an inertia or Handraulic starter. These are charged up by hand winding or pumping and the power is then released to give several powerful starting turns. Only routine maintenance is normally required to these components.

An overhead shaft with starting handle is a useful safeguard on a small marine engine even when electric starting is fitted. The equipment needs little care except lubrication and an occasional check to see that the ratchet pawls are not sticking, that the chain tension is correct, and that the chain links are

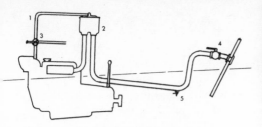

*Drawing 26.   This popular type of
exhaust system needs careful handling.*
*1. Cooling water through this pipe dis-
charges into the exhaust system.*
*2. Water injection silencer where water
mixes safely with exhaust gases.*
*3. A few minutes before shutting down
this two-way valve is turned to direct
all cooling water overboard, thus drying
out exhaust pipes.*
*4. Where lack of space prevents a swan
neck bend being fitted near to transom,
a seacock may be substituted. Make
sure this is open before attempting to
start engine!*
*5. Drain cock to ensure that water
cannot freeze inside exhaust pipe
during winter.*

*Picture 54.   Bent and worn propeller
shafts like this example are by no means
uncommon. Partial withdrawal is
simple to check the condition and repair
is often possible without complete renewal.*

not stretched. One frequently sees installations where the
starting handle is so inaccessible that it would be impossible to
use. Items like this should go on one's list of future improvements.

Marinized vehicle diesel engines do not often have decompressors and are therefore impossible to start by hand. However, many of them do have cylinder heater plugs which may
be essential for easy starting on yachts or work boats which are
kept in commission all the year around. These plugs can be
checked occasionally by removing them to see if they glow
when switched on.

The winter starting of obstinate engines can often be improved by using one of the Aerosol sprays which are fired into
the air intake as the engine is cranked. This may mean removing the air cleaner. By removing the sparking plugs of
either two-stroke or four-stroke engines and introducing a
squirt of commercial di-ethyl ether, awkward starting can often
be eliminated completely, provided there is no unseen
mechanical defect causing trouble.

Electrical Equipment

Components such as starter and dynamo will often run for many years without overhaul. A Bendix drive between starter and engine flywheel can cause trouble by jamming though the fault may be mostly due to the fact that this part is starved of oil.

The most frequent dynamo repair jobs are renewal of brushes and bearings. Excessive bearing wear is often caused by having the drive belt too tight. Rewinding and skimming commutators on a dynamo or starter would not normally be undertaken by an amateur but commutator cleaning is simply effected by spinning the armature while a special stick of glass fibres is held against the copper segments. The alternators now frequently used for engine generators do not necessarily have a longer life than D.C. generators, and there is in addition a built-in rectifier. Always learn how to start your engine should the ignition switch or starter solenoid fail. Keep the charging panel free from corrosion and label everything with a borrowed Dymo (Rotex) labeller.

Batteries play an important part in the majority of modern marine power installations, varying from single units (similar to those in a car) for engine starting and lighting duties to the complex double or triple bank sets used on large ocean-going yachts. In the latter instances separate generating plants may be used to feed the batteries and changeover switches are incorporated so that a fully charged bank of batteries may be available at all times.

Metal-cased alkali batteries are preferred for the highest specification yacht work, for although expensive and heavy, they are almost indestructible. The common lead/acid battery used in cars is quite satisfactory for most small yacht work, provided one unships it for attention during the winter and takes care not to charge or discharge it too rapidly.

Such cells are happiest when used frequently under light load and must never be allowed to reach anything approaching a fully discharged condition. Only distilled water should be used for topping up the electrolyte. When this proves to be necessary at frequent intervals it may mean either that the battery is nearing the end of its useful life, or that the charging rate is too high.

Always keep the tops of batteries clean and dry with petroleum jelly (Vaseline) smeared liberally over all exposed lugs and connexions. Check occasionally to ensure that terminal clamps are tight. Before replacing a clamp, scrape the contacting surfaces to bright metal.

Sterngear

Except in the case of Z-drives and hydraulic drives, nearly all inboard marine engines have a sterntube or shaft log to take the propeller shaft through the hull. This has a stuffing box or a special form of seal (to prevent ingress of water) as well as bearings.

Where the outboard bearing is metallic the whole sterntube may be filled with grease supplied from a Stauffer (screw-down) greaser just abaft the inboard bearing, or fed remotely by a long pipe from a lubricator at a convenient position some distance away. Where a cutless rubber bearing is used at the outboard end of the sterntube, this is lubricated by water only (via special scoops which must always be kept clear) and the grease supply is fed only into the space between the inboard bearing and the water seal.

Other types of sterntubes have patent water seals at each end, the space between being filled with oil fed automatically from a small tank situated well above the boat's waterline. How to renew the packing rings in the stuffing box (or gland) is described in the next chapter. When running, the gland should not become hot. If excessive tightening is necessary to prevent leakage of water, additional or new packing is required.

Another cause of overheating may be that the shaft is not truly in line with the engine or with an intermediate plummer block. The engine bearers may shift slightly when a vessel is moved from the laid-up position to the water, so it pays to check the alignment by slackening the flange coupling bolts and testing all around between them with feeler gauges.

As well as a possible error in this axial direction, the whole shaft may be incorrectly aligned sideways or up and down. If there is a spigot and socket in the centre of each coupling, by drawing the flanges apart it should be possible to ascertain whether the spigot is registering concentrically.

When coupling bolts have no tab washers or other locking devices, an occasional check for tightness throughout the season is prudent. Flanges are always keyed on to the shaft and may be secured either with Allen grub screws, or on a taper with recessed nuts, rather like a propeller. If you find a brass spring touching the shaft and connected by wiring to a keel

209

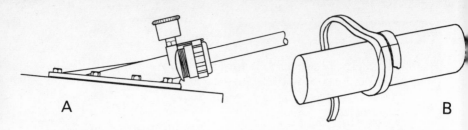

Drawing 27. A – Internal shaft log showing the important stauffer grease cup and locking spring engaging in notches to prevent gland nut from turning back.

B – How to cut packing rings for a sterntube gland. Note direction of knife cut. The actual shaft can be used as a mandrel, though a piece of hardwood turned to exact size is kinder on the knife.

bolt, this may have been fitted in an attempt to stop radio interference by static electricity.

A few propeller shafts incorporate universal joints to eliminate the need for accurate alignment and where flexible engine mountings are used special resilient couplings must be incorporated. Such parts may not require lubrication at all but make sure no nipples or greasers have been ignored, perhaps for years!

Vibration at the stern may be caused by a buckled propeller or a bent shaft, so a thorough check is advisable when a yacht is hauled out. Through lack of a zinc sacrificial anode the propeller and shaft may be corroded or dezincified into a weak and porous condition demanding renewal, while the propeller tips may be jagged, through striking underwater objects and one or more blades may be twisted enough to alter the pitch.

Jagged tips may be straightened up with a hand file, but any further damage means returning the propeller to a maker for repitching and balancing. Folding propellers may get fouled with barnacles and fail to close, a useful point to check if your boat dries out on a sandbank one day!

A small amount of slackness where the shaft runs in an outboard metal bearing is not important, but when the shaft can be wobbled the time has arrived for new bearings and shaft. As only a short length of the shaft will be worn it might be possible to have this repaired by building up with brazing, then turning in a lathe to the original diameter, followed by truing, if warped, during the brazing operation.

To remove a propeller, when no puller is available the nut should be slackened (after removing the cotter pin) and a dolly

Picture 55. A folding propeller in-creases sailing efficiently on certain types of auxiliary, but the pivots can sieze up, especially in the open position.

Picture 56. Cavitation and electro-lytic corrosion make propeller blades rough. Lying idle on moorings leads to barnacle growth. Polishing can be done in situ, but a return to the makers will enable the pitch and balance to be checked also. Note sacrificial zinc anode on deadwood.

of heavy metal held to the nut while the forward end of the propeller boss is given sharp blows with the heaviest hammer available, using a short piece of hardwood packing to prevent damage.

As soon as the propeller moves slightly on its taper the nut can be removed completely and the propeller pulled off. If the shaft key refuses to come out of its recess in the shaft, it may be taped around and left in place. When the key is loose, see that it has corresponding centre-pop marks at one end and remove it for safe keeping with the nut and pin.

When a craft is laid-up ashore or in a shed it may be wise to remove any bronze propellers and rudders immediately, as metal thieves frequently carry hacksaws with them! If this seems too much trouble, one should at least make a note of the dimensions engraved on the propeller boss.

A typical marking would be LH 17 x 12, which signifies left-handed rotation (anti-clockwise when viewed from aft)

17 in diameter, 12 in pitch (or the corresponding dimensions in millimetres may be used). To be even more fully armed in case replacements must be ordered, one should really keep a paper template of the blade outline with a similar template of a bronze rudder.

Cutless rubber bearings may not last more than a couple of seasons in muddy or sandy water, so keep a spare one in stock. The renewable bush should fit snugly into the sterntube casting (or into an independant A-bracket) secured there with stainless steel Allen grub screws.

Portlights and Windows
The glass in portlights is normally secured with a screwed bezel ring which can be eased and removed for renewal in the case of a breakage. The hinged light seats on to a rubber sealing ring set into a groove on the frame. When the rubber hardens with age, exceptional pressure on the screw clamp is necessary to achieve a good seal. Chandlers should stock standard sizes of square rubber strip, but make sure you get *Neoprene* (synthetic rubber) as a replacement, this having a much longer life than natural rubber.

Clear all old rubber from the groove before inserting new and stick the strip in with Bostik (or a similar rubber adhesive) making a neat butt joint at the top.

Large windows in grp coachroofs are sealed with special rubber mouldings in similar fashion to car windshields. Perspex (acrylic sheet) is often used instead of glass. This wears rough in time unless kept bright with metal polish.

When renewal is necessary, try to order the builders' correct size rubber moulding in one piece. This should arrive with fitting instructions, but any car body repair man will tell you how to do it. When the moulding must be made up from a coil, place the joint at the top and seal it with Bostik.

Summary
Clearly we cannot deal with every known type of mechanical equipment in this limited space, but from these general notes, with the aid of a complete set of maker's literature the keen amateur should be able to ensure that all his machinery is kept in reliable working order.

Water jet propulsion systems; gas turbines; centrifugal clutches; reversing propellers; hydraulic drives; electric;

steam; Wankel and orbital motors, are all found in the marine field and have their own specialized maintenance schedules. Mathway; Edson; Morse; Teleflex and various hydraulic steering gears and control systems for gearboxes and engines are in use, and the owner does not need to be a mechanical genius to understand the workings of these devices and to diagnose any possible faults.

Most equipment is incredibly reliable, but this should not deter one from studying the maintenance instructions and fault-finding charts to make ready for an emergency. With all types of control system there should always be an alternative manual method of operation to enable one to limp home in case of trouble.

The same should also apply to much of an engine's ancillary equipment. For serious deep sea cruising, parts such as ignition system; fuel pump; fuel filters; water cooling pumps; starting gear; and battery charging arrangement, should be duplicated in some way.

With regard to engine maintenance, remember to keep a jump ahead of the need to decarbonize and renew worn parts in a two-stroke. Leave well alone with a four-stroke, but check and recheck the ancillary equipment regularly, as this is more likely to prove the cause of a breakdown than the basic engine. Ensure that the correct grade of fuel is used at all times, adhere to a rigid maintenance schedule, and just because the air at sea is clean, do not neglect to check engine air filters. It may be a good idea to test peak revs with a tachometer to check whether full power is being produced and whether the propeller pitch is correct.

Keep a record of hours run (or a note of the amount of fuel consumed) as one tends to loose track of running time after a few years and this information can be essential for knowing when a part should need renewal or when communicating with the makers on any matter.

CHAPTER 10

PUMPS, HEADS AND GALLEY

Although racing dinghies manage without bilge pumps by using self bailers, drain plugs, and buckets, even the smallest motor tender or keel boat normally has at least one pump.

With increasing sizes of craft the number of other pumps also increases. Not counting the four or five pumps incorporated in the engine, a 30 ft (9 m) motor sailer may have a hand and a power bilge pump, two pumps on the toilet, one at a hand basin, and two in the galley.

In addition to these, a 45 ft (14 m) motor cruiser may have one more engine with five pumps, a shower bath fed by twin electric pumps, draining to a septic tank emptied by one electric pump, also perhaps a pressurized water supply system plus other pumps to fill gravity header tanks on deck for water and fuel oil.

As no two pumps on board a craft may be of equal design or size, some experience is needed to understand them all, while the prudent owner will keep instruction sheets describing simple maintenance and repairs, with spare parts lists and a stock of the items most frequently needing replacement.

Types of Pumps
Hand operated bilge pumps may be of the semi-rotary, plunger, diaphragm, bucket, or geared type.

A semi-rotary pump consists of a circular housing containing a paddle which is rocked to and fro by the operating handle with four simple pivotted clapper valves, two set in the paddle and two in the lower part of the housing. Although marine semi-rotary pumps should be made throughout of brass, many yachts have the cheaper type with brass paddle and valves running in a cast iron casing.

214

Whereas the maintenance requirements on brass pumps are almost nil, it proves essential to remove the cover of an iron-cased pump to dry it out completely at laying-up time, then to smear all working surfaces with water pump grease before assembly. Unless this is done, the pump will be found to have seized up due to rusting when fitting-out time comes around.

Plunger pumps may be single-acting or double-acting. The former is similar to a simple country well pump with a clapper valve at the bottom of the cylinder barrel and a second valve in the plunger. The top of the cylinder may have a cover with a gland in the centre to seal the piston rod. Proper double-acting pumps lift fluid on the downward as well as the upward movement of the piston rod, so the piston (or plunger) is solid and the valves duplicated. Galley pumps which deliver a continuous stream of water are usually differential pumps, taking in water only on the upward stroke.

Diaphragm pumps have (instead of a plunger) a flexible membrane (sometimes of reinforced *Neoprene*) which is depressed by the operating lever and rises under the action of a spring (or *vice versa*) to provide a pumping action with the assistance of inlet and outlet valves.

As all fluid is below the diaphragm, there is no necessity for a gland. The successful range of *Henderson* bilge pumps are of this type, and so are most of the mechanical and electric fuel pumps used on engines. Double-acting diaphragm pumps have a gland, and duplicated valves.

Bucket pumps are similar to plunger pumps except that the top of the barrel is left open. These pumps are sunk into the deck so that the discharge water flows out over the deck instead of via a hose and skin fitting through the topsides. For yacht use, bucket pumps usually have a screw-on cap to make a flush fitting with the deck when the pump is out of use, the operating handle being stowed separately, sometimes inside the pump barrel. The bucket (plunger) may have leather washers (like a bicycle pump or garden syringe) which can cause failure if allowed to get dry and hard.

Geared pumps (such as the Simpson-Lawrence *Vortex*) have a slow-turning rotary handle coupled through gearing to drive a high speed impeller pump at the foot. There are no valves and as the pump unit is often submerged, priming is no problem.

Unusual types of bilge pumps, such as those built into a

length of hose for emptying dinghies, and those that operate by the movement of one's foot, all work on the same principle as one of the above. Maintenance requirements to bilge pumps are minimal, consisting chiefly of removing debris from valves and renewing gland and piston packing.

Pumps like the *Whale* and *Henderson* have flick-open shutters over the valves to enable these to be inspected or cleaned in a trice. This could be important in an emergency as some of the older types of pumps may take nearly an hour to strip, clear, and reassemble.

The fouling up of valves becomes quite a rarity when an efficient *strum box* (strainer) is fixed to the end of the intake pipe in the bilges. Strum box gauze should not be too fine as most pumps will pass quite large particles without fouling. The gauze must be readily accessible for clearing, as the paper wrapper from a food can or a gash polythene bag can stop a pump without warning. Any yacht larger than an oversized dinghy should have two completely separate bilge pumping devices, at least one situated below decks for emergency use when the ship is battened down in a storm.

Gland Packing

Gland leakage around the piston rod is not normally a serious matter on bilge pumps, but the discharge pump glands on toilets must be kept tight at all times. Similar glands are used on rotating shaft pumps, such as the semi-rotary and *Jabsco* types.

Gland leaks are normally cured by a one-half turn of the nut, but if the nut will not turn, or the shaft binds as soon as tightening is attempted, the packing certainly needs renewing. When after renewing the packing, a plunger rod feels tight in the gland towards the ends of its stroke and slack in the centre, the rod is worn and must be renewed if the gland is ever to be satisfactory.

These pump glands are constructed similarly to the stern-tube stuffing box mentioned in the last chapter. A cylindrical space is formed around the shaft of the exact size to hold several turns of standard packing material. A bush fits over the shaft and presses on top of the packing, while a nut or other tightening device bears on to the bush, so allowing the pressure on the packing to be adjusted. The nut and bush may be combined into one piece.

Standard packing is supplied wound on to spools or card-

Picture 57. Renovating the head is simpler than generally imagined. This picture shows a clapper type valve at the base of the soil pump. The valve requires a new washer.

Picture 58. A different sort of base valve consisting of a bronze ball on rubber seating. This is the time for external cleaning and painting to last a further 5 years.

board tubes in the following sizes:- $\frac{1}{16}$ in (round like string); $\frac{1}{8}$ in (sometimes round, sometimes square in section); $\frac{3}{16}$ in; $\frac{1}{4}$ in; $\frac{5}{16}$ in; and $\frac{3}{8}$ in. All the larger sizes are normally square, and sizes above $\frac{3}{8}$ in are only required for the sterntubes of very big vessels. Corresponding metric sizes are also made.

The packing most frequently used for water pumps is of woven flax or hemp (rather like a braided rope) and impregnated with tallow or similar lubricant. So little packing of any one size is normally needed by the amateur that it usually pays to get a short length from a boatyard instead of buying standard spools.

If the correct packing proves unobtainable when needed in a hurry, graphited asbestos steam packing will do the job almost as well, being made in the same sizes and shapes. In an emergency, a gland can be packed quite successfully with many turns of smaller packing, so it pays to keep a fairly large quantity of, say, $\frac{1}{8}$ in in stock. This comes in useful at home for repacking the leaky glands of domestic taps (faucets). Plumbers normally keep this size so there should be no difficulty in obtaining a supply.

217

Although an extra turn or two of packing can be inserted on top of old packing, a much more satisfactory job will result if all the old material is raked out first. Worn out dentist's probes of various shapes are useful for hooking out old packing though the work is very much simplified if the shaft can be removed beforehand. Special extractors are made for grabbing old packing of the larger sizes, but the amateur should be able to get by without such tools.

Domestic packing is normally wound straight into the space between the shaft and the gland in one continuous length, and tamped down with a skewer as work proceeds.

For larger glands and all sterntube work, the packing must be inserted as a series of separate rings. Each ring should be made with a diagonal cut in preference to a straight butt joint. The simplest way to do this accurately is to wrap the packing around the shaft, and make a diagonal cut with a sharp trimming knife across two adjacent turns together. Discarding any offcuts, this leaves a perfect ring which will butt together tightly when pressed into the gland.

When inserting the rings, stagger the joints to minimize leakage. It may be a good idea to cut one extra ring which can be inserted later when the other new ones have settled down.

The packing supplied by the makers of Jabsco rotary pumps is not in rings, but arrives in the form of a cylinder ready to slip into the gland after removing the old packing. Other makers supply packing in ready cut rings, while some modern pumps use one or more Neoprene 'O' rings which are let into a recess in the bearing wall. On expensive rotary pumps one may find a patent spring-loaded seal (similar to the oil seals used on engine crankshafts) and this kind normally has a very long life.

Rotary Pumps

Centrifugal pumps are rotated at high speed by the engine or an electric motor and are very useful for water supply and deck wash duties. Some of them have a plastics impeller which is not suitable for pumping bilge water contaminated with engine oil or fuel. Centrifugal pumps are happiest when handling large quantities at a low head and they have the great advantage of not being harmed unduly if starved of fluid.

Engine cooling water pumps are often valveless Jabsco types with a relatively slow-moving Neoprene impeller, which is unsuitable for tackling fuel or oily bilge water. Other rotary power pumps include the internal eccentric cog and the meshing gear wheel pump. The latter type is frequently found inside the sump of an engine to circulate the oil through the bearings and in this position it should not need attention until about the time that crankshaft regrinding is necessary.

Cooling pumps handling silty or sandy sea water may wear out quite rapidly, so when frequenting such waters it may be advisable to carry a spare pump. Failing this, one can keep aboard a maker's overhaul kit, which may consist of spare diaphragm, valves, impeller, bearings, packing, and gaskets, as applicable.

One other type of pump not so far mentioned is the swashplate type used for supplying high pressure oil to hydraulic windlasses.

These pumps and the motors they propel are normally replaced as exchange units when any fault develops, but maintenance checks on the system should consist of observation of the piping for damage causing restrictions or leaks, slack unions, cleaning filters, and topping up the hydraulic fluid reservoir.

Pump Valves

The inlet and outlet valves of an engine-driven plunger pump may need grinding in after many years of use. Fitters grinding paste is useless for this job, being much too coarse. If a little 550 or 400 grit powder can be obtained, add this to a smear of oil on the valve face to make a suitable grinding paste.

Use a magnifying glass to ensure that all pitting and scoring has been removed and then lap the surfaces by continuing to grind in with metal polish. If fine grit powder cannot be obtained, use metal polish throughout. This would take too long by hand, so it may pay to improvise an extension spindle on the valve to enable an electric drill (running at slow speed through a *thyristor* speed control) to be used.

No pump in good condition should fail to prime immediately on starting provided the head, or lift, is below about 10 ft (3 m). One sees all sorts of devices to enable a quantity of water to be poured into a pump for priming, or a swan neck may be formed in the intake pipe to keep a quantity of liquid inside the pump at all times.

It may be necessary to operate a hand pump with rapid strokes at first to make it prime, but if the valves are in good order leakage past the piston is the most likely cause of trouble. Although some large pistons rely on being a good fit inside the bore, others have rings, or grooves to hold hemp packing or 'O' rings, all readily renewable. When the plunger is made entirely from plastics or rubber, or when leather or rubber cup-shaped washers are used, spares can be kept.

Water pumps are not normally intended to be lubricated though hand plunger and semi-rotary pumps function more smoothly if given a smear of white underwater grease on the plunger and rod occasionally. The Neoprene impellers of Jabsco pumps can be lubricated with glycerine and rubber plungers with soft soap, but this should be done only at laying-up time to prevent seizure before wetting.

Toilet Treatment

The enormous range of yacht heads includes simple chemical ones with no mechanism, those flushing by vacuum (like the *Lavac*), neat but expensive electrically operated types, and the most popular models which operate by hand pumping.

In the latter category, most makes follow the principles adopted by either Simpson-Lawrence or Blake. The line drawings explain the differences between them. The Simpson-Lawrence type has one double-acting pump A, the lower half of which handles the soil discharge while the upper section pumps sea water to flush the basin via the valve chest B. The cam C shown in the centre of this chest is connected to a lever (or pedal) with ON and OFF positions.

The cam is horizontal in the ON position allowing sea water to be drawn up through pipe D and fed to the basin rim via pipe E. With the lever OFF, the cam holds the lower valve on to its seating and raises the upper valve so that the top section of the pump works freely in air, enabling the basin to be discharged completely, through the two large flap valves in the basin pump, and out via pipe H. With the lever in the ON position the basin level tends to rise during pumping. Any leakage at the pump valve gland will not be contaminated.

In the Blake system, two single-acting pumps are used. The soil pump A has a bucket type plunger, the valve in its centre consisting of a rubber covered metal ball resting on a brass seating. As well as the normal flap valve at the base of the pump some models have a third valve at the pump outlet pipe H, as a precaution against siphoning back and to improve

220

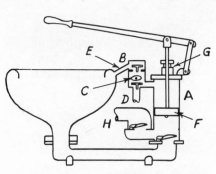
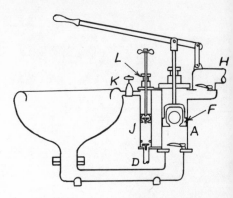

Drawing 28. Diagrammatic section through a Simpson-Lawrence single pump yacht toilet.
A – double acting pump. B – valve chest. C – On/Off cam. D – intake pipe. E – flushing pipe. F – solid plunger. G – stuffing box. H – soil pipe.

Drawing 29. Diagrammatic section through a Blake twin pump yacht toilet.
A – soil pump. D – intake pipe. F – plunger with valve. H – soil pipe. J – flushing pump. K – flushing pipe stopcock. L – stuffing box.

pumping action should the other valve be held partly open by paper.

Flushing water is provided by the smaller pump J, drawing sea water through the pipe D and delivering it via the stopcock K to the basin. Some models have a twin barrel flushing pump operated by a foot pedal.

Designs change over the years, and some toilets (such as the SL 400) adopt a double-acting diaphragm pump, the ON/OFF control being actuated by a sideways movement of the pumping lever. Most other makes adopt the single pump system with modifications. The *Lavac* has a hard nylon coated aluminium alloy basin and may be fitted with an additional non-return valve in the soil pipe to eliminate any risk of flooding when the seacock is open. In the *Hydra* the OPEN/CLOSED control is operated by a foot pedal.

The *Lavac* toilet works on a different principle with only one single-acting pump. The seat and cover make an air tight seal over the top of the basin, so that when the Henderson discharge pump is operated a vacuum is created in the pan, drawing in the flushing water automatically.

Toilet treatment throughout the season need only consist of keeping everything clean and oiling the pump handle pivots occasionally. As sea water is quite a good disinfectant powerful chemicals need not be used. The makers of the *Lavac* suggest

Picture 59. Complete pump plungers from a Baby Blake. Flushing pump with bronze poppet valve on left; soil pump with rubber coated ball valve on right.

Picture 60. Blake soil pump plunger dismantled showing ball, twin rubber cup washers and retaining ring.

that only alkali based cleaners, such as *Harpic* or *Domestos*, should be used.

Even when working properly, it pays to take a closet ashore every three or four years for a thorough check and clean. Unshipping is normally a simple matter of releasing the pipe unions and base bolts. If the latter are of steel the nuts may have rusted solid, necessitating the use of either a hack-saw blade in a pad handle, or a nut splitter. Needless to say, when replacing steel bolts, use stainless or brass ones.

Spare parts for most makes of yacht toilets are easy to obtain, but unless the basin has cracked, or unless water has been allowed to freeze, damaging one of the castings, the ingenious handyman should be able to repair or make new any of the working parts, including valves, gaskets, piston rod and lever pins. If the unit is dismantled immediately, one should have all the winter to order or make spare parts.

If the glazing on a vitreous basin has crazed or cracked the appearance of the unit can be completely rejuvenated by ordering a new basin (costing about £6 in the UK or $25 in the USA) while a new seat and cover costs about two-thirds this amount. To complete the renovation two coats of topside enamel may be necessary, though the more modern units with all plastics and stainless steel parts should only need cleaning.

Blakes will do a 24-hour overhaul service on any except the very oldest of their models. Yards frequently carry spare parts for certain makes to enable them to carry out emergency

222

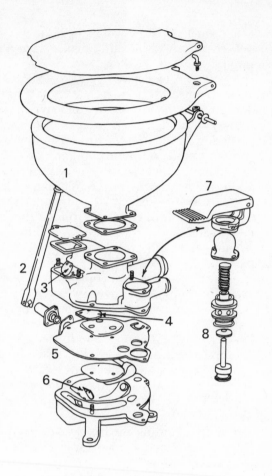

Drawing 30. *Exploded view of the Hydra toilet widely used on yachts built between 1955 and 1968. All nuts, bolts and washers have been excluded.*

1. *Nylon coated alloy pan.*
2. *Pumping lever.*
3. *Soil discharge valve.*
4. *Soil inlet valve.*
5. *Pump diaphragm.*
6. *Flushing inlet valve.*
7. *Control pedal.*
8. *Control valve.*

repairs. Simpson-Lawrence will rebore their pumps and supply oversize pistons, while other makers favour the renewal of worn pumps.

Get a quotation for extensive repairs to a very old toilet as it may prove wiser to invest in a completely new unit. This may mean new piping (as the unions are unlikely to match) though existing seacocks can often be adapted.

When ordering new parts, try to find the maker's number which is often stamped on the top pump cover. If the wrong parts arrive, it may be necessary to return the original parts for identification. When writing for the first time, ask the makers for data sheets covering repair work and spare parts.

The maintenance of toilet pumps follows the same lines as already described for bilge pumps. Although the older models have conventional piston rod glands, newer types (like the SL400) have self-adjusting glands consisting of two packing rings held apart by a spring, sometimes with a lubricator in the centre. Blake soil pumps have two rubber cup washers back-to-back with one similar washer with its rim uppermost on the flush pump.

The *Waterloo, Headmaster* and *Hydra* toilets have a solid metal piston with one Neoprene 'O' ring let into the centre of its periphery. The SL400 and the Hydra have double-acting diaphragm pumps. A new diaphragm may cost over £2 ($9) but it pays to keep a spare one as an improvised repair is unlikely to be satisfactory.

Reaming and re-pinning the operating lever pivots should not be delayed, as wear becomes rapid once these parts get noisy. When very badly worn the holes may have to be filled by brazing and then drilled and reamed to the original size.

The valves used on the soil pump side are quite different from those normally found in bilge pumps. Three types are to be found—ball valves, flap valves and joker valves. Blakes use the first type with a solid brass ball resting on a renewable rubber seating for the lower soil valve and a rubber covered metal ball working on the brass seating of the plunger. The size used in both cases resembles that of a table tennis ball. Smaller stainless steel balls are used on the flushing side of the *Headmaster*.

Two sorts of flap valves exist: those with metal hinges, pins, and clapper, and those in which the hinge and flap are formed from a single sheet of rubber, leather, or Neoprene, with a circular metal weight riveted or screwed on top. The metal valves are often double hinged to enable the flap to lift bodily when choked. Most repairs consist of the renewal of washers or fabric flaps, though a time may come when valves with metal hinges require the reaming of holes and the fitting of oversize pins.

Joker valves (sometimes called reed valves) are made entirely from Neoprene (synthetic rubber), the shape resembling a short piece of tubing, one end of which has been squashed flat in a vice. Fluids are readily forced through in one direction, but the slit end closes firmly whenever pressure is applied the other way.

Toilet repairs can be carried out on board though it takes much longer in a cramped space and some small parts are sure to find their way into the bilges. The making of special spanners and keys may sometimes prove necessary for dismantling and assembly, and when gaskets are made from plumbers' jointing rubber, check whether the thicknesses have any effect on the alignment of unions and brackets.

When installed, see that a copy of the maker's operating instructions is attached to the bulkhead for all to read. This will probably advise against using the toilet to dispose of oil or gash from the galley, against pumping when the seacocks are closed, and perhaps against using chemical cleaners and the soft varieties of toilet paper.

Thorough flushing is always advisable to keep the valves clear. Even when the unit is installed above the waterline siphoning back can occur if the seacocks are left open when the boat is rolling and the pump valves are not seating properly. The fact that the soil discharge pipe takes a swan neck bend well above the waterline (as it always should) is not a foolproof precaution against siphoning back.

Note that a macerator/chlorinator unit can be coupled to any pumped closet to ensure that only clean effluent is discharged when in a marina or other restricted waters.

Seacocks and Skin Fittings

Although any type of seacock can be used for toilet skin fittings, tapered barrel large bore seacocks are favoured at least for the soil outlet. The only maintenance these should require is annual greasing at laying-up time.

Dismantling and greasing should not take longer than five

minutes, but if the job has been ignored for many years, the *thrust ring* (keep plate) screws which hold the barrel in place may have corroded and the inner surfaces may be scored. When in this condition the thrust ring has to be screwed down tightly to prevent leakage and the valve becomes so stiff to operate that no one attempts to turn it off.

Heavy duty seacocks of this type have an internal flange on the casting through-bolted to another flange on the outside of the planking. Be suspicious of seacocks which have no proper chock between the inner flange and the planking. A cheap installation may have cheap brass bolts which dezincify in sea water, so try turning the nuts with a spanner and renew all the bolts immediately if one shears off.

On grp hulls, there should be a substantial reinforcement on the inside. If the fitting is moulded permanently into this, inspect every year for cracking and looseness. Make the normal check on bolts where the fitting is fastened to a timber pad inside.

Engine water intake fittings are normally through-bolted as above but lighter duty valves such as sink outlets and cockpit drains normally utilize ordinary plumbers' *gate valves* (wheel valves) attached to simple tubular skin fittings, which look similar to the waste outlet on a sink. The tube is threaded externally for its full length and has a flange cast to the outside end. A broad backnut screwed down the tube holds the fitting securely through the planking, while the gate valve screws to the inner end of the tube. Wheel valves should need no maintenance for five years, after which time a strip down, clean, grease, and renewal of gland packing is well worth while.

Skin fittings and even complete seacocks are now being made of plastics (such as *Delrin*) and owing to the prohibitive cost of copper and brass such materials are bound to become increasingly popular. They are too resilient for moulding into grp skins, but are admirable for all other purposes.

Skin fittings to steel hulls may take the form of internal flanges welded into place with four studs protruding for the attachment of a seacock, or a short length of pipe with external thread may be welded on. Rusting of these parts must be prevented.

If water tends to surge into the cockpit through the self draining pipes, the trouble may often be cured by fitting simple rubber or leather flaps (trailing aft) to the outside of the

Picture 61. Seacocks for the head need annual attention, especially easy when the toilet has been unshipped for overhaul. Corroded flange bolts have caused many a good boat to sink unexpectedly!

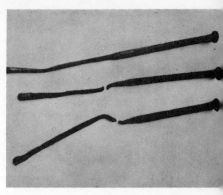

Picture 62. Three keel bolts taken from a 7-ton yacht after 23 years service. Losing a ballast keel in rough water is not funny!

skin fittings, or with proper non-return (check) valves plumbed into the internal piping.

There may be many other types of skin fittings on a yacht. Speed and distance indicators sometimes have a retractable impeller housing sliding inside a backnut type skin fitting of large diameter. The water sealing is normally provided by 'O' rings as mentioned above, and these must be kept greased.

Make sure the screw-on cap for the end of the skin fitting is attached close by with a piece of small chain, for this cap may be needed in a hurry one day when the impeller housing has to be withdrawn for repairs while in the water. Try to remember to withdraw the impeller when not in use to obviate unnecessary wear and damage.

On a big vessel the exhaust pipe skin fittings may be either the bolted flanged type, or the screw type. With dry exhaust systems, a periodic check to ensure that the surrounding woodwork has not been damaged by heat is advisable.

Inaccessibility is a fault affecting many seacocks. The wheel valve types are most prone to this as they may be too close to some fitment, restricting space for proper movement of one's knuckles or elbow. Where a screw skin fitting is used it may be possible to rectify the faults by inserting a 45° or 90° elbow on top of the fitting, or with flange types to make the inside chock tapered, setting the seacock on a slight angle. Failing this, extending the stem of the valve is not an insuperable job.

227

Plumbing Repairs

Almost every type of pipework imaginable can be found on a boat and the owner of a sizeable craft is likely to become quite a competent plumber if he carries out many repairs and alterations. The types of piping used may include black or galvanized steel for exhaust systems, copper for engine cooling as well as for fresh and seawater supply purposes, rubber hose, and a variety of plastics materials (including polythene, PVC and nylon) largely used for bilge pump connexions and waste pipes.

Sets of dies for cutting pipe threads can be obtained from most of the tool hire stores, but it may be simpler to ask a boatyard, plumber, or garage to cut the odd one. Once threaded, any of the common pipe fittings (available black or galvanized) can be screwed on to alter the length; provide junctions and bends; to reduce or increase the pipe bore; to insert a control valve, or to plug the end. Other fittings are made to permit a transfer from steel to copper or from steel to polythene tube.

The $\frac{1}{2}$ in and $\frac{3}{4}$ in (12 mm and 18 mm) bore steel pipes can be given a slight set or bend when long enough by gripping one end in a strong vice or through a hole bored in a baulk of timber. The larger sizes can be bent by heating to redness locally with an oxy-acetylene torch, but normally standard elbows and bends of various angles are used to alter direction.

All screwed joints in steel tube must be sealed, using PTFE tape or jointing paste. With the latter, depending on the tightness of the thread, a certain number of strands of plumber's hemp should be wound neatly into a smear of paste on the male thread before the joint is made.

For dry exhaust systems that run very hot, plain graphite jointing paste without hemp may be used. Where there is any risk of leakage, fit a backnut at each joint with a turn of asbestos string and graphite paste underneath it.

Copper piping for hot or cold water is easy to run as almost any shape can be imparted by means of a *Hilmor* or similar bending jig obtainable from tool hire stores. Compression fittings can be attached by simply inserting an olive and screwing up a nut. Soldered fittings are neater and cheaper, the *Yorkshire* range having the correct amount of solder built in. As long as the pipe surface and the inside of each fitting is correctly scoured with steel wool or fine sandpaper before fluxing, perfect results can be guaranteed. For yacht work, using the $\frac{1}{2}$ in (12 mm), $\frac{3}{4}$ in (18 mm), and 1 in (25 mm) sizes, soft tube in coils is more convenient to run than the straight hard tube used for domestic plumbing. Note that modern thin-walled stainless steel water pipe is cheaper than copper and is equally simple to work.

Rubber or Neoprene hose is ideal for many marine duties such as on engines, sink wastes, and toilets. Periodic examinations for defects leading to failure are essential, but where the correct grade of canvas-reinforced rubber is used (and is kept away from sunlight) the life should be at least six years. Always use stainless steel hose clips, two at each joint for high pressure. Proper spigot fittings for standard hose sizes in brass and Delrin are available for connecting to skin fittings; sink wastes; steel and copper pipe fittings; also straight hose connectors and ones reducing from one hose size to the next.

For engine circulation water, even when this is utilized for heating radiators (especially useful on board yachts which are cruised all year round), hoses may be connected direct to copper pipes. It pays to swage a slight bellmouth on to the ends of the copper to prevent the hoses from pulling off.

Rubber elbows and connexions with stainless steel *Jubilee clips* are used throughout on the Hydra Yacht toilet. Soft lead pipe (with plumbers' wiped solder joints at each end) is never used nowadays for toilet soil pipes. Instead, polythene tubing is popular. The opaque stiff black domestic pipe hides the contents better than transparent polythene and also takes paint better.

Low pressure polythene pipe fittings consist of a spigot which is forced into the end of the pipe after heating the latter in boiling water. On cooling, the polythene shrinks on tightly and no clip is required. For high pressure work, the compression fittings made for the next size larger in copper pipe are used but before putting on the nut and olive, the tube is again heated in boiling water and a short copper ferrule is pressed inside the tube. Permanent bends may be made in polythene by inserting a plumber's spring, heating locally with boiling water and then holding the pipe into the correct position until it cools. Springs have an eye on one end to enable a lanyard to be attached for easy withdrawal from the centre of a long length of pipe.

Note that copper tubing in sizes smaller than $\frac{1}{2}$ in (12 mm) is measured to the outside diameter and is stocked by motor factors in 25 ft (8 m) coils. This soft annealed pipe is used for engine oil, fuel, or cooling water piping. The correct brass unions and fittings are normally brazed on. All the necessary bends can be applied by hand, but if for any reason an exceptionally sharp bend is necessary, one should fill the pipe temporarily with molten solder or sealing wax to prevent distortion.

Polythene and PVC tubing is not suitable for hot water supplies, but the more expensive nylon tube (which is similar to handle) may be used up to the boiling point of water. Union end fittings for the smaller bored plastics pipes (such as for fuel lines) can be fitted in a few minutes by a garage having the necessary press. A ferrule is slipped on to the tube, the union with spigot is forced into the hole, and the ferrule is then crimped tightly with the press.

Soft plastics tubing is not suitable for the suction side of a pump, but excellent flexible corrugated plastics piping is made for this purpose and it may also be used for the delivery piping on pumps and toilets. Some of this is wire-wound armoured hose and a short length of the internal wire spring must be cut out before a spigot with hose clip can be fitted.

With all pipe work, sharp bends and kinks must be avoided and where many similar pipes run closely together it may be a good idea to code these with paint marks for easy identification when repairs become necessary. The periodic annealing of copper piping in the engine space was mentioned in Chapter 9. If such pipes are clipped to the hull or bulkhead to lessen vibration, work hardening will occur much more slowly. Suitable clips can be made quite easily from strips of copper bent around a former the same size as the pipe. They should be secured with screws to facilitate removal for annealing and cleaning out. For long pipe runs in a grp or metal hull, it may be necessary to fit wooden battens behind to take the clip screws.

Big yachts have complicated plumbing systems when there is central heating and pressurized water supply. Many water heating appliances are independent diesel fuel units with automatic spark ignition, and similar equipment is available for ducted hot air space heating.

Butane (LP) gas water heaters are popular, especially in the smaller sizes. Although all these devices are trouble free for the relatively few hours they are used each year, makers' instructions must be followed precisely where running, maintenance, or repair works are concerned.

Many modern hot water systems work in conjunction with an automatic water supply pump. When a hot tap (faucet) is opened, the electric pump starts and at the same time the gas water heating unit ignites. When pressurized cold fresh water is also required on demand a separate pumping unit is used. Should pressurized sea water be needed also, a third unit will be employed. Most pressure supply units are actuated by the pressure drop on demand, but in the *Bee* system electrical contacts are built into each tap so that the motor starts as soon as each one is opened.

Stoves

Solid fuel stoves (except the small bulkhead mounted charcoal stoves) are little used on modern yachts. For serious cruising, solid fuel stoves provide an ideal form of heat, not only out of season, but also for drying out the ship and clothing during stormy summer weather. Lighting such stoves is simple if there is a butane gas supply on board.

With the smokeless fuels normally used these stoves require little maintenance except cleaning soot deposits every two or three years according to the amount of use. With the exception of very old stoves, it should still be possible to buy new firebars, lining bricks, or an ashpan. Ordinary fire cement (such as *Kos*) can be used to repair holes and cracks in the lining for many years before fire brick renewal is necessary and the same cement can be used to bed and seal the new bricks. Always moisten the absorbent surfaces before using this cement and avoid lighting the stove until it has cured and dried out.

Some oil-fired stoves and cookers (e.g. the *Perkins* and *Kempsafe* makes) are quite complicated and the instruction leaflets need to be followed explicitly to ensure reliability.

Rippingill, Pithers, alcohol (meths) and all bottled gas stoves require little maintenance except regular cleaning. Extreme care must be taken to ensure that all butane gas piping, unions, flexible hoses, and control taps, are in first class condition and checked frequently for leaks with a smear of soft soap. Remember that a burner left turned low should be watched continuously in case the flame blows out, filling the bilges with an explosive mixture. A gas detector (e.g. Tannoy *Sniffa*) is a valuable insurance against such dangers.

Leakage can be minimized if burners are lit the instant gas is turned on. Gas refrigerators can be extinguished when the supply is turned off at the cylinder and could leak when this is turned on again. For extra security when leaving the boat, turn off the cylinder valve with the burners lit, thus emptying the pipes of all gas. Remember to keep a suitable spanner for the big union nut on the gas bottle.

On some cruisers the gas cylinder is stowed on deck or in a special locker vented overboard. Wherever the bottle is kept, all crew members should be trained to turn off the main cylinder cock whenever the stove is extinguished. Bottled gas may also be used for lighting, hot water supply, and space heating.

Much of this equipment is less likely to deteriorate if taken home for storage in the winter. Proper cleaning can then be carried out at leisure.

Primus (pressurized kerosene) stoves are widely used on yachts of all sizes. Running maintenance requirements follow those described for blow torches in Chapter 2. One should always carry a set of essential spare parts, including a burner head joint washer; a leather cup washer for air pump; a jet nipple, and perhaps a complete burner head. You will need a jet key and a few prickers, plus a spanner to fit the burner head nut. For those models with a regulator and self-clearing jet (and these are vastly superior for cooking purposes) you should keep some spare gland packing.

The Primus principle is also used for space heaters and cabin lamps, both these having incandescent mantles. Several spare mantles should be kept handy.

Wick kerosene lamps are still used for cabin lighting and navigation lamps on small yachts without batteries and need occasional wick trimming and glass cleaning.

All oil heating stoves and lamps are best taken ashore at laying-up time, but some owners like to keep a stove on board for heating soup, coffee, or washing water, during the winter. Fuel should be emptied, all parts cleaned, any faulty components replaced, air pump plungers greased, and rustable metal lightly oiled. Remember to keep gimbal pivots oiled on stove, lamps, and compass.

Tanks

On the the older yachts, fresh water tanks are normally of galvanized steel, sometimes built in so completely that they cannot be removed easily for cleaning or renewal. Similarly, the tanks in many glass fibre boats are moulded in, utilizing the hull skin as part of the tank. Whereas the majority of galvanized tanks have a removable inspection cover to assist cleaning, few grp tanks are so equipped, and rectifying this mistake can be a useful job for the amateur handyman to tackle.

Generally speaking, yacht fuel tanks never need cleaning out, so inspection covers are not necessary as long as a proper sump or a drain plug at the lowest point is incorporated. Correct filtering ensures that only clean fuel reaches the engine and unless contaminated fuel gets aboard at some time, only water from internal condensation should ever need to be drawn from the drainage plug.

During the laid-up period fuel tanks should be either completely drained or topped right up to avoid condensation. Although the latter method does the job best, the former may have to be used (leaving each tank completely sealed with a pack of silica gel suspended inside to absorb all moisture) to eliminate the fire hazard.

Some boatyards use household bleach to clean out water tanks and prevent them from getting foul, while others sometimes use *formalin* (formaldehyde) solution. Phenolic (carbolic) disinfectants should never be used as they require even more rinsing to get rid of the taste than the two milder chemicals.

A much better idea is to avoid this chore by using built-in tanks only for washing water, keeping all drinking and cooking water in clean plastics breakers. For long distance cruising additional drinking water may be carried in one or more of the large flexible tanks which are now available in various shapes to fit into the bilges.

Note that unless plastics containers are made from thick dark coloured material, they must be covered or kept in dark cool lockers to prevent fresh water from turning foul.

Many glavanized water tanks tend to rust inside after about ten years of use. This can be tolerated for washing water for, perhaps, another five years, and then complete renewal becomes necessary. If special paint (such as International *Tantectol* or *Water Tank Black*) is applied as soon as the rust appears, and repeated when necessary, the life of a tank can be prolonged

233

enormously. Two coats of good black bitumastic paint will do the job satisfactorily for a washing water tank, but it will affect the taste of drinking water for two years. Only tanks with adequate inspection ports should be treated internally, for although a small removable tank without this provision can be treated by pouring a little paint inside and rotating the tank slowly, this proves a chancy job which is best avoided.

The making of a new grp tank to any desired shape is by no means an insurmountable task for the enthusiast. As the inside should be smooth and glossy (leaving the outside rough) the two halves may be laid up over a plug fabricated from wood and plaster with well rounded corners. Leave flanges around the edges to enable the two halves to be bonded together on completion.

A large tank will need external ribbing or corrugation for rigidity. Remember that flat internal baffles must also be stiffened and although these may be bonded readily to one half of the tank they may require protruding tenons to mesh into slots (glassed over after assembly) through the wall of the other half. If a drinking water tank has an inspection plate, this will allow access to the inside for bonding baffles, but remember that the opening must be arranged to permit all internal compartments to be reached for cleaning.

Water tanks do not normally need separate venting (as described for fuel tanks in Chapter 9) as when equipped with a proper raised neck filler pipe, the cap need not be sealed. A deck filling plate should never form the tank cap also, as contamination by sea water might then occur. Remember to keep a spare two-pronged key for filler plates, and always fit them with lanyards to check the possibility of loss overboard.

CHAPTER 11

DINGHIES AND TRAILERS

We live in a peculiar era, the idiosyncrasies of which affect yachting more than some other pastimes!

A man will buy himself a boat with which to escape the tension and noise of city life, but will ensure that she has a pair of noisy engines capable of whisking him from harbour to harbour in the shortest time possible and he will moor her in a spot where the blaring of radios is only interrupted by the sounds and smells from charging plants!

Much the same thing applies to dinghies used as tenders to the parent vessels. Inflatable boats are ideal for stowing on board and lightweight grp dinghies can be loaded on the car roof and taken home after use. However, many yachtsmen who buy these useful types of tender have never experienced the enjoyment of rowing a well proportioned clinker dinghy. Finding their own boat almost impossible to row (as she blows about in the wind and tends to stop dead as soon as the oars leave the water) an outboard motor becomes a permanent fitting and the accompanying noise ruins the peace of many an anchorage late into the night.

Choosing a Dinghy
Although pottering under sail is too slow for many modern yachtsmen, much enjoyment can sometimes be added to a cruise (especially with children on board) if the yacht's tender has a fairly efficient sailing rig.

The type of dinghy one chooses also depends upon the method of stowage. A rigid dinghy must be towed behind a yacht shorter than about 22 ft (7 m), so, unfortunately, the craft least able to deal with this additional drag is forced to do so.

Naturally, such owners favour inflatable boats which can be stowed aboard during a long passage.

Transom sterned craft longer than about 28 ft (9 m) sometimes fit Scandinavian type stern davits enabling a rigid dinghy to be stowed directly above the water, simplifying launching considerably. However, this system lends itself only to those craft with sufficient freeboard aft to enable the dinghy to be hoisted clear of the highest seas likely to be met.

Other methods of dinghy stowage include upside-down or right-way-up positions on the foredeck; on the cabin top; fore-and-aft, athwartships, or diagonally on the after deck; leaning up against the guardrails or cabin top along the side deck, or in other similiar positions.

In addition to their light weight, another advantage of inflatable boats is that they can be stowed on deck or down below neatly after deflation. However, to avoid the tediousness of filling them with air, most owners leave them inflated throughout the season. A further advantage of rubber dinghies is that provided no damage occurs, they are safer when swamped than a rigid boat with built-in buoyancy. In most other ways a sectional rigid dinghy (the components of which nest one inside the other) is a better proposition for a small yacht's tender.

Where davits are available a class racing dinghy may be used as a tender with the advantage that her sailing performance will aid the exploration of backwaters or creeks, while class and handicap racing can also be tried at opportune moments. Preferably, the dinghy class chosen should be without side decks or after deck (more space for use as a tender and easy to row or fit an outboard motor) and the mast should be sectional for easy stowage, perhaps with a gunter rig as in the *Heron* Class. Conventional $\frac{3}{4}$-decked racing dinghies are too heavy for small davits and Bermuda masts perhaps 20 ft (6·5 m) in length are difficult to stow on any but the largest yachts.

For the owner with davits who does not wish to have a rigged dinghy, a small tender with a silent running inboard engine may well be the ideal choice.

Although glass fibre is by far the most common material used for new dinghies, those of moulded wood, glued clinker plywood, or aluminium alloy may be slightly heavier but are more satisfactory to row. Chine or flat bottomed plywood dinghies are cheaper than the other types though often not so robust.

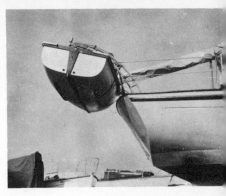

Some ways of avoiding the problem of towing a tender when the parent boat is big enough. Picture 63. On the after cabin top of a g.r.p. ketch. The mizzen boom can be used as a davit.

Picture 64. Scandinavian-fashion on fixed davits abaft a transom or short counter stern.

A glass fibre dinghy can be made to take care of herself, but if a smart appearance is required throughout her life she will demand nearly as much maintenance as a wooden dinghy with a good catalyst finish.

When a newcomer decides to purchase a sailing dinghy purely for racing the correct choice can prove a difficult matter with such a bewildering range of classes. The problem is usually resolved by discussions with other club members and by crewing for them. Generally, a secondhand boat is the best first choice. The handyman should be able to find a boat at the right price, and have an interesting time experimenting with the fittings and adjustments currently in vogue, perhaps selling at a profit when a conclusion about his ultimate choice has been decided!

Picture 65. This design of motor/sailer has a commodious foredeck. There is still room to sunbathe on the starboard side!

Picture 66. Athwartships between mast and windlass. Good way to batten down a leaky forehatch! Staysail boom makes a suitable davit.

The modern skimming dory or sea sled type of craft is extremely stable for heavy loading. These boats can be driven at high speeds when necessary and can be towed quite successfully, but they are more conveniently stowed in davits than on deck.

Some owners try to drive an ordinary dinghy at impossible speeds by fitting an oversized outboard motor. Not only is this dangerous, but unless the transom is properly reinforced it could be torn right out. A $1\frac{1}{2}$ hp motor should be adequate to propel a tender up to 10 ft (3 m) in size while a 3 hp motor can cope up to 14 ft (4·5 m). Such powers will give a dry ride with great economy and a minimum of noise, while children will come to no harm when left in control.

Repairs

Major repair works to dinghies for all types of construction are treated in *Boat Repairs and Conversions*, but much of the minor damage which occurs (mainly to racing dinghies) in the course of a season may be treated as additional maintenance work. The handyman is well advised to tackle such small jobs himself to avoid the inconvenience of dealing with insurance claims and possible delays while the work is handled by a boatyard, and neat repairs should not diminish the value of a boat.

Racing dinghies are most vulnerable to gunwale damage during collisions as they are very rarely equipped with any form of all-round fendering. The outside gunwale may range from a small half-round beading to an elaborate wide laminated anti-spray guard.

If a beading is screwed on, the best solution is to remove it completely (the damage may be confined to the short length between the chain plate and the stem) and obtain a new piece of moulding from a boatyard or sawmill in the same species of timber.

To avoid removing an old beading which is glued into place it may pay to scarf a short piece of new wood into the damaged section. Note, however, that a short piece may prove difficult to pull in fair to the curved edge of the deck. If brass pins will not do it (and screws are not suitable) it should be possible to fix props or wedges from a nearby wall.

Removing a glued beading is not too difficult if an old but sharp chisel is employed to shave it away in layers between the pins, finishing flush to the planking with a *Surform* plane which will not object to cutting through brass pins if necessary.

Wide laminated gunwales can be shaved down in similar fashion and new pieces of the same thicknesses scarfed in. Although scarfs in rails are traditionally faced aft, scarfs pointing in opposite directions at the ends of short pieces prove easier to make.

With a little care, resin glue, and some matching stopper, these joints can be made almost invisible when varnished. If the results look a bit rough, it may even improve the appearance of the dinghy if the finish on the gunwales is changed from varnish to paint.

Other minor repairs which racing dinghy enthusiasts may be faced with include stem and transom damage similar to the above; deep scratches in the planking (see Chapter 4 and later in this chapter); broken rudder pintles or gudgeons; loose keel band fastenings; torn centreboard slot rubbers, and perhaps fixing a leaky seam on a glued clinker ply dinghy.

The best way to deal with the latter problem is to wedge the seam apart, clean it out with a knife or small hacksaw blade, then inject some resin glue and secure with a few fine copper nails and roves. If this would look unsightly, small screws may be used, perhaps made more secure by fitting a false foot grip on the inside.

Dealing with keel bands is very similar to mast track as

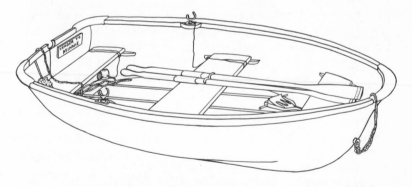

Drawing 31. Few yacht tenders are fully equipped or seamanlike. This glass fibre dinghy has no buoyancy and would sink like a stone, but she does have the following good points – all round fendering, sculling notch, name board, bailer, painters fore and aft, oar lock, rowlock lanyards correctly rove, Trident anchor, seat swab, transom reinforced for outboard motor. If equipped with buoyancy she should also have hand grips fitted to the bottom.

239

described in Chapter 6. Slot rubber may be replaced either as a single full-width strip which is severed down the centre after fixing, or in two separate strips meeting in the middle. Tight screws through the half-round brass strips clamping the rubber to the keel are essential. If the original strips are re-used it may be advisable to use slightly longer screws or to plug the holes in the wood to ensure tightness. If new brass strips are made the hole positions can be shifted slightly from the original. Always punch holes through the rubber where the screws come before fixing as this prevents the rubber from puckering between fastenings. Do not stretch the rubber fore-and-aft.

Improvements

As racing dinghies are intended to be complete and competitive when new, the only improvements ever likely to be undertaken concern newly discovered gadgets and fittings.

On the contrary, few new rowing dinghies or yacht tenders are equipped to the satisfaction of experienced yachtsmen. Some of the defects are quite minor but important. Very few dinghies have an eyebolt in the transom to enable an aft painter to be rigged for securing the dinghy alongside a yacht and one has to improvise by making fast around the after thwart or behind a riser.

Some new dinghies have no all-round fender. It would be a good idea if all racing dinghies had these (plus an effective bumper at the stemhead), then perhaps insurance companies could lower their premiums considerably and the damage which such boats do to unattended yachts at moorings might be halved!

Not only must yachts' tenders have good fendering to prevent damage when coming alongside, but all rowing dinghies, launches, runabouts and sailboats which are ever moored at popular landing stages or pontoons must have proper fendering to prevent them chafing their neighbours.

A coir rope fender is the cheapest and the easiest to fit. Another cheap form can be made by filling lengths of white canvas fire hose with granulated cork. This method has the added advantage that by stitching lengthways, continuous tabs can be formed to take screw fastenings with washers under the heads.

With large enough hose, one of the continuous tabs can be

made to fit right over the top of the gunwale and another tab can be formed for securing to the planking. Very few dinghies have any padding on top of the gunwale, though this is a useful thing for obviating chafe when the dinghy drifts under the counter stern of a yacht or underneath a short boarding ladder.

Coir rope fenders are usually made in one length to pass right around the stem. For neatness, the ends should be thinned down to a small thimbled eye to take a lashing across the transom. If such a lashing would foul an outboard motor separate eye plates can be fitted on either side.

Alternatively, each rope end may be cut off square, whipped, and then clamped with two sheet brass stirrups screwed or bolted to the transom.

To get the rope tight all around, secure the ends, hold the middle over the stemhead and then, with some help, stretch each part of the rope outwards over the gunwale. Ties of copper wire sunk into the lay of the rope are normally fitted at about 6 in (150 mm) centres to fix the rope in place. Each wire passes through two holes in the planking, but when twisting the ends together on the inside, endeavour to house the sharp points right up under the gunwale where they can never cause injury.

Few people know how to twist two ends of plain wire together neatly and the process is frequently used on boats, as when mousing shackles and wiring up rigging screws. The wires should be crossed at right angles and given two even clockwise turns together with the fingers. Using heavy pliers, tighten these turns, pulling towards you at the same time.

Continue twisting with the pliers making sure that the turns are even (avoiding the situation where one strand remains straight while the other winds around it) until six turns are complete. With wire cutters, nip half-way through each wire close to the last turn, then make a seventh twist with the pliers. By rocking the untwisted ends slowly with the fingers, they should break off cleanly at the nips leaving a neat finish. Especially when using copper wire, a little practice may be necessary to determine just how much tension to apply to the first turns to avoid breaking the wire.

White rubber 'D' section fendering is generally secured to the boat with woodscrews which are fed through prepared holes in the nose, then through smaller pilot holes in the inner

241

wall. In the best quality fendering (and in all the largest sections used for big vessels) a brass strip (with corresponding screw holes bored through it) is fed into the fendering to act as a continuous washer under the round-headed screws.

Rubber fendering of other shapes is available, including some to give protection to the top of the gunwale. The rubber should not be over-stretched when fixing. Any fastenings which shear off during use should be replaced as soon as possible by boring new holes close by.

Coir rope fendering can be wired to a grp dinghy much as described for wood. Stainless steel self tapping screws may be used into hollow gunwale grp sections while in the places where the screws would protrude inside, nuts and bolts are suitable, the threads being treated with *Loctite* to stop them working loose. Locking washers are not suitable where the bolt heads seat on to rubber.

For a motor tender or launch, small square canvas covered fenders filled with Kapok or foam rubber are a possible alternative to all-round fendering. Each one should be mounted on two padded canvas straps screwed to the inside of the planking or to the under side of the inner gunwale allowing the fenders to hang inboard when not in use. They can be flipped over the gunwhale to hang in the correct outboard position at a moment's notice. These fenders are very easy for the amateur to make at home during winter evenings; see Chapter 8.

Buoyancy

Built-in buoyancy is a useful adjunct for a yacht's tender and is an important safety measure. Some grp rowing dinghies have buoyancy tanks built-in below the thwarts or under a false floor, but clinker, plywood, or moulded wood tenders are rarely so equipped when new. The matter may be rectified by boxing in blocks of rigid expanded urethane or polystyrene at the ends of the boat and under the centre thwart. Be careful to judge that there is sufficient leg room for rowing before installing a bulkhead across the stern sheets, as trying to row with one's knees fouling the oars is most annoying. Space for a pair of feet can usually be contrived with a little ingenuity.

The buoyancy beneath the centre thwart should be kept about 4 in (100 mm) deep instead of extending right to the bilges to allow clearance for removal of the bottom boards. If, however, complete bulkheads must be used, it should be possible to alter the bottom boards to fit the two compartments.

When building buoyancy tanks into a grp hull at least three methods may be used. If plywood bulkheads are used as above, chocks may be bonded to the inside of the hull with epoxy adhesive. This method lends itself especially to grp dinghies with wooden thwarts.

In the second method, hollow grp tanks can be bonded to the hull and thereby permanently sealed. Drainage bungs can be incorporated in case any leakage does occur.

In the third method grp bulkheads are bonded into place but each tank formed is filled with liquid catalyst foam which becomes permanently rigid on curing.

The bulkhead panels for methods two and three may be made up over a sheet of glass, thus providing a glossy outer surface. Cellophane laid on top of the glass surface will ensure easy release and can be peeled away after cutting out the shape of the bulkhead from a cardboard template tested for accuracy inside the hull.

Note that the panels for Method 2 must be three times the thickness of those for Method 3 unless they can be webbed or reinforced on the inside. Both these methods lend themselves especially to dinghies with grp thwarts. When the thwarts are of wood, it should be possible to remove these, fit a complete grp box beneath, and then refix the timber on top.

As an aluminium alloy dinghy (in similar fashion to a glass fibre one) can sink without trace unless equipped with buoyancy, the need for improvement in this respect may be even more urgent than for a wooden boat. Rigid expanded foam plastics boxed in with plywood panels makes the simplest job for the amateur and alloy or hardwood fixing lugs may be bonded to the hull with epoxy adhesive.

For safety reasons a yacht's tender should have bilge keels with slots cut through them to provide hand grips in the event of a capsize. These slots are also most useful when securing the dinghy upside-down on deck as *gripes* of webbing or cordage (perhaps crossed diagonally) can be used to lash the boat down. A motorized tender must always carry oars while a sailing dinghy should have paddles on board.

Sculling and Rowing
One rarely sees a sculling notch in the transom of a modern

dinghy. This enables the boat to be propelled with a single oar, sometimes imperative when an oar is lost and also useful for enabling one person to ferry a boat-load of bulky gear which might preclude the use of two oars.

Sculling notches are omitted partly because few people know what to do with them and partly because grp and other lightweight boats do not have sufficient grip on the water. They yaw while the oar blade remains almost static when sculling!

The most efficient wrist and arm action for sculling is readily mastered after a short demonstration followed by occasional practice. A heavy dinghy about 16 ft (5 m) long is best for practice. Smaller boats are made easier to scull with several occupants aboard or with a few pigs of ballast in the bilges. It may be a good idea to line the sculling notch with leather (as described for gaff jaws in Chapter 6) as the leathering on an oar never corresponds with the sculling notch position.

Whether one prefers old-fashioned thole pins or swivelling crutches (rowlocks) this is often a department where improvements can be made. Moulded plastics crutches are lighter to carry and less noisy than the common galvanized or bronze variety and some of them will float on water making the use of lanyards less essential. Avoid crutches that are intended to be left shipped permanently as they can cause damage when coming alongside and create snarl-ups with the painters of other dinghies at a pontoon mooring or tidal quay.

Captive rowlocks which fold over to hang below the gunwale when not in use are popular, but many makes of these have no provision for removing the rowlocks completely as an anti-theft measure.

In another system rowlocks are permanently attached to the oars and once the pins have been dropped into the sockets they can be locked there with a circlip or split ring. The idea is useful for hired craft on boating lakes but is not practical for a yacht's tender.

On some inflatable dinghies the crutches are fixed rubber eyes. To prevent the oars coming adrift some makers supply oars which are a tight fit in the eyes. Unfortunately this makes the oars creep inboard when in use, a fault which can be dangerous when continuous hard rowing is needed in an emergency. To overcome this it may be necessary to reduce the diameter of the oars with a spokeshave in the spots concerned, taking care not to overdo this and create weakness.

Inflatable boat oars are frequently jointed for easy stowage and it pays to keep the metal sleeves smeared with petroleum jelly and to oil the spring-loaded ball catches.

Lanyards must be fitted to all new rowlocks (including any spare ones) before they are used. The lanyards can be of quite thin codline or Terylene cordage but the length must be adequate. Having spliced the codline tightly to the groove around the neck of each rowlock (never through the small hole at the end of the shank which is there expressly for wiring a pair of rowlocks together for storage) seize the eyes with twine if at all loose. At the other end of the lanyard make an eye splice large enough to pass the rowlock through with ease. The lanyard can then be attached to the nearest thwart rapidly by forming a noose.

When leaving a dinghy briefly the lanyards (with the rowlocks attached) may be wound around the oars as they lie across the thwart. When the boat is left unattended for longer periods oars and rowlocks should be taken away, or an *oar lock* fitted. Oar locks consist of a stem with a ramshorn-shaped top (like a double boathook head). A hole is bored through the centre thwart, the stem is passed between the two oars with the ramshorns holding them down, and a padlock is inserted close underneath the thwart through a hole in the stem.

Any dinghy moored at an isolated landing place should have a painter of light but strong chain with a large enough end link to take a sizeable padlock. This will at least discourage vandals from casting the boat adrift for amusement.

Some rowlocks are made with both horns the same height. For use on a yacht's tender where the oars need to be shipped and unshipped rapidly, rowlocks with the for'ard horn higher than the after one should always be used. With this type, each rowlock spins around into its correct position as soon as the oar touches it. With equal tops it may be a two-handed job to get each oar into its crutch.

The leathering on oars must never be allowed to wear right through due to chafe at the crutch. When re-leathering, each new piece is cut out 1 in (25 mm) longer than the old one to cover the end nail holes, with an overlap of about $\frac{3}{8}$ in (9 mm) circumferentially for the scarf joint.

A proper leather skiving knife is the best tool for tapering down both edges along the joint and also around the ends. Having left the leather submerged in warm water for an hour it can be nailed on to the oar with $\frac{3}{8}$ in (9 mm) copper tacks spaced about $\frac{1}{2}$ in (12 mm) apart. Once the leather has completely dried out a coat of neatsfoot oil should be applied every day until the leather is saturated.

Notice that the joint on oar leathers should be made roughly in line with the blade to prevent it from bearing against the rowlocks when rowing. Note also that the skiving around the ends should be made on the inside of the leather, while along the scarf joint the hidden skive is made on the outside of the leather while the overlap is skived on the inside.

Modern oars sometimes have moulded plastics sleeves with *buttons* forced on to make an almost permanent alternative to leathering. Buttons (which rest against the rowlocks) are ideal for novices and are simple to laminate from leather strap wound on and nailed through.

Towing the Tender

As mentioned previously a tender is best stowed on deck. Although towing is simple enough in calm weather, dangerous situations can arise with heavy following seas. Drag may be minimized by keeping the painter short, but in rough weather towing a bucket over the stern of the dinghy and increasing the painter length may prevent the dinghy from charging towards the parent vessel periodically.

Although the painter is referred to above as a single rope, a dinghy must never be towed at sea with less than two warps rigged. The second rope may have to be made fast around the for'ard thwart as it would be unwise to rely on the security of a single eyebolt. If a stem dinghy has its painter attached low down to the outside of the stem this will have a lifting effect when towing, keeping spray and the wash from the parent ship out of the dinghy.

If the boat rides best with the main painter kept taut, the additional warp may be kept slack merely as an emergency measure. However, yawing at speed is less likely to occur with the painter taken to one quarter of the ship while the lesser rope is taken to the opposite quarter with equal load on both ropes. Both must have anti-chafe wrapping wherever they touch and (especially on yachts with a central wheelhouse) a crew member should be told to keep a regular eye on the towed craft.

When a taffrail log is streamed, fit this from the windward

Picture 67. How to fit a rope fender tightly. This fender is lashed workboat fashion across the stern transom. Do not use this method if an outboard motor has to be fitted.

Picture 68. Bath night for the dinghy. In muddy harbours this may become a weekly chore. Note the use of thole pins instead of rowlocks.

quarter. Windage on the dinghy will keep her to leeward and prevent her fouling the log line.

If the oars or any other items are left in the dinghy they should be securely lashed while under way. A close fitting waterproof cover is worth getting for a dinghy which is habitually towed behind a fast yacht and which could become swamped, creating a troublesome or even dangerous situation.

To prevent forward surging from causing a collision some enthusiasts make a rigid towbar to fit from transom to dinghy with a universal coupling fitted to each end and perhaps a telescopic length adjustment. Spinnaker boom spring-loaded end fittings are suitable, but the size chosen for a towbar 9 ft (3 m) long needs to be the type normally used for a spinnaker boom 20 ft (6 m) long. Whenever this method is used, a preventer rope which is left slack is a wise precaution.

Running Maintenance
As most dinghies are hauled out when not in use, antifouling paint is not required and a good gloss paint or varnish finish is

suitable on wood. Craft which are left in the water (or brought to a tidal landing stage) will grow a fair amount of weed and barnacles, but scrubbing is normally simple. Antifouling paint would be sure to get rubbed off whenever the dinghy had to be hauled up a beach during the various trips of the parent vessel. Most racing dinghies are stored in a pen ashore and are not likely to get fouled.

All sea-going dinghies benefit from a regular hose down with fresh water, drying off completely with a sponge or wash leather on completion. When these facilities are not available, a rowboat may be sluiced down with sea water inside to keep her clean.

To do this, remove the bottom boards and loose gear, stand the dinghy on its transom leaning against a wall or supported by a helper and throw several buckets of water into the bilges. If necessary, scrub down as well and finish off with a few more douches. Lean her over to scrub the bottom, then wash around the topsides and the transom to remove any mud or grit accumulated during the previous operations.

When a sailing dinghy is left ashore, fit chocks or old car tyres under the bilges to prevent her from blowing over and to give her a tilt for drainage through the stern bungs. Always fit a waterproof cover if there is one and equip this with some sort of ridge pole to prevent heavy pools of rain water from collecting in it.

The bungs and inspection covers to the buoyancy tanks should be removed to prevent internal condensation even where no leakage occurs. Some plywood dinghies have little or no paint inside the tanks and moisture can work through causing the external paint or varnish to blister.

If the boom is used as a ridge pole, see that some protection against chafe is provided where it rests upon the after deck or main sheet track. The sponge or a rubber bailer may be improvised where nothing better can be found.

Ensure that a swab is kept aboard a yacht's tender to enable rain, spray, dew, or muddy footprints to be wiped off, especially when the occupants are on an excursion ashore in respectable clothing!

Additional running maintenance jobs on a racing dinghy can include the periodic flatting down of a graphite bottom finish; the application of wax and other mysterious preparations; adjustments to rigging, shockcords and fittings; smoothing the tips of rudder or centreboard roughened by abrasion, and washing sails and sheets. Such items can all make slight improvements to performance and must be treated as routine maintenance by the enthusiast who intends to win races.

Safety requirements should take priority and for a racing boat this means constant checks on rigging, rudder, and buoyancy, especially when winter (*frostbite*) sailing is undertaken.

Most buoyancy bags are made from welded PVC material, and although some makers will supply patches and adhesives to seal small punctures, repairs directly on a welded seam are generally unsatisfactory, indicating immediate renewal to ensure safety.

An anchor with ample nylon cordage is essential. All gear (including paddle and bailer) must be equipped with lanyards secured on board.

Since Frank Dye cruised from England to Norway and Iceland in a 16 ft (5 m) *Wayfarer* dinghy, the popularity of miniature camping cruisers has increased. Safety precautions on such craft are, of course, more important than for racing. Experience is essential for dinghy cruising; not only general sailing experience, but prolonged experience with the same class of boat.

Careful stowage is necessary to ensure that gear and stores are kept dry, secure, and out of the way. Close attention to safety is imperative. A compass may be scorned by some, but proves essential when fog descends at the same time as a wind shift, even for coastal cruising and certain races. Make sure that rudder fittings are bolted to the transom, not screwed, and check the centreboard pivot bolt for wear, fracture, or seal leaks.

Winter Work

With the exception of clinker boats, dinghy surface preparation, painting, or varnishing, follows the instructions given in Chapters 3 and 4.

Clinker boats (especially those of traditional construction with steamed timbers inside) need a little extra care to prevent the planking from drying out, while treating the interior is more troublesome if one wishes to do it properly.

If such boats must be laid up out-of-doors, the hull should be placed upside-down on chocks and sheeted over, preferably in the form of a tent to keep direct sun from heating the wood.

With all painting and varnishing completed and the hull the right-way-up, the inside can be kept hosed down during warm dry weather to prevent the seams from opening up. Water should not be left in the bilges when there is any risk of sharp frost at night.

Similar precautions apply to carvel planked hulls for launches and larger vessels. If these can be stored in a shed the planking will not shrink appreciably between November and April in the UK. Outside these months regular hosing down will be advisable, though leaving a large quantity of water in the bilges may do more harm than good by reversing the stresses on the hull and forcing the caulking outwards.

Small clinker and carvel boats may be seen submerged and filled with water to hasten the process of taking-up seams. This is perfectly satisfactory provided the water is bailed out before the dinghy sits on the bottom in tidal waters.

Stripping the interior of a traditional clinker hull is a formidable task as the surface can be assumed to consist of perhaps four hundred separate panels, most of these being obstructed by the presence of riveted copper nails. One needs a range of scrapers of varying widths to avoid scratching adjacent parts and power tools are of little value with so many obstructions. However, with this treatment, an ancient dinghy can be given a satisfying new lease of life.

An old hacksaw blade is handy for scraping dirt and paint from the numerous tapered slots behind the steamed timbers, but for cleaning these places during the annual refit, a test-tube brush or bottle brush is kinder on the adjacent paintwork.

A vacuum cleaner is ideal for clearing all the debris from the bilges. A dinghy can usually be housed where an electrical power outlet is handy. If not, it may be possible to borrow a small 12-volt vacuum cleaner. Dust can find so many hiding places that wiping over with a tack-rag is essential.

Treating the exterior of a clinker hull is in many ways simpler than for a smooth surface. The division into narrow panels (without obstruction this time) makes rubbing or scraping less tiring and enables paint or varnish to be laid off more neatly with only one drying edge to watch.

With the hull upside-down run marks from the lands should be minimal. For painting inside, any convenient position may be adopted as long as one works outwards from the hog to the gunwale to avoid reaching over wet paint.

Note that when rejuvenating an old varnished dinghy it may prove impossible to shave down throughout to bright new wood as the customary discolouration around fastenings may persist to a considerable depth. In such cases conversion to paint is expedient, leaving thwarts, gunwale capping, rubbing strake and perhaps the transom, rudder, tiller and centreboard, as varnish work, these parts being easier to revive as new than the remainder.

Plastics and Alloy Repairs
Being so small, runabouts and dinghies of alloy and glass fibre are more likely to receive the burnishing they deserve than large yachts in these materials. This means that painting to keep up a smart appearance can sometimes be delayed for a much longer period. A power operated mop can always be wired up if the boat is brought home, thus ensuring that the job is done speedily as well as thoroughly.

Hair cracks on a glass reinforced plastics surface are not always detrimental if the boat is to be painted. When the cracks radiate in a star formation this may be due to a collision, and internal examination is advisable to check whether the skin has been shattered right through, needing reinforcement on the inside. A hollow sound on tapping the surface often means that the outer gel coats have parted from the glass reinforced core. If found over large areas it would be advisable to return the boat to the makers for extensive reconstruction.

The dirt in cracks can be removed by wiping over with acetone, and newly mixed gel coat resin can then be rubbed into the cracks to seal them.

Deep scores in the gel coat are best filled with a good quality resin putty (such as *Isopon* or *Crystic Stopper*) which need not be pigmented if the hull is to be painted. Ream out narrow scores and cracks with an old wood chisel to ensure a good key for the putty. Leave the putty proud and cut it down flush after curing with a Surform Plane, finishing with fine abrasive paper.

Holes through aluminium alloy boats of all sizes can be repaired by fitting a large grp patch on the inside, flushing off the surface with resin putty when this has cured. More extensive damage should be repaired by riveting a sheet of the same gauge alloy as the skin on the inside (with the rivet heads countersunk into the outer surface) while resin putty may again be used to flush off outside.

Small holes and leaking bolt heads in wooden craft are traditionally repaired with *tingles*. To apply a tingle, cut a rectangle of sheet copper about 24-gauge (0·6 mm) and pierce around the edges with small holes to receive closely spaced copper tacks. Cut out a piece of calico a little smaller than the copper. Soak this with paint, stick it to the hull, then tack the copper into position and paint over.

Temporary repairs of minor leaks on hulls of any material may be effected by sticking a canvas patch to the outside with epoxy glue such as *Araldite*.

Many of the above notes apply equally well to small multi-hulled sailing and power craft, though the larger of these craft may be too beamy to transport readily by road to one's home.

Inflatable boats cannot normally be repaired reliably by the amateur but most makers will service them annually for a modest charge plus additional costs where more extensive work proves necessary.

Rubber liferafts are normally kept packed in special containers and are self-inflated only when jettisoned from the yacht during an emergency. The amateur has no means of testing them and most makers recommend returning them to the works annually for testing and repacking, including the renewal when necessary of sealed rations and other equipment stored inside. The annual cost is small in relation to the importance of the service they could one day provide.

Self-inflating liferafts are compulsory aboard ocean racing yachts and should be considered most valuable cargo for any craft straying far from coastal waters, especially when the dinghy carried would prove an inadequate lifeboat in rough weather for the number of persons on board.

Trailers and Trolleys

The majority of racing dinghy owners possess a road trailer nowadays to enable them to transport their boats readily when attending race meetings in strange waters. As road trailers are not normally intended for use on a soft beach or for submersion in water, a launching trolley is also considered a standard piece of equipment.

The road trailers used for transporting shoal draft sailing boats and motor cruisers behind their owners' cars are of much heavier construction and usually have two pairs of wheels with brakes. Boats up to about 2 tons dead weight can

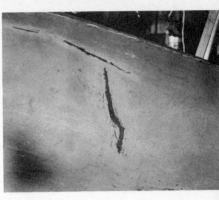

Plastics dinghy repairs. Picture 69. Stippling polyester resin on to the first layer of glass cloth inside the boat.

Picture 70. Finally, the cracks are filled with resin putty from the outside.

be towed over average road gradients with a big car, but for heavier boats, or over a hilly route, it pays to enlist the services of a Jeep, or similar towing vehicle.

Towing at night can be dangerous and even during daylight precise regulation requirements concerning brake-lights and direction indicators are a wise precaution to avoid any needless collision from behind which could result in several weeks without a boat while repairs are carried out. An overhanging mast must have some rag or a reflecting sign attached to it.

Launching trolleys are of simple construction and quite easy to fabricate at home. The wheels normally run on plain bearings which should receive frequent oiling to prevent squeaks and unnecessary wear. Suitable wheels are obtainable from yacht chandlers. If the solid rubber type with no central metal bush is used, the axles should be of brass to reduce friction and the excessive wear which can occur on sandy beaches.

Experienced club members should know the best type of wheels to adopt for their launching conditions. Small diameter cheap wheels are quite suitable on a hard ramp while the larger pneumatic tyred wheels are preferable on beaches.

Good padding is essential for the bilge supports on all types of trailer and some support for the keel is advisable when a heavy boat is towed on the road. Commercial trailers generally have specially made white rubber pads for this purpose but the amateur can improvise quite well by tacking thick canvas over several layers of old truck inner tube rubber. Thin leather makes the best covering for these pads, but old canvas fire hose cut open makes quite a hard wearing alternative.

253

Where the pads are fitted to metal brackets without wooden chocks it may be necessary to sew new canvas or leather into position around the brackets instead of using closely spaced copper tacks or screws with washers.

When trailing a boat over a long distance, it pays to carry a spare trailer wheel (or perhaps a tyre and tube) as some tyre sizes are not readily available. A trailer wheel blow-out may not be noticed immediately so that repairs usually involve renewal of the inner tube.

Few cars nowadays carry tools or a tyre pump, but the yachtsman towing a boat needs to be much better equipped in this respect than the normal motorist. A tyre inflator that screws into a spark plug mounting on the car engine is ideal in emergencies though with the standard length of air line it may be necessary to unhitch and move the car within reach of the trailer wheels.

For loads heavier than a sailing dinghy a bottle jack should be included in the tool kit.

Small road trailer wheels have ball bearings built into the hub and these slide off the stub axle with the wheel after removing the retaining nut. On larger trailers with brakes the wheels are bolted separately to the drums as on a car. The hub races in the latter type are sealed for immersion and the packed grease rarely needs renewal.

There is no point in renewing the seals if the shaft is pitted with rust. With the former type, however, grease can leak out and water may leak in so that attention with a grease gun is advisable before and after using the trailer as a launching trolley. Keep wheel nuts and all other threads greased or they will eventually rust solid.

Good trailers are galvanized or zinc sprayed at the works so when repainting the steel work, avoid the use of a scraper which could damage the zinc.

Although most modern dinghy trailers have bonded rubber or torsion bar springing, many of the older types utilize coil springs which may rust badly in sea air and eventually fracture. Painting the inside of coil springs is difficult, so when a trailer is dismantled for a routine overhaul, it may be well worth while to send the springs away for shot blasting and zinc spraying.

Dinghy trailers take quite a pounding on the road so it pays to check the tightness of all bolts and chock adjusters before

Picture 71. A two-wheeled road trailer is quite man enough to take this 23 ft (7 m) twin bilge keel sloop to the owner's home at laying-up time.

Picture 72. Once you can get her up there, almost any dinghy without side decks will trail comfortably on the properly equipped roof of a small car.

embarking on a trip. Tyre pressures are most important for safety as well as tyre wear and while checking lubrication points, a little grease on the surfaces of a ball and socket hitch should not be forgotten. Arrange the weight distribution so that a small downward pressure is exerted at the hitch.

Dinghies under about 60 lbs (27 kg) in weight may be carried with safety upside-down on a car roof if a suitable roof rack is fitted. Unless sufficient help is always available, a rack with rollers on the back is useful enabling a dinghy to be loaded single-handed.

When a boat has to be moved from the beach to the car single-handed, sets of wheels made to clamp to the transom (with the boat upside-down) are useful. Similarly, for launching on a soft or steep beach, *Sea-Esta* and other makes of inflatable rollers are invaluable. Two of these will do the job although three simplifies the operation by keeping the boat on an even keel throughout. Inflatable rollers can be utilized as buoyancy bags if secured firmly inside a dinghy after launching!

CHAPTER 12

BERTHING, MOORING, AND LAYING-UP

It takes a few years of experience and observation, as well as a lot of reading, for newcomers to catch up on the knowledge of older hands with regard to the safest procedure when berthing a yacht. Manoeuvering to come alongside under all conditions of wind and tide is described in other books, but safe maintenance when berthed is in many ways even more important.

Yachtsmen are liable to encounter at least six different methods of berthing. Making fast to a swinging mooring marked with a buoy is usually a simple matter of hauling in the buoy rope (perhaps followed by a length of small chain) until the main bridle chain is brought on board and secured to the samson post, bitts or windlass.

To make fast reliably, take a couple of round turns to check any immediate surging, then take a bight of chain under the standing part and loop it over the post, finishing with another two round turns. In some waters it may be advisable to fit a padlock across the links.

If the chain does not pass over a proper roller fairlead make sure that adequate anti-chafe packing is provided and always rig a proper bow fender to prevent the chain from scraping the topsides during wind-against-tide conditions.

Mooring to a large floating buoy is normally a temporary arrangement, and once the ship has been made fast with rope, the anchor cable should be shackled to the ring on the buoy or rove endless through the ring handy for slipping later. Similarly, when a yacht is moored fore-and-aft between two big buoys, chain is advisable. If rope lines must be used the ends should have thimbled eyes with shackles to the buoy ring.

Berthing stern-to-quay (as in many Continental ports) usually means dropping the anchor in just the right position (perhaps $\frac{1}{2}$ cable (100 m)) from the quay and dropping back into the appropriate space until a heaving line can be passed ashore. This type of berth is normally well attended so that anxiety concerning damage caused by warps carrying away is minimized.

Conditions in a well run marina are similar, though craft are generally moored to keep dead still in the centre of four radiating warps, usually bow-to-jetty. Yachts in a marina may be well cared for and most of the owners may be wealthy, but good seamen are sensible folk who provide their warps with full anti-chafe gear to avoid needless wastage.

The fourth common berthing arrangement is the *trot* where three or four yachts lie abreast with fore-and-aft warps leading to driven piles ahead and astern, or to some type of quay. Much more vigilance is necessary to maintain a boat safely at a trot than with the previous methods. Customarily, each boat arriving to berth provides all the fenders and warps necessary. All craft should point in the same direction (normally up-ebb in tidal waters) with rudders secured amidships. As well as breast ropes and springs to her neighbour, each yacht must run her own heavy warps to the piles, ensuring that these are made fast to sliding rings or *kites* where provided to overcome the effect of tidal range on the rope tension.

Fenders need to be large, especially when your neighbour has a rubbing strake which protrudes further than your own. In general, fenders are best hung quite close to the water on small boats, for, if high up, the rubbing strake of a rolling neighbour may come down on top of a fender and snap its lanyard.

Breast ropes should be left with a little slack, but the two springs need have only the slackness required to allow for shrinkage after rain if ordinary hemp rope is used.

The fifth common berthing situation is alongside a quay or wharf. If the yacht is liable to touch the bottom at low water she must be ballasted to prevent her from falling outwards, but not too much or the fenders may get squashed.

Although one long warp in each direction may suffice to hold her, secondary warps (or preferably wire ropes) should be made fast to separate places on shore unless the berth is continuously under surveillance. Very long warps are an advantage in tidal waters, for when taut at low water they will not be too slack at high tide. If necessary, a heavy weight (an

257

angel) can be suspended from the centre of each warp to keep the ship close to the quay at all times.

Heavy duty shockcord *snubbers* (with a thimbled eye moulded into each end) are available, providing the same benefits as weights in a more convenient way. Note that snubbers are never made fast to the bitter end of a warp in case they part under load. Instead, part of the continuous rope is knotted through each eye on the ends of the snubber.

The anchor cable, a few filled water breakers, or some pigs of ballast (according to the size of craft) will usually list her adequately towards the quay. For a short stay with the yacht attended, a halyard or other guy from the mast to the shore can be adjusted at low water to provide the necessary amount of heel. By suspending a weight from this rope it may be possible to arrange a reliable system which needs no attention.

A guy from the mast is more certain to keep a boat close to the quay than listing her with ballast, for without a guy, severe wash from a passing craft could cause her to list outwards shortly after her keel had settled on the bottom. However, there must be no possibility of malicious interference when a guy is used.

Although ordinary fenders are satisfactory when a yacht is berthed to a stone harbour wall, they are useless against an ordinary timber piled quay. For a short stay it may be possible to leave a crew member in charge of fending off, but for a permanent stay one must hang a pole or plank fore-and-aft at least 9 ft (3 m) long between the yacht's fenders and the quay. Few yachts carry a plank on board, but many harbour authorities keep these handy for the use of visitors.

Another common type of berth used widely on rivers is the *stage mooring,* consisting of two almost vertical poles with a ladder between them and a catwalk extending from the ladder to the bank. In tidal waters the poles are driven sufficiently far from low water mark to prevent the yacht touching bottom, while the tops of the poles extend well above highest flood level.

Fore-and-aft warps of considerable length are advisable to keep a yacht close to the stage at all river levels. These ropes should be made fast to stakes driven into the river bank, well below bank top in a concealed and muddy location to minimize interference. At unattended stage moorings additional wire ropes must be rigged from separate stakes, with the

Picture 73. Cutting off one fluke to make a mooring anchor. In shallow water a protruding fluke could sink a moving boat or cause the anchor to trip if fouled.

Picture 74. Old Fisherman anchor prepared for a mooring with one fluke bent to touch the shank.

ends locked on board. Wire rope is very resistant to chafe but synthetic or natural fibre cordage can fail due to chafe after only an hour or two of rough weather.

In some locations a *running mooring* is most satisfactory for small boats. An anchor is bedded offshore with a single sheave block shackled to it. A light chain is rove through the block in a continuous length (like a conveyer belt) and belayed to a stake on shore.

A bridle is shackled to the chain at one point. Having stepped ashore from the boat, the bridle is made fast to her, and by pulling on the ground chain the craft is moved out into deep water.

With a *hypotenuse mooring* there are two stakes on shore, one where the single ground chain meets the shoreline at 90° and another some distance away to reduce the angle to about 30°.

When the boat on her bridle comes close inshore at 90°, she is transferred into deep water at the 30° position with full chain scope paid out.

Other types of mooring are in use, such as sitting on the

hard (or perhaps on soft mud) in a harbour which dries out. Most small shoal draft yachts will lie happily in this situation. Deep draft vessels should be equipped with *legs* to keep them upright, moored all fours, or with one heavy chain cable at bow and stern.

Many deep keel cruising yachts carry a pair of legs on board, for even if they normally lie at a deep water berth it may be essential to rig the legs when a snug berth is required in some small port. Legs should be bolted roughly amidships to adequate chocks inside, and this may be difficult to arrange on a grp hull which was not properly equipped for legs during manufacture.

The legs must be just the right length (slightly shorter than the depth to underside of keel) to allow the vessel to sit lightly on one leg when the keel sinks in. Swellings or chocks at the bottom end of each leg are essential to prevent it from sinking into a soft bed. Fore-and-aft guys must be rigged to prevent the legs from swivelling and causing the yacht to fall over.

Telescopic light alloy legs can be made, simplifying the stowage problem. These are sometimes attached to the chain plates when rigged. Legs of square timber (with padded curved chocks attached to conform to the shape of the topsides) having a slight outward splay from the vertical, generally make the soundest job.

Drawing 32. Legs are very useful on a deep keeled yacht when visiting small ports which dry out. Legs must be of exactly the correct length, well padded, well bolted, with big feet and guyed fore and aft for safety.

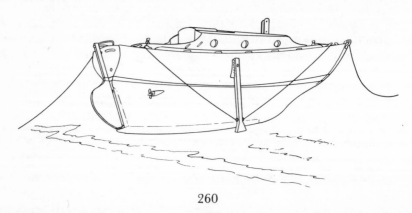

Picture 75. Bilge keelers do not necessarily always sit upright on the putty!

Picture 76. Using a dockside crane for launching. Note how old bunk mattresses are used for packing. Fenders at the ready before she goes in.

Laying Moorings

Moorings are often sold outright and although local authorities and harbour boards like to take over control of all waters there are still places where a yachtsman can make arrangements with a landowner to lay his own mooring.

Variations are possible, but the usual procedure is to lay a heavy *ground chain* at right angles to the tidal flow (or prevailing wind) secured at each end to a sinker or anchor, with a rising *bridle chain* attached to the centre point. The ground chain needs to be massive and is commonly made from $\frac{1}{2}$ in (12 mm) chain for boats under 16 ft (5 m) in length; $\frac{5}{8}$ in (15 mm) up to 22 ft (7 m); $\frac{3}{4}$ in (18 mm) up to 29 ft (9 m); 1 in (25 mm) up to 36 ft (11 m); $1\frac{1}{4}$ in (31 mm) up to 49 ft (15 m); $1\frac{1}{2}$ in (37 mm) up to 60 ft (19 m).

Using these sizes, and with the ground chain as long as possible, only the middle part of the chain should ever move. The bridle chain should be galvanized, a size larger than the yacht's anchor cable. Its length may be governed by the amount of swinging room permitted to avoid collision with neighbouring craft, but a length of twice the high water depth should be reckoned as a minimum.

There must always be a *swivel* in the bridle, and renewal of this and the chain will be much simplified if a short piece of heavy chain is fitted between the ground chain and the swivel, sufficiently long to come above water at low tide. In sandy waters it may be a good idea to fit the swivel higher up the bridle to reduce wear as it rotates with the swinging of the yacht.

261

Heavy old anchors with the top arms and flukes cut off or bent over are ideal for fitting at each end of a ground chain. Ideal *Fisherman* or *Stockless* anchors for the above range of ground chains would be of the following weights in lbs with kilogram equivalents shown in brackets: 40 (18); 60 (27); 100 (45); 160 (72); 220 (100); 300 (135). If *Plough* anchors are available and the ground is suitably holding for them, they may be 60% of the above weights.

Concrete block sinkers may be cast to use in place of anchors, the size required varying considerably. On impacted sand or shingle, double the Fisherman weight would be necessary, but at a mooring which dries out one may be able to dig the sinkers in. If this is done, the sinker need weigh no more than the Fisherman.

For light moorings on mud, circular concrete discs with concave bottoms are made. They can be lighter than ordinary weights as they hold to the mud by suction. Steel mud anchors (shaped like mushrooms with long stems) work well, and screw anchors (shaped like corkscrews) may be wound into mud by turning with a wooden pole through the eye at the top.

When a deep trench can be excavated at low tide, each anchorage may be a *deadman* made from a length of old steel girder. Whatever form of sinker is used, try to keep the eye and other protruding parts as low as possible.

Chains permanently below water do not normally corrode very rapidly and black chain is frequently used. To avoid having to lift the mooring for inspection every three or four years it may be possible to get a skin diver to examine it.

The threads of all shackle pins should be smeared with graphite grease before assembly and moused with thick galvanized wire. The chain on a mooring which dries out may rust more rapidly, but regular inspection is then simple.

The best way to lay a heavy chain mooring below water is to use a powerful motor workboat, preferably flush-decked and equipped with a derrick. Flake down the chain on deck (with bridle, buoy rope and buoy attached), drop the first anchor at its allotted location, then motor powerfully in the proposed direction paying out the ground chain over the stern. Dump the bridle on the way, but before the final anchor or sinker is ready to let go, sling a strong rope under it, lower it over the stern and keeping the boat forging ahead, pay out more rope until the anchor settles. Then slip the rope.

In winter, it may be advisable to replace the buoy rope with a length of flexible wire rope and fit a large steel buoy. The bridle chain and swivel can also be removed to keep them in good condition. If the buoy is lost during the winter, it usually takes an hour with one man rowing and one trailing a grapnel on a nylon line to pick it up. On a sandy bed a chain can become deeply buried if left too long. With the yacht moored at a certain state of tide, try to establish a transit on shore to provide a future check against dragging.

Other arrangements for the ground chain on a swinging mooring are feasible, sometimes three anchors being used. Customary local practice is usually sound, based upon long experience of the various wind and tide effects.

The only other type of mooring that the amateur is likely to install himself is the stage mooring. These are simplest on lakes where only the wind and a small range of water level may have to be considered. On tidal rivers (or ones subject to high flood levels) the ladder may be as much as 25 ft (8 m) in length.

In its simplest form, the stage mooring consists of a ladder supported away from the bank for a boat to rest against, but unless the mooring ropes can be kept permanently taut, one end of the craft may swing towards the bank and run aground

Drawing 33. For up-river mooring, especially in tidal waters, a stage mooring is ideal and simple to erect. Tubular steel scaffolding can be used, but timber poles are kind to the boat and can last ten years, Boy scouts delight in carrying out such a project.

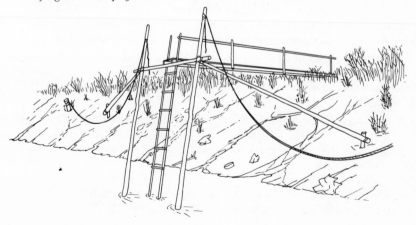

on a falling tide or strike a supporting strut to the ladder on a rising tide. Therefore, a superior method is to erect a post either side of the ladder the distance between the posts being about half the length of the boat. Local practice can be followed reliably in this respect.

To avoid the necessity to drive the posts as piles into the bed whenever renewal becomes necessary, a wiser procedure is to drive short piles of long-lasting hardwood (such as oak, Jarrah, or Greenheart) into the bed, protruding sufficiently above low water mark to enable each post to be bolted on. The piles may be driven with a sledge hammer or maul, but if a two-man post driving tool is used it may be necessary to use longer piles and cut them off to length after driving.

The posts should be made from springy pine (sawn square or in the round) and a simple system of struts should be nailed, bolted, or wired on to hold the posts, ladder, and catwalk, firmly into place.

Any craft lying at a stage mooring should have either an all-round rubber fender or a rubbing strake surmounted by a metal band. If round poles of larch, spruce, or pine, are used in the construction, all bark should be stripped off with a draw-knife to ensure maximum life, and to facilitate examination over the years for rot and cracking.

Leaving Her Afloat
Although many yachts are laid up at the highest point on a beach or in a mudberth, the boat will suffer less and fitting-out work will be easier if she is hauled out (on a slipway or into a shed), or lifted by crane on to a wharf.

Many small craft (especially near certain marinas) live permanently on shore and are transported to the water during the season by means of a mobile crane. Such craft may not need to be moved at all for laying-up, though some may be trailed home to avoid unnecessary winter rentals and to simplify fitting-out.

Many of the largest yachts stay afloat continuously, while a few hardy souls in British and North American waters follow the example of the frostbite dinghy racing enthusiasts and remain cruising during the winter!

Some yachtsmen consider that a wooden hulled vessel should never be allowed to dry out, but although there are a few ancient vessels about which might break their backs if hauled out of the water, wintering ashore is definitely beneficial to yachts of all materials. If the seams of a wooden yacht show any sign of opening up during the laid-up period, this nearly always means that she was hauled out too early or launched too late.

Laying-up in a mudberth is a little safer than in deep water, but it should not be forgotten that when gales coincide with high tides there can be trouble. Access to a mudberth and across to the yacht may be difficult, but this has the advantage of deterring vandals.

Most antifouling paint is ineffective by laying-up time but it should not be forgotten that some mudberths harbour teredo, gribble, and other infestors of underwater planking. These menaces tend to increase as the winter water temperature is raised slightly by industrial cooling water effluents in many rivers and harbours.

Condensation and damp bilges limit fitting-out work on many craft laid-up afloat or in mudberths, but where a power line can be run from the shore a small heater may be left running on board. The cost of this is sure to prove cheaper than hauling out and storing under cover. Insurance premiums for laying-up afloat are frequently no higher than on shore as most boatyards do not carry insurance cover for laid-up vessels.

The fitting of steel wire mooring ropes is a most important precaution during the winter and in some waters it may be advisable to attach timber packing along the waterline (especially at bow and stern) to prevent ice from damaging the hull.

With power available a *Bubbler* can be installed. This consists of an air compressor feeding a perforated weighted hose sunk below the boat. The rising bubbles prevent surface ice forming.

In a mudberth, four radiating mooring wires or stout ropes are necessary to ensure that the yacht always settles into the same depression (or *wallow*) after a high tide. When laying-up in a fresh mudberth it may be advisable to dig a trench for the keel and part of the bilges to assist the boat to settle down snugly without listing. Mooring rope stakes can be driven as described above for stage mooring piles.

Hauling Out
When your boat is lifted out with a crane, make sure that old mattresses or similar paddings are used to protect the topsides

265

from the strops (slings). In addition, *spreaders* of adequate length must always be used to prevent the strops from pinching the gunwales. If the boat has a rockered keel, tie both sets of strops together near the keel to prevent them sliding fore-and-aft when under load.

To haul boats out, shipyards use slipways with steel cradles running on track, and motor winches. Small yards have *greased ways* with timber cradles. Each cradle consists of two planks to ride on the greased way planks and a grid of baulks across these to support the keel. Vertical legs braced to the baulks are used to keep the boat upright.

The cradle is moved to the bottom of the ways at low tide and is weighted with iron ballast called *kentledge* to prevent it floating. At high tide the boat is moved on to the cradle and winched out.

Once ashore, a yacht of almost any size can be moved considerable distances on wood (or steel tube) rollers into a shed or other favourable position for laying-up. Although this work would normally be done by a boatyard, amateurs trail quite large vessels to their homes or to plots some distance from the water for laying-up, thus some knowledge of the procedure when moving a vessel about on dry land is useful.

Craft smaller than about 25 ft (8 m) in length may be lifted (one end at a time) by means of a lever, enabling chocks to be placed under the keel. For larger craft, a *bottle jack* may be used in the same manner.

The lever for lifting a 25 ft (8 m) boat would need to be about 9 ft (3 m) long, of tough sound timber about 3 in × 3 in (75 mm × 75 mm) in section at the business end (tapering if necessary towards the handle) or of thick steel tube with an outside diameter of about 2 in (50 mm). A large range of chocks (offcuts of plank) between $\frac{3}{4}$ in (18 mm) and 3 in (75 mm) in thickness will be necessary, plus, perhaps, some chunks of 9 in × 9 in (230 mm × 230 mm) timber and a few wedges.

These requirements depend very much on the type of boat, and the distance between keel and ground. An ideal size of wedge is about 12 in (300 mm) long, 4 in (100 mm) wide, tapering from 1 in (25 mm) at one end to about $\frac{1}{16}$ in (2 mm) at the other end.

For a fulcrum under the lever, build up with chocks to the required height, placing a narrow strip of timber on top to allow the lever to rock. Keeping the fulcrum close to the keel

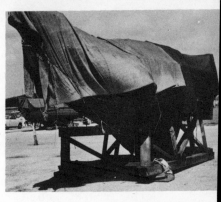

Picture 77. Good system of ridge pole and struts with permanent guardrail, ready to receive the winter sheet.

Picture 78. If a tarpaulin is permitted to blow about in the wind, a couple of winter gales will chafe it like a sieve or tear out the eyelets.

for maximum leverage, it may be impossible to gain more than about 1½ in (37 mm) of lift.

Having raised the keel chocks to gain this, the fulcrum must be raised for a fresh bite. Unless the lever is kept almost horizontal, a smooth keel can slip off the end, so it pays to keep to small lifts. A team of two people is ideal for the operation. When using a jack, lifting and chocking can be almost continuous until the jack reaches the end of its travel and must then be readjusted on chocks.

As the keel is raised, adjustment of the supports preventing the yacht from falling over must be watched. With extra help, this operation is simple as props under the rubbing strake can be shifted as required, keeping the boat dead upright all the time. Bilge keels of any size are most convenient for chocking under.

Raising the keel above ground makes bottom fitting-out work simpler. Once chocked up, it may pay to add extra supports underneath a long keel using *folding wedges* (two wedges driven towards each other) to obtain even support at each point. Chocks (called *squats*) under the bilges must be linked together by timber dogs or nails into athwartships baulks beneath the keel, while struts (unless nailed to the planking) will need regular attention to prevent slackness. Short keeled yachts with long overhangs are particularly awkward to shore up safely to prevent pitching when a heavy person is moving about on deck.

Striking over

The process of moving a boat sideways on land is called *striking over*. Small craft weighing less than about 2 tons can be inched along by means of a crowbar or lever under the keel while the keel is supported on two athwartships baulks.

For striking over heavy boats, some professionals use greased ways under the cradle and a motor winch. When the winch is remote, a system of *snatch blocks* is used to keep the rope feeding in the required direction.

The amateur without equipment can strike over by using rollers between the planks instead of grease. Rollers of scrap thick walled steel tube with outside diameter about 3 in (75 mm) are ideal. The ground planks may be in quite short lengths, passed around with the spare rollers as the boat moves along.

Instead of the windlass, a powerful rope tackle will do, with a party of friends heaving on the fall. A three-fold rope purchase can probably be borrowed from a boatyard or contractor. Remember that massive steel blocks (if properly lubricated) work better than neat but strong blocks with cordage too small to hold comfortably in the hands. Sometimes it may be possible to utilize a Jeep in low gear (or a farm tractor) to pull the boat about.

Even without rollers boats up to 10 tons can be moved slowly by using a hydraulic jack angled at about 45° under a keel edge, operated first at one end of the keel and then at the other.

An old vessel could be damaged if moved about in a jerky fashion on land, especially if ballast is stowed in the bilges. Some yards might not worry about this, but the careful owner will empty water tanks; unship ballast; anchors and cable, and all radio and other sensitive equipment as soon as the boat reaches the top of the slipway or even sooner.

Scrubbing Off

If the yacht can be left a while at the top of the slipway, this is an ideal position for scrubbing the bottom. Even with antifouling paint in good condition, scrubbing off is so much easier while still wet that the opportunity must never be missed. The aim is to scrub off most of the antifouling paint as well as the marine growth, with long handled scrubbers and copious douches of sea water, finishing with a good squirt from a fresh water hose. This may prove a messy job, but is much healthier than having to breath the poisonous paint dust when rubbing dry at a later date.

Any barnacles are best scraped off with an offcut of plywood which is less likely to damage the surface than a steel scraper. Barnacles must not be scraped off a depth sounder transducer. The tops can be pinched off with pliers, but the remainder should be dissolved by brushing on dilute *spirits of salts* (hydrochloric acid).

If there is sufficient delay before transferring a boat from the slipway to the shed, this is an excellent opportunity to wash out the bilges, as her trim will urge all water to flow rapidly to the pump well or drain plugs. A bucket full of water and bilge cleaning fluid should be mixed up according to the maker's instructions, and scrubbed on to every part accessible from beneath the cabin sole, or under berths and lockers, with special attention to any oily regions near the engines or fuel tanks. A hose down with fresh water working aft should then leave the bilges sweet.

Some launches and fin keeled or shoal draught sailing boats have no proper sump from which to pump bilge washing water and residue has to be mopped out to make a thorough job.

Care of Spars and Rigging

As soon as a mast has been unstepped for the winter (see Chapter 6) all rigging should be stripped off, pulling *gantlines* of thin terylene cord through the mast as internal halyards are removed. Label every coil of rope; block; tackle; rigging screw; chafe pad; spreader and other fitment. As most of these parts should be washed in fresh water before storing it pays to use waterproof labels (such as those made for gardeners) and waterproof ink. The notebook should be handy at this time so that as each piece of equipment is taken off and examined, notes can be made of defects such as broken strands of wire; damaged servings; worn clevis pins; bent shackles; chafed cordage and worn sheaves. These items can then receive attention in good time to avoid panic when fitting-out. Permanent notes covering the lengths and sizes of all ropes and wires may prove most useful one day.

When dry, coils of cordage can be hung from a pole high in

a shed roof. A sheet of polythene loosely draped over the ropes will keep them free from dust. Covering coils of wire rope is especially important to prevent dirt rubbing off on to sails next season.

With modern materials little deterioration occurs if proper spar laying-up procedure is skimped, and many sailing dinghy owners with alloy spars and stainless steel fittings are inclined to leave the whole lot draped on a rack until the following season. However, even anodized alloy masts deserve a wash down with detergent and fresh water once a year and this operation at least may bring some defect to light which could eventually have led to dismasting and stranding.

When spars are suspended from a roof or laid on trestles some care is advisable to prevent a permanent bend occurring, especially in long solid masts. It may pay to give each spar a half turn once a month.

Remember that some long racing masts are quite frail when ashore without the support of their rigging and their own weight could damage them when a single point lift is applied to the centre. Such masts are best stored along a wall to which four or five aligned brackets have been fixed.

Aluminium spars which have not been anodized eventually get a patchy white patina on the surface which feels rough to the touch. If not left too late this can be removed with *Brillo* pads or fine steel wool used with water and detergent.

To prevent oxidation, these spars can be coated with good quality car wax, and if alloy spars must be stored in the open air throughout the winter, a coating of machinery preservative such as *Plus Gas Formula B* or *Shell Ensis Oil* is ideal. These lacquers should be kept out of the luff groove and away from sheave pins. They are readily removed when required with cellulose thinners. A smear of anhydrous lanoline will do the same job more cheaply.

To preserve wooden spars greasy coatings should be avoided and if for any reason the surface cannot be rubbed and revarnished (giving the final coat in the Spring) wrapping with polythene sheeting is a suitable alternative.

Winterization

The main requirements for the hull consist of dismantling and taking away every movable part; draining all water from tanks and plumbing systems; winterizing engines and other mechanical equipment; general spring cleaning below decks, and the rigging of winter covers where necessary.

Stripping all movable gear and stores from a cruising yacht may take a considerable time, though the wise owner will have started doing this with non-essential parts some weeks before laying-up.

There is always a strong temptation to leave aboard such items as spare ropes; cans of food; water breakers; crockery and cutlery. A few of these items may, of course, be needed during the Winter, but otherwise everything should go, including locker doors; hatch covers and washboards. These can be varnished at home.

Whenever there is risk of frost, all water must be drained away to eliminate damage by freezing. This must include the small amount of water trapped inside the pumps on toilets, sinks, engine etc, as well as all loops of piping under cockpit flooring, cabin sole, and bunk boards. With all unions and hose connexions undone any water inside the piping can be blown out.

Water held in the bowl trap of a yacht toilet must be removed with a syringe or mop while any residue in the pumps can be released by lifting the suction valve with a wire probe, operating the handle at the same time. To drain the chamber of a rotary or semi-rotary pump the coverplate must be removed or slackened away.

Engine Lay-up

The water jackets of engines, heat exchangers, and intake filters, must be completely drained. Although car anti-freeze solution can be added to some water-filled components, it may prove impossible to distribute this properly to all parts, so complete draining is a more foolproof procedure.

External cleaning is the next task, followed by cleaning of the drip tray. All electrical equipment should be removed for storage in a dry place at home, leaving labels on the disconnected wires and leads. A small fold of masking tape will suffice for this, a code number on each one corresponding to a master list to be kept in a safe place.

When batteries are on shore, try to arrange for an occasional slow discharge (as well as a trickle-charge) to ensure they are kept in ideal condition. Batteries can freeze when in a state of low charge.

Sparking plugs and injector nozzles should be removed. Insert a small dose of light oil into each cylinder, rotate the engine a few times, insert a little more oil, then seal the holes using corks, old spark plugs, or old injectors.

Tank treatment was described in Chapter 10. If copper fuel piping is taken ashore for annealing the ends of any disconnected pipes or unions left on board should be sealed with PVC tape.

Fuel pumps and injector pumps can be left in place, but carburettors (including those on two-stroke engines) are best stripped and cleaned prior to storage at home. Seal the induction hole with a piece of oily rag.

A wet exhaust system must be drained and unless flexible rubber tube is used one can run the engine for a few minutes with the water injection union disconnected to dry the system completely. If the exhaust outlet is sealed for the winter, it might be a good idea to insert a pack of silica gel to absorb any latent moisture. This will prevent corrosion of exhaust valves or the piston rings of two-stroke engines.

Sump oil should be pumped or drained out, the oil filter element renewed, fresh oil inserted, and the engine run briefly to circulate this. Some makers recommend changing gear oil in a similar manner and some recommend using special Winter inhibiting oils. Whatever type of oil is used, this should really be renewed again just before the start of the new season.

Slack away the shaft couplings on old boats or those liable to flex while hauled out. Grease chains and sprockets on hand starting gear and wipe other bright steel parts with thick oil. As an alternative, the entire engine can be sprayed with one of the many makes of preservative oil supplied in Aerosol cans.

Engines should, if possible, be rotated a few turns every week during the winter, taking care that pieces of rag filling orifices are not sucked in.

When laying-up an outboard, run it briefly in fresh water to clear salt from the jackets. Rotate rapidly by hand when ashore to pump the water system dry, then drain and replenish the gearbox oil.

The threads on the clamp bolts should be treated with white stern gland grease (called *water pump grease* by some makers). The swivel bearing ought to be oiled as this too can seize up completely when not moved frequently.

If the engine will not be touched for six or seven months, oil the cylinder bores as described above. Drain the fuel system completely (including the carburettor) and clean the fuel filter. Alternatively, when the engine is kept at home it can be rotated by hand once a week and given a short dry run every six weeks.

Aluminium parts should be treated as described above for alloy spars. Chromium plated parts are best protected with one of the Aerosol lacquers used for this purpose on automobiles, as chromed parts are by no means immune from corrosion on a neglected outboard motor. Finally polish all enamelled parts with car wax.

Cleaning Below Decks

Just as a dinghy deserves a good internal scrub at the end of the season, cabin craft of all constructions deserve at least a wipe over on all below-deck surfaces with one of the magic household wall and floor cleaning fluids.

When such work has been neglected, scouring powders may have to be added to revive paintwork. For scrubbing out food lockers, some household disinfectant or formalin (formaldehyde) should be added to the water. Lockers and doors (including the icebox) must be left open during the lay-up period.

Some influence from the distaff side is valuable at laying-up time and usually ensures, at least, that the cushion covers and portlight curtains (drapes) are properly dealt with at home!

With commencement of laying-up, one should start a note book or list of all work required before next season. This can later be divided into two parts, one for the boatyard and one for the owner. The yard list should be presented to the manager at the earliest opportunity.

While cleaning below decks, some items for the list are sure to come to light, including locker doors and drawers that jam; badly fitting cabin sole boards; a bubble in the compass; loose plastics sheeting in the galley; radio repairs; an overhaul for the cooking stove; adding a metal tray to the bottom of the anchor chain locker, or lining the engine compartment with sound deadening material.

These lists can extend to all parts of the boat. It may be a good idea to have a survey made while hauled out ashore, and the results of this could provide some more items to add to the list. In any case, with certain craft it may be wise to draw one or two keel bolts for examination, not forgetting that bilge keel fastenings are almost equally important.

The gudgeons and pintles used for supporting rudders are similar on grp, metal, and wooden craft. Severe wear in these parts can lead to danger, as well as sleepless nights due to the rattling noises. Temporary repairs can be made by building up such parts with epoxy resin, but the matter is so important that it pays to have new parts made or the existing parts built-up to original size by brazing or welding.

Damage to sheathing, keelband, and worn out sacrificial zinc anodes are all typical external items for the list.

Sheeting over

More harm is caused to varnish work (especially on flat surfaces) during a few weeks of frosty weather than throughout a season of sun and rain, while topsides and other vertical surfaces are not affected too badly. Sheeting over is therefore essential when a yacht is laid-up in the open.

Although covering may be unnecessary inside a shed, the roof could be leaky. If other enthusiasts intend to use power sanders or spray painting equipment in the shed, some form of light-weight sheeting may be advantageous to keep the dust at bay.

Ordinary cotton duck canvas is considered better than plastics as it can breath slightly and does not form condensation inside. Nylon (Dacron) coated with PVC has a longer life, and is probably more resistant to chafe, but its cost is higher.

Sheets of transparent or translucent film plastics have a more limited life with the advantage of excellent illumination below. The fitting of transparent windows into opaque sheets means that much more work can be done during inclement weather.

It pays to have a good quality purpose-made cover, for with a life of at least ten years the cost is but a small addition to the annual lay-up bill. Thinking that the boat might be sold next year, there is a temptation to improvise with standard rectangular sheets, but a properly fitted cover and framework should add correspondingly to the boat's value.

Whether the cover is made at home or professionally, accurate measurements will be necessary. Before taking these, the proposed ridge pole and framing required to support the cover free of obstacles (and with good drainage) must be erected. Athwartships measurements at each frame should then

274

Picture 79. Yacht on cradle at the end of greased ways awaiting the flood tide. Cradle can be dismantled to fit under the next craft to be launched.

Picture 80. Any safety conscious sailor should ensure that his boat has some sort of permanent step below water to enable a man overboard to climb up. With a transom hung rudder this is easily contrived as illustrated.

pick up all changes of angle and the proposed edge of the cover around the topsides. Fore-and-aft dimensions between frames and to the extreme ends will be needed also.

In making the framework, the first necessity is to fix the ridge pole (or *strongback*) into position temporarily, lashed, cramped, or wedged at convenient places such as the bow and stern pulpits, mast tabernacle and main hatch top.

A mainmast can sometimes be made to serve in this capacity, but attaching struts is never easy and without these the waterproof cover is sure to blow about needlessly in a wind or trap pools of rain water. Flat planed pine timber set on edge makes the best strongback. Suitable sizes are $\frac{3}{4}$ in × 3 in (18 mm × 75 mm) for vessels up to about 25 ft (8 m) in length; 1 in × 4 in (25 mm × 100 mm) up to about 39 ft (12 m); 1 in × 6 in (25 mm × 150 mm) up to about 70 ft (22 m).

The struts may be of similar timber some 30% smaller in section than the ridge pole set on edge and screwed to chocks to facilitate dismantling. More space is made available beneath

275

the cover if the struts are notched to fit over a rigid guardrail or wired to the top eyes of lifeline stanchions. All timber edges and corners must be well rounded and padding should be lashed around any suspicious places.

If the ridge pole is made to overhang the hull at each end the waterproof sheet can overhang also with open ends for ventilation. When using ordinary tarpaulins, a ventilation opening can be formed by screwing an old bottomless plastics bucket to the underside of the ridge pole and lashing the edges of the tarpaulin together beneath the bucket.

A specially made cover can have additional vents built in like a big tent. It can also have an access hatch formed in one or both sides fastened by lacings through eyelets.

Large waterproof covers are normally handier if made in two or three sections with overlapping double laced athwartship joints. This not only simplifies handling and stowing, but it also enables one to throw open the sheets during spells of fine weather.

To fasten a sheet securely with a good overlap down the topsides, usually means fixing a *guest warp* around the hull close to the waterline. Small wooden chocks can be screwed to the planking of a wooden boat to secure this, while on steel and plastics hulls several lines from rail to rail passing under the keel can be rigged. Bowline-on-the-bight knots formed in the correct positions on the lines will create loops through which to pass the guest warp.

The eyelet positions on a new cover must be exceptionally well reinforced. The eyelets are usually the first parts to fail on plastics film covers for stresses on the lanyards are very high in a gale. Shockcord lanyards allow some elasticity while cordage needs occasional checking to ensure tautness.

Treating the Bilges

The well organized owner starts fitting-out as soon as his vessel is securely laid-up. The lists mentioned above are all part of this and should be augmented continuously until every item needing attention is recorded. Many owners derive great pleasure in striking through the items as soon as completed and one can then tell from a glance at the notes whether the fitting-out program is well advanced or whether there will be a mad rush shortly before launching time!

It may take a few months for the bilges to dry out completely, but when ready, a vacuum cleaner or tack-rag can be used to clear out all loose dirt prior to painting. A piece of wire and a bottle brush may be handy at this time to clear the *limber holes* where bilge water flows underneath the frames. If small chains or knotted Terylene cords are rove through the limber holes (perhaps with shockcord or a spring at one end) these must be unrove before any bilge painting is started.

This is a good opportunity to check for rot in wooden frames, for deep rust in steel, and for galvanic action where copper fastenings fit through steel floors. If any rot or softness is discovered, the timber should be impregnated with a pentachlorophenol preservative, such as *International PCP*.

A few small holes into the wood may be expedient; certainly many applications of the fluid will be necessary to ensure saturation. Treating rot in bilges is often simpler than trying to get a preservative into some member close under the deckhead, such as a shelf or beam.

This may sometimes be done by boring $\frac{3}{16}$ in (4 mm) holes into the suspect part, pressing into the hole a length of wick (cut from any type of oil lamp wick), and dangling the end of this into a jar of preservative suspended close by.

On many glass fibre yachts the bilges are moulded in white plastics. This is an advantage when attempting to find a nut or some other missing part, while dirt which could eventually cause evil smells can be identified at a glance.

Wood and steel yachts can have bilges coated with white lead or white bitumastic paint (so changing the colour from black or dark gray) if thought worth while. Changing from paint to bitumastic (or black varnish) or *vice versa* is never advisable. Similarly, some wooden racing yachts may have polyurethane bilge paint (in an endeavour to prevent any moisture soakage into the planking) and this should not be changed.

Internal Ballast
There are still many yachts afloat with 100% inside ballast plus vast numbers of sailing and motor craft with small amounts of trimming ballast in addition to their external ballast keels. Most of this is of cast iron, but lead is common for Class (a) yachts, while concrete blocks are sometimes used.

Iron ballast varies from old sash weights and firebars to cast pigs weighing 150 lbs (68 kg). Well rounded pigs of about 75 lbs (34 kg) weight are ideal, and heavier ones should be cast with a hole through the centre enabling a strop and pin to be used when lifting them overboard.

When unshipping ballast for the first time it pays to make sketches of the arrangement, as the distribution of trimming ballast is important. Where the bilges are full to cabin sole level there may be difficulty in getting it all back in place.

When the amount of ballast is small, one can obviate taking it all ashore by laying each piece on chocks across the floor bearers (or on bunk boards) for painting. Although it may be possible to treat a large quantity of ballast in similar manner by shifting one panel at a time, this makes the operation of cleaning and drying out bilges very protracted.

Lead ballast requires little treatment except cleaning. Concrete is similar but can be given a few coats of swimming pool paint. Traditionally, iron ballast has always been coated with red oxide or black varnish. These usually show rust after two years and then tend to peel off and block the limber holes and strum box. Two coats of epoxy pitch will last almost indefinitely if applied in a warm atmosphere. A cheaper alternative is the thick plastics dope used for cocooning machinery parts, such as *Avigel 300* made by Corrosion Ltd, Warsash, Southampton.

Ballast must not be allowed to shift when a boat heels sharply on drying out and although very little *dunnage* is normally necessary to keep it in place, large pigs should be supported on the hog, keelson, or frames, and not directly against the planking.

Storing Gear

Many boatyards provide sheds to store all removable gear from clients' yachts plus separate storage for masts and spars. The keen amateur will probably take home everything movable in order to keep the equipment dry and to ensure an early start on fitting-out.

Storing ropes was mentioned earlier and sail treatment was described in Chapter 8. Mattresses are best stored on edge and turned over occasionally. After a thorough hosing down, rubber dinghies should be left inflated, resting on some padding and standing up against a wall.

Delicate equipment such as a windvane, anemometer, or self-steering gear, needs special care in stowage to avoid accidental damage. All electronic equipment is best stored in

278

the house. Be careful to remove dry batteries from these (also from torches and sextants with reading lights) as even the metal-cased cells can ooze corrosive chemicals when left in a discharged condition.

Coat the working parts of electrical switches and deck sockets (outlets) with petroleum jelly (Vaseline) to prevent verdigris. Clean and oil the working parts of winches and roller reefing gears, dismantling these if necessary. Clean and polish all brass fittings and lacquer them for protection using aerosol *Britect* or anhydrous lanoline for winter protection.

If brass fittings such as ventilators and winch drums can be removed, polishing will be simpler if these are taken home and buffed by using polishing compound on a linen mop in the electric drill. Brass and bronze can sometimes be revived by rubbing with a mixture of salt and vinegar prior to polishing with *Brasso* or *Bluebell,* but badly corroded fittings may need reviving with fine emery tape (used dry) before polishing.

Clean up adjustable jib sheet fairlead tracks, removing dirt from the stop holes by twiddling a twist bit between the fingers. Check that the mounting brackets for a taffrail (Walker) log are fixed securely and not fouled up with dried varnish. See that you have adequate sound anchorages for safety harness clips, such as a taut fore-and-aft wire rope along the centre of the coachroof.

Inventory
An inventory list is especially important for big boats. If no inventory list can be found at change of ownership, laying-up time (when all loose gear is taken ashore) is the best time to make a new list.

Stowing at fitting-out time will be made much easier if the inventory list also mentions which locker holds what. Although two owners rarely see eye to eye with regard to stowage, the previous owner might have had good reason for his method of stowage. For example, if food cans are shifted towards the steering compass, serious deviation errors could arise. One empty beer can or a safety harness near the compass can cause an error.

If all items on the inventory list are ticked off when stowed at fitting-out time one will at least know that everything is back on board and if any item cannot be found easily one should know that it has not been left at home.

TABLE 9
Typical Inventory for 30 ft (9·2m) Auxiliary Sloop

Compartment	Location	Inventory Items
Forepeak	Sail rack Chain locker Port bin S'board bin	5 sails in bags 30 fthms chain Sea anchor; boom awning; spare oilskins and lifejackets; weed scrubber Black ball (folded); navigation lamps; spare blocks; spare winch and windlass handles
	On hooks Clipped to bulkhead	Shrimp net; spare ropes; spare lifebelt 2 water breakers; kedge anchor; legs; spare dinghy oars; fire extinguisher
Fore Cabin	On berths Port aft drawer S'board aft drawer	2 mattresses with covers; 4 blankets in 2 bags; 2 sleeping bags; 2 cushions with covers Taffrail log; spare rotator and line; 3 towels Fishing tackle; flash lamp; spare batteries (3 types); spare bulbs (9 types); 3 boxes with parts for radio, sounder and all spare fuses
	For'ard drawers Under sole Fixtures	Keep empty for clothing 18 cans beer Mirror; 2 sets curtains; 2 coat hooks; emergency lamp in gimballs with smoke bell
Hanging lockers	Port locker S'board locker	Mop; deck scrubber; squeegee; dusting pan and brush; 1 galv. bucket; 1 plastic bucket; 1 set oilskins; 4 coat hooks Dinghy anchor with nylon rope; anchor buoy with nylon tripping line; dinghy bilge pump; 2 sets fishing rods; 2 fenders; 4 coat hooks; 6 coat hangers in silent stowage pocket
Toilet	Cabinet Fixtures	2 spare packs paper; nail brush; sponge; toothpaste; shampoo; spare soap Sanitary bin; magazine rack; deodorizer in holder; mirror; 1 coat hook; 2 towel rings; 1 towel; toilet paper with holder; brush and disinfectant in rack; emergency lamp in gimballs
Galley	Drawer	4 of each – big knives and forks; small forks; small knives; dessert spoons; teaspoons; eggspoons. 6 small knives. 2 serving spoons. One of each – carving knife and fork; fruit knife; cook's knife; potato peeler; fish slice; wooden spoon; can opener; corkscrew; beer can/bottle opener

TABLE 9—*continued*

Compartment	Location	Inventory Items
	Shaped racks	4 large plates; 6 small plates; 4 bowls; 6 mugs; 6 tumblers
	Behind stove	3 saucepans; fry pan; meths (alcohol) dispenser; kettle
	Behind sink	Asbestos mat; toaster; cheese board; milk jug; cream jug; coffee pot; tea pot; thermos flask; chopping/bread board; detergent; scouring powder; soap dish and soap; dish mop; scourer; swab
	Top cabinet	Jars of sugar; coffee; tea; salt; butter; jam; marmalade. Standard packs of maize oil; pickles; dried milk; honey; extra jam. 2 sandwich boxes; cruet
	Bottom cabinet	Boxes for salad; cheeses; extra butter; fruit; vegetables; long-life milk; dehydrated and canned foods
	Sink locker	Gash bucket; 2 trays; old newspaper; disinfectant; spare soap and detergent
	On bulkhead	Oil lamp; cleaning paper roll; 1 dish towel and 1 hand towel on rails; 1 set curtains; extinguisher
Main Cabin	Port settee/berth	Mattress with cover; 2 cushions with covers; 2 sleeping bags and 2 blankets (stowed in foot sponson)
	Lazarette under	Signalling lamp; paint cans; spare foghorn; 2 fenders; handybilly; canvas bucket
	Drawer under	Keep empty for clothing
	Shelf over	Books; medicine box; burgee on staff; torch; shackle key; marline spike; duster; ashtray; box of flares; box of cleaning equipment (including metal polish and furniture wax)
	S'board berth	Mattress with cover
	Lazarette under	Bosun's chair; leadline; fender inflator; radar reflector; emergency rations; spare rowlocks; skipper's spare clothing in duffle bag (including jerseys and deck shoes)
	Drawer under	Keep empty
	Shelf over	2 hanks codline; 1 roll PVC tape; sail repair kit; fire extinguisher; alarm clock
	Locked cabinet	All liquor and wines; 6 whisky glasses; 6 wine glasses; extra flares; main and hand compasses
	Locker under steps	Engine toolbox; 2 spare V-belts; oilcan (thick oil); oilcan (light); box engine spares; box packing and spares for pumps; bosun's toolbox; cleaning rags; greases; bottle distilled water; spare log impeller, skeg and housing; bosun's storebox with shackles; slides; hanks; wire rope grips; thimbles; hose clips; split pins; assorted screws and bolts; marline; seizing wire; shockcord. 1 small funnel; 1 medium funnel; 1 can engine oil

TABLE 9—*continued*

Compartment	Location	Inventory Items
Oilskin locker	Fixtures	Table; stove; 3 coat hooks; clock; 2 emergency lamps in gimballs; 4 sets curtains
	On hooks	1 set oilskins; 3 safety harnesses; 2 deck filler plate keys
	Clipped to bulkhead	Boarding ladder; 1 pair waders; water breaker; 2 fuel cans; 1 kerosene can
	Fixtures	5 coat/hat hooks
Navigation	Berth sponson flat	Radio/DF receiver; barograph; books (including almanac; traverse tables; tidal atlases and pilots)
	Behind radio etc.	Rolled charts
	Under table	Charts stored flat in case
	On aft bulkhead	Code flags in rack; racks for binoculars; DF attachment and hand bearing compass; chart light
	On fore bulkhead	Emergency oil lamp; speed/distance recorder; depth sounder; rack for log book and pad; rack for 2 thermos flasks, 2 mugs, 1 sandwich box
	Shelf	Ashtray; parallel rules; eraser; pencils; chart magnifier; course plotter; rule; dividers
Cockpit	On bulkhead	Compass mount; fire extinguisher; ashtray; binocular rack
	Port seat locker	Kedge warp; 3 fenders; 2 fuel funnels; sponge; swab; 1 bucket; ensign with staff; cockpit cover and ridge pole
	S'board seat locker	1 can fuel; 1 can lamp oil; 1 bottle meths (alcohol); 1 water breaker; 4 mooring warps
On Deck	Port aft lazarette	Butane cylinder in service; 2 heaving lines; 2 sheet winch handles
	S'board lazarette	Spare butane cylinder; anchor windlass handle; 2 nylon towing warps
	After deck	Lifebuoy with light in chocks; liferaft in casing
	Cabin top	Dinghy oars; boat hook; deck mop; 1 lifebuoy
	Fore deck	Bower anchor; dinghy (in gripes); fore hatch cover; whisker pole

Safety

Special importance must be attached to all safety equipment. Spare lifejackets or personal buoyancy sets should always be kept on board in case crew members or passengers arrive without one. Inflatable jackets are especially prone to failure when most needed unless checked by the makers each year. Careful stowage is important to avoid damage.

Inexperienced passengers may not have suitable wet weather gear with them and as dampness and coldness can lead to inefficiency and sickness, owners should make sure that spare sets of oilskins and neck towels are available.

Although lifebuoys need little maintenance, they must have suitable quick release mountings on deck and if the safety lights attached to them are dry-battery operated, frequent testing is wise.

Flares must always appear in first class external condition and should be renewed in accordance with the maker's instructions. Outdated flares are only of use in firework displays!

The same precautions are necessary with Very cartridges, rockets, and smoke signals. Some owners like to clip a white flare inside the main hatch or close to the helmsman, providing instant warning when a nocturnal collision is imminent. This stowage can be another job for the winter list. If *Terry Clips* are used these must be of stainless steel or plastics-coated.

The large motor cruiser may have automatic fire extinguishing nozzles in the engine compartment and at other strategic places. The small craft owner must rely on hand operated dry powder extinguishers and these must always be provided in any case to augment an automatic system. Even on the smallest cabin boat try to keep one extinguisher near the fo'c's'le and one right aft, with a third one near to an auxiliary engine or to the galley.

Examine all safety harnesses with special attention to the condition of the lanyards and spring carbine hooks. Remember to inspect a radar reflector at laying-up time, for these devices will not function at peak efficiency if the plates are buckled.

Some radios and other electronic instruments have a *desiccator* fitted behind a screwed plug in the casting. If the silica gel crystals have turned pink they are saturated with moisture and should be kept in a warm oven until they turn blue. Wash, clean, and oil a patent log before stowing it away. Make a note to remind you to send charts away for correction in the spring unless new ones are to be ordered.

When a cruising boat is equipped with a foghorn of the Aerosol type it would be wise to keep a hand operated or mouthpiece horn in addition. Although the Aerosol type is ideal for signalling purposes and emergencies, one may always be caught out in prolonged foggy conditions when too few spare canisters are carried or when an electric horn might drain the battery on an auxiliary sailing vessel.

Damage by lightning is rare at sea but as a precaution one should fit a thick copper strap from one masthead chainplate bolt to a keel bolt. With a through-deck alloy mast it proves better to strap from the mast head to a keel bolt.

The navigation lights on many small craft have insufficient brilliance (or are incorrectly positioned) to comply with the regulations. Such faults can place a boat in jeopardy. Although one may never intend to sail at night, unforeseen happenings are common on the water and the knowledgeable owner in a well-found yacht has a far better chance to combat the whims of the sea than the ill-prepared tyro in a tore-out!

INDEX

285